New Writing Explorations

This book, *New Writing Explorations: Researching Creative Writing,* investigates creative writing as an area of research, building from a recognition of its qualities as a creative human practice. It presents a critical examination of current methodologies and highlights many of the latest advancements in the field of creative writing studies.

This book's contributors examine writerly knowledge and action, places and spaces, tested methods and an array of associated concepts. Chapters draw not only on critical ideas formed by examining the works of creative writers but also on a range of individual writing activities and the lively and fluid dynamics we frequently encounter when we seek to use writing for both communication and art. The chapters in this volume provide excellent examples of the many avenues of inquiry seen in both practice-led and critical research in creative writing. This volume is relevant for students and scholars interested in the field of creative writing and cognate fields.

The chapters in the book were originally published as articles and editorials in the *New Writing* journal. They are accompanied by a new Introduction and Conclusion, as well as a Foreword by award-winning poet and critic, Dan Disney.

Graeme Harper is Editor of *New Writing: The International Journal for the Practice and Theory of Creative Writing.* He is the author of such books as *Critical Approaches to Creative Writing* (2018) and *Creative Writing Analysis* (2022) and, as Brooke Biaz, the novel *Releasing the Animals* (2023) and the forthcoming *Robots,* among many others.

New Writing Explorations
Researching Creative Writing

Edited by
Graeme Harper

LONDON AND NEW YORK

First published 2025
by Routledge
4 Park Square, Milton Park, Abingdon, Oxon, OX14 4RN

and by Routledge
605 Third Avenue, New York, NY 10158

Routledge is an imprint of the Taylor & Francis Group, an informa business

Foreword © 2025 Dan Disney.
Introduction and Conclusion © 2025 Graeme Harper.
Chapters 1–20 © 2025 Taylor & Francis

All rights reserved. No part of this book may be reprinted or reproduced or utilised in any form or by any electronic, mechanical, or other means, now known or hereafter invented, including photocopying and recording, or in any information storage or retrieval system, without permission in writing from the publishers.

Trademark notice: Product or corporate names may be trademarks or registered trademarks, and are used only for identification and explanation without intent to infringe.

British Library Cataloguing-in-Publication Data
A catalogue record for this book is available from the British Library

ISBN13: 978-1-032-85462-5 (hbk)
ISBN13: 978-1-032-85463-2 (pbk)
ISBN13: 978-1-003-51829-7 (ebk)

DOI: 10.4324/9781003518297

Typeset in Myriad Pro
by codeMantra

Publisher's Note
The material in this volume has been reproduced in facsimile. This means we can retain the original pagination to facilitate easy and correct citation of the original essays. It also explains the variety of typefaces, page layouts and numbering.

The publisher accepts responsibility for any inconsistencies that may have arisen during the conversion of this book from journal articles to book chapters, namely the inclusion of journal terminology.

Disclaimer
Every effort has been made to contact copyright holders for their permission to reprint material in this book. The publishers would be grateful to hear from any copyright holder who is not here acknowledged and will undertake to rectify any errors or omissions in future editions of this book.

Contents

Citation Information		vii
Notes on Contributors		x
Foreword		xi
Dan Disney		

Introduction: prying with a purpose: the prose poetics of creative writing research 1
Graeme Harper

1 Performances in contradiction: facilitating a neosophistic creative writing workshop 4
Ben Ristow

2 Creative writing: a Newtonian thought 12
Graeme Harper

3 'Unconscionable Mystification'?: Rooms, spaces and the prose poem 14
Paul Hetherington and Cassandra Atherton

4 Thoughts are creative writing 31
Graeme Harper

5 Screenwriting studies, screenwriting practice and the screenwriting manual 32
Craig Batty

6 Creative writing, as it happens: the case for unpredictability 44
Graeme Harper

7 The writer and meta-knowledge about writing: threshold concepts in creative writing 48
Janelle Adsit

8 Flight 60
Graeme Harper

9 Cognitive poetics and creative practice: beginning the conversation 62
Jeremy Scott

CONTENTS

10 Structuring empathy
Graeme Harper
68

11 Creative work as scholarly work
Nigel Krauth and Peter Nash
69

12 Why our responses matter
Graeme Harper
91

13 Shifting the power dynamics in the creative writing workshop: assessing an instructor as participant model
Donovan McAbee
92

14 Creative writing on other planets
Graeme Harper
101

15 Different ways of descending into the crypt: methodologies and methods for researching creative writing
Francis Gilbert and Vicky Macleroy
102

16 Forms of illumination
Graeme Harper
121

17 Retooling workshops of empire: globalising creative writing with an edge
Khem Aryal
123

18 New types of intelligence relevant to creative writers
Graeme Harper
133

19 English-language creative writing in a Chinese context: translation as a supplement
Xia Fang
135

20 An agreeable crest: the *New Writing* 20th anniversary year
Graeme Harper
154

Conclusion: intentional echoes
Graeme Harper
157

Index
159

Citation Information

The following chapters in this book were originally published in various volumes of *New Writing*. When citing this material, please use the original page numbering for each article, as follows:

Chapter 1
Performances in Contradiction: Facilitating a Neosophistic Creative Writing Workshop
Ben Ristow
New Writing, volume 11, issue 1 (2014), pp. 92–99

Chapter 2
Creative Writing: A Newtonian Thought
Graeme Harper
New Writing, volume 12, issue 3 (2015), pp. 263–264

Chapter 3
'Unconscionable Mystification'?: Rooms, Spaces and the Prose Poem
Paul Hetherington and Cassandra Atherton
New Writing, volume 12, issue 3 (2015), pp. 265–281

Chapter 4
Thoughts are creative writing
Graeme Harper
New Writing, volume 13, issue 3 (2016), p. 349

Chapter 5
Screenwriting studies, screenwriting practice and the screenwriting manual
Craig Batty
New Writing, volume 13, issue 1 (2016), pp. 59–70

Chapter 6
Creative writing, as it happens: the case for unpredictability
Graeme Harper
New Writing, volume 14, issue 1 (2017), pp. 1–4

Chapter 7
The writer and meta-knowledge about writing: threshold concepts in creative writing
Janelle Adsit
New Writing, volume 14, issue 3 (2017), pp. 304–315

Chapter 8
Flight
Graeme Harper
New Writing, volume 15, issue 1 (2018), pp. 1–2

Chapter 9
Cognitive poetics and creative practice: beginning the conversation
Jeremy Scott
New Writing, volume 15, issue 1 (2018), pp. 83–88

Chapter 10
Structuring empathy
Graeme Harper
New Writing, volume 16, issue 2 (2019), p. 127

Chapter 11
Creative work as scholarly work
Nigel Krauth and Peter Nash
New Writing, volume 16, issue 3 (2019), pp. 281–302

Chapter 12
Why our responses matter
Graeme Harper
New Writing, volume 17, issue 4 (2020), p. 355

Chapter 13
Shifting the power dynamics in the Creative Writing workshop: assessing an instructor as participant model
Donovan McAbee
New Writing, volume 17, issue 3 (2020), pp. 244–252

Chapter 14
Creative writing on other planets
Graeme Harper
New Writing, volume 18, issue 1 (2021), p. 1

Chapter 15
Different ways of descending into the crypt: methodologies and methods for researching creative writing
Francis Gilbert and Vicky Macleroy
New Writing, volume 18, issue 3 (2021), pp. 253–271

Chapter 16
Forms of illumination
Graeme Harper
New Writing, volume 19, issue 3 (2022), pp. 251–252

Chapter 17
Retooling workshops of empire: globalising creative writing with an edge
Khem Aryal
New Writing, volume 19, issue 2 (2022), pp. 240–249

Chapter 18
New types of intelligence relevant to creative writers
Graeme Harper
New Writing, volume 20, issue 2 (2023), pp. 121–122

Chapter 19
English-language creative writing in a Chinese context: translation as a supplement
Xia Fang
New Writing, volume 20, issue 4 (2023), pp. 420–438

Chapter 20
An Agreeable Crest: The New Writing *20th Anniversary Year*
Graeme Harper
New Writing, volume 21, issue 1 (2024), pp. 1–3

For any permission-related enquiries please visit:
http://www.tandfonline.com/page/help/permissions

Notes on Contributors

Janelle Adsit, English Department, Humboldt State University, Arcata, USA.

Khem Aryal, Department of English, Philosophy, and World Languages, Arkansas State University, Jonesboro, USA.

Cassandra Atherton, Faculty of Arts & Education, School of Communication & Creative Arts, Deakin University, Geelong, Australia.

Craig Batty, University of South Australia, Adelaide, Australia.

Dan Disney, Sogang University, Seoul, South Korea.

Xia Fang, Department of Translation and Interpreting, Yangzhou University, People's Republic of China.

Francis Gilbert, Department of Educational Studies, Goldsmiths, University of London, UK.

Graeme Harper, The Honors College, Oakland University, USA.

Paul Hetherington, Faculty of Arts and Design, University of Canberra, Australia.

Nigel Krauth, School of Humanities, Languages and Social Science, Griffith University, Gold Coast and Nathan, Australia.

Vicky Macleroy, Department of Educational Studies, Goldsmiths, University of London, UK.

Donovan McAbee, College of Liberal Arts & Social Sciences, Belmont University, Nashville, USA.

Peter Nash, School of Humanities, Languages and Social Science, Griffith University, Gold Coast and Nathan, Australia.

Ben Ristow, Department of Writing and Rhetoric, Hobart and William Smith Colleges, Geneva, USA.

Jeremy Scott, University of Kent, Canterbury, UK.

Foreword

Which myriad forces contribute to the event and phenomena termed "creative writing"? What is it that compels writers to write, and how might our considered responses to these irritatingly general questions open onto new vistas of possibility for non-humans, humans, and extra-humans alike? Over the last 20 years, *New Writing: The International Journal for the Practice and Theory of Creative Writing* has formalized a field – the practice-based study of creative writing – which has, at least since Modernity, otherwise been largely only peripherally fascinating to thinkers.

Under the aegis of the visionary Graeme Harper, two decades of effortful and deeply eclectic scholarly attention from across the planet lead now to a globally significant, emergent theoretical canon.

To bring creativities from the echelons of unconscious, untheorized (and arguably elite) processes and into clear critical light: this seems not only germane but quite possibly Promethean. Which unimagined dimensions of futurity are opened when new tools and technologies are thrust into the hands of the masses?

This remarkable anthology posits a number of possible answers. Continuing the work of framing Creative Writing as not only a *bona fide* academic discipline within those edifices we call Humanities Faculties, *New Writing Explorations: Researching Creative Writing* also shows how this domain in particular remains an area of study that stands to humanize its constituents. Salient, perhaps? In an era of increasingly intelligent machines, emerging in a moment of dire ecological precarity, this book of research, methodologies, pedagogies, and ethics proffers a resounding *yes!*

It seems to me that, in highly rigorous and diversely compelling ways, the papers in this book set about making sense of creativity as a vast autoethnographic archive; from the micro to the macro, the individual to the communal, the historical, and the ideological, even, this book parlays creative writing and its manifold creative processes as not only central but, indeed, defining.

Dan Disney
Sogang University (Seoul)

Introduction

Prying with a purpose: the prose poetics of creative writing research

Graeme Harper

"For I have laughed," writes Zora Neale Hurston, in her poem "Passion" (1922).

Hurston's "Passion" begins with an evocation, a looking back on life: "For I have laughed / With the dew of morn / The calm of night"; and it ends with a vision of existence beyond life, a dream wandering in the astral: "To touch my feet on cloud / And wander where none / But souls dare climb."

Enhancing the linearity in the poem is an integrity founded in the conversation between emotion and reason. Hurston is feeling while she is thinking. One aspect is not present without the other. Their connection resonates.

Because creative writers employ an organized collection of linguistic signs and symbols, arranged in a way to make sense to others as well as themselves, and which rely on such shared meaning and agreed definition, they cannot draw only from the realm of emotion. They need the systematized nature of the intellect in order to do this linguistic work.

Because creative writers use this method – these written words – to express emotions, not downplaying their feelings but using them as guides for their subjects and themes, the strength of their views and their reaching out to others, they need the speculative, explorative, and inclusive approach of the imagination. They cannot work only within the realm of reason.

Action. Interaction. Resonance.

Creative writing *research* echoes creative writing *practice* by embracing both thinking and emotion. It is one of the reasons we have now and then found higher education institutions and government funding agencies struggling to define what creative writing research entails. The conversation between ordered written language and inventive expression challenges ideals of research as a series of organized linear steps often along single disciplinary lines – steps and lines that are seen as necessary to ask informed questions, create and test hypothesis, and analyze the results. Alternatively, the actions and interactions in creative writing research (as in creative writing) tend to be reverberant and can be irregular.

The questions and hypotheses in creative writing research (as in creative writing) draw on multiple avenues of knowledge and, frequently, are not restricted in the ways in which they do that. Creative writing research takes many forms – some of it practice-led, some of it practice-focused, and some of it practice-informed. That is not to say creative writing research cannot sometimes concentrate primarily on completed works of creative writing. Rather, it is to say creative writing is fundamentally writerly action and creative writing research therefore distinguishes itself by its recognition and attention to that fact in its forms and modes of delivery. Creative writers similarly choose the mode of delivery they favor, and while completed writing forms and genre carry the weight of tradition, convention, and reproduction, the newness and originality that creative writing entails encourages action-based and resonant choice-making.

For these reasons, the types of knowledge explored and used in creative writing research (much as in creative writing) include both the tacit and the explicit. Such tacitness, which incorporates perceptions and intuitions, reflects the nature and behaviors of human creativity, and its highly personalized, experiential disposition is customarily difficult to express. Such explicitness is often obtained through a variety of formal educational activities; in particular, when it comes to technical writing skills, those associated in a literate culture with each of us becoming literate. We normally begin acquiring these skills in early childhood. This explicit knowledge is also highly codified, appearing in books and other media and in representations of communal behaviors (of reading and writing, and discovering and communicating in these codified ways), and this has historical breadth and depth, representing and solidifying such explicit knowledge in terms of societal norms and cultural intentions.

Indeed, creative writing research draws on and explores both the codified and the informal. The informality comes about through social interaction (whether that social interaction is in live, real time with others, or whether it dwells generally in the linguistic agreements that are needed in any culture for its members to use a shared language). Such research can be personal, and it can be descriptive. It is frequently procedural and sometimes conceptual. Procedural in that actions that take place over time develop some shared procedural understanding among any population, as well as individual procedural interpretation, and conceptual in that classifications (for example, genre, form, semantic meaning), models (completed works, records of writer's activities, such as in diaries or memoirs), and concepts (abstract ideas such as those connected with beauty or sometimes with intention) provide guides for writerly action and understanding. Creative writing researchers have been known to note that their research is provisional (founded on their practice-led discoveries perhaps, on work they want to further undertake and consider). Not least, a creative writing researcher will frequently acknowledge the contextual and include reference to some aspect of the emotional. This is not to suggest other forms of research do not do this, but the clarity with which creative writing research does it is distinctive if not unique.

This research can be *a priori* (that is, proceeding from theoretical deduction, in creative writing terms often based on literary, cultural, or linguistic theories) and it can be *a posteriori* (that is, based on experience or personal observation, which is a primary driver for many creative practice researchers). Because creative writing is so human-centered, many times based in an exchange between an individual writer and an individual reader, the way it is learnt also is a focus of creative writing research and therefore produces and investigates meta-knowledge about creative writing – questions of how we know what we know about creative writing, how we teach what we know, and ultimately how we acquire knowledge that can assist our own (and others) practice in creative writing.

The ability to travel between, and resonate and engage with a variety of knowledge types is an attractive aspect of creative writing and creative writing research, as evidenced by the fact that other fields of research and study have noticed that research in and *through* creative writing has benefits. For example, Daniel Paiva, writing in the journal *Emotion, Space and Society* observes: "Poetry as a research method has received a significant amount of attention by geographers in recent years." (Paiva: 1) He adds that he wants to explore: "poetry as a method by addressing the potential of poetry for attuning to and expressing resonance in multi-sensory geographies."

Multi-sensory indeed! And resonant. Like a prose poem where prose has poetic qualities and distinctive rhythm, is metrical and lyrical, and contains engaging imagery, the figurative as well as the literal. Creative writing research has the qualities of prose poetry, and not necessarily in the technical sense of its frequent combining of conventions and formatting of written academic research with those stylistic, evocative approaches of poetry but in a broader aesthetic sense where thought and feeling are in constant and integrated communication and the knowledge that is explored, discovered and exchanged is therefore public and personal, communal and individual. Further, such knowledge is concrete and it is transcendent, it is rational and it is visceral.

In essence, the resonance in creative writing research, the prose poem qualities, produces an active and energetic embodiment of what Zora Neale Hurston once succinctly called "formalized curiosity." This is Hurston's alliterative poetic evocation:

> Research is formalized curiosity. It is poking and prying with a purpose. It is a seeking that he who wishes may know the cosmic secrets of the world and they that dwell within. (Hurston, *Dust Tracks on a Road*: 127)

When we set out on creative writing research we are "poking and prying with a purpose", combining outward looking (drawing on our observations, and/or observable practices, our sources, what we read and so forth) with dwelling within (seeking explanation, consideration, response within ourselves, encouraged by our emotions, our memories, our imaginations, and our personal psychology). We go about doing so in a way that traverses knowledge types and research actions (which can be more, or less, structured research methodologies). This research reverberation impacts the discoveries we make and the way in which we express those discoveries.

By equally embracing both thinking and emotion, we echo the practices of creative writing in our creative writing research, empowering the possibility of approaching a more complete, holistic understanding of the themes and subjects we explore.

References

Hurston, Zora Neale, *Dust Tracks on a Road*. 1942. New York: Harper Perennial, 1991
Hurston, Zora Neale, "Passion", *Negro World*, April 15, 1922
Paiva, Daniel, "Poetry as a resonant method for multi-sensory research", *Emotion, Space and Society* 34, 2020, pp.1–6.

Performances in contradiction: facilitating a neosophistic creative writing workshop

Ben Ristow

This article examines the ways that creative writing instructors may willingly (or unintentionally) suppress contradiction and indeterminacy in workshop feedback conversations. By suggesting that contradiction and indeterminacy may be fruitful and dynamic sites to investigate craft practice, aesthetics, and authorship, the essay argues for a reassessment of the way teachers facilitate workshop. In addition to drawing on experience in the classroom, the author suggests that workshop become a site where rhetorical and artistic invention are intermeshed in the sophistic pedagogical tradition of *antilogikê* and *dissoi logoi* (rhetorical strategies emphasising contradiction and doubt, rather than certainty). The concept of *antilogikê* is connected to workshop pedagogy through an analysis of William Covino's *Magic, Rhetoric, and Literacy: An Eccentric History of the Composing Imagination*. In the book, Covino suggests that *generative* magic (rather than *arresting* magic) provides a lens to analyse language and institutional structures. Using the sophistic concept of *antilogikê* from Andrea Greenbaum's *Emancipatory Movements in Composition: The Rhetoric of Possibilities* and Covino's analysis of magic, the essay argues that teachers can better encourage the development of apprentice writers by facilitating conversations in the sophistic, rather than the Socratic tradition.

One of the great challenges for the academic discipline of creative writing in the 21st century will be to remain connected to the extra-institutional knowledge that makes art possible. Does the institution of the creative writing workshop in higher education facilitate art making? Yes, or, potentially. The workshop should be a context where pedagogy is diversified and where experiments are run. The traditional workshop, often referred to as 'The Iowa Workshop' in the States, has given birth to two dominant strands of instruction. First, workshop instruction may be cast as a Socratic enterprise whereby the workshop instructor ultimately determines the revision suggestions (and the final judgement) on a submission piece for workshop. The second brand of instruction is more closely aligned with a pseudo-democratic or Aristotelian system. In this system, the instructor takes a consensus-based approach whereby students dictate the trajectory of suggestions while instructors provide comments that reside in the non-committal or superficial.

Both forms of workshop instruction outlined above represent each end of the spectrum in creative writing workshop, and the conversation on a workshop submission may exhibit shadings of one side or the other. In both forms of instruction, the position of contradiction or indeterminacy among peers is observable but quite often suppressed. By ignoring these points of friction, the instructors may brandish their authority throughout the conversation or they may wield it at the moment when final judgement must be passed. In this pedagogical method, the instructor ultimately dictates the course of action for the workshopping author through more or less explicit means. Alternatively, and as a second method, the instructor may try to distance themselves from suggestions on the submission piece and attempt to coalesce the peers' feedback through consensus gathering. In this role, the workshop facilitator leans away from personal opinion on the piece and attempts to represent the will and sentiments of the collective of peers (Figure 1). In contrast to the first method, the second method is in danger of becoming awash in an engagement that becomes innocuous or given over to the malaise of group consciousness. Individual feedback by peers may be gathered and stored only to be later taxonomized by the facilitator. The effect of the first approach, what I am referring to as the *Socratic method* of workshop, and the second approach, what I am calling the *Aristotelian method*, leaves the workshopping author with a peer readership that has been blunted by an overly prescribed task. Through the course of this essay, I will argue that a third workshop method is achievable and may displace the traditional workshop method with a *neosophistic altern-ative*. The neosophistic method identifies the contradictions of verbal student feedback and utilises these sites and the experience of the workshop leader to frame workshopping through contradiction, not consensus. Figure 1 provides a visual representation of the workshop methods outlined above.

The function of the creative writer as an instructor often plays a pivotal role in developing the craft practices and teaching of apprentice writers, and I propose that the workshop leader reject their role as dignitary, or authoritarian. In a similar vein, I believe that the workshop leader must also consider shedding their role as the one who conducts workshop as a pseudo-democratic affair built upon consensus gathering. An alternative to these identities might cast the workshop leader as a discerning sophist who pushes students to articulate their revision suggestions through *antilogikê* and *dissoi logoi*.[1] Both terms originate in the classical sophistic tradition and are rhetorical strategies that emphasise *aporia* 'doubt' rather than certainty in argumentation. *Antilogikê* 'contradiction' and *dissoi logoi* 'double argument' allow for the possibility that opposing proofs (*logos*) may be true simultaneously (Greenbaum 2002). My objective in this essay is to unite scholarship on the sophists from rhetoric and composition studies with creative writing studies, and I will propose an alternative to the traditional workshop method, what Wallace Stegner calls 'mild[ly] Socratic'.[2] It might distress Plato and Aristotle to hear so, but there is no measure of certainty provided in the verbal feedback on a workshop submission – there is no resolution, no winner – and it is my argument that the

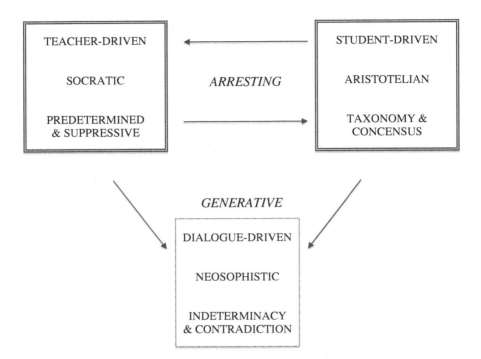

Figure 1. Arresting vs. Generative creative writing workshop methods.

workshop facilitator should invest in contradiction and indeterminacy by making it the site in which writers can advance their teaching through the pedagogical techniques employed in sophistic rhetoric.

In providing verbal feedback to peers on their workshop submissions, writers often carve out conflicting or meandering paths in their commentary. Peers dispute the particulars in their reading experience and disagree in principle about how best to revise. These contradictions place focus on the commentary of workshop and the microcosm of peer responses. It is also central to identify the historical macrocosm and the legacy of workshop as observed in its progenitors in guilds, salons, and societies from the classical to postmodern period. Throughout the history of workshop and its various instantiations, there is an observable tension between institutional and extra-institutional contexts. Histories of workshop also vacillate between inclusive or exclusive motives, depending on the governance of the workshop and the goals of its participants. Anne Gere charts the evolution and epistemological framework of workshops that function inclusively in *Writing Groups: History, Theory, and Implications* (1987) and, in contrast and more recently, Joshua Gunn has identified the ways that subculture groups employ more esoteric and exclusive rhetorics.[3] The contemporary workshop is born of a historical tradition of workshopping where broader arguments define craft practices, aesthetics, and determine who is called the 'artist'. Points of confusion, tension, and frustration arise and are articulated in class, and the teacher must do more than participate in workshop, they must facilitate an interrogation of art making.

Along with recognising the way workshop conversations operate, instructors must also be attentive to issues of power. Authority and power are themes in Anna Leahy's edited collection *Power and Identity in the Creative Writing Classroom: The Authority Project* (2005). In her essay 'The Value and Cost of Nurturing', Leahy points to the fact that authority is not a matter of *if*, but *how* instructors wield it in workshop. Leahy writes that 'we may too easily think "I don't have any authority – it's a workshop". I find, though, that even in a workshop circle, students tend to raise their hands or seek organization of the conversation from me and that students often address comments to me' (Leahy 2005, 18). The workshop leader functions as the ballast in classroom instruction, and this power brings forward the pivotal question: How do instructors manoeuvre their authority in a workshop without impinging on the artistic practice of the writer? The influence of the instructor may be unavoidable, however, creative writing teachers should imagine themselves as a fluid character, an almost amphibious figure that moves between roles as a publishing writer, constructive mentor, workshop facilitator, and more. It cannot be assumed that each writer may excel in every role in the university and publishing world, but I argue that the writer-teacher will benefit students most when their ethos is embedded in sophism.

Magical (Re)Visions to Workshop Leadership in the Creative Writing Workshop

In *Emancipatory Movements in Composition: The Rhetoric of Possibility*, Andrea Greenbaum (2002) reimagines the historiography of classical rhetoric through the lens of Plato and Aristotle's contemporaries, the sophists. By focusing on the sophistic concepts of language and argumentation, Greenbaum is able to contrast Platonic and Aristotelian argumentation in the form *logos* (proofs) with sophistic forms of argumentation and knowledge in the form of *antilogikê* (contradiction) and *dissoi logoi* (double argument). Plato believes knowledge lies beyond, in an eternal sphere, and that argumentation should lead toward (and from) a degree of certainty and truth. Proofs eliminate possibilities and interlocutors create a measure of probability where from a winner is named, usually Plato. In contrast, Greenbaum characterises sophistic argumentation as context-based and dependent upon audience's *aporia* (doubt). For the sophists, proofs in argumentation could be brought into *antilogikê* (contradiction) and more than one proof could be true simultaneously. This constructive relativism toward truth in argumentation assumes, as the sophists did, that knowledge was conditioned by the time and space of its articulation, or *kairos* (timeliness). For the sophists, there is no absolute truth.

The scholarship on the sophists by rhetoric and composition scholars has helped to displace Plato's marginalisation of rhetoric. Neosophistic scholars have written a counter-narrative in the midst of the prevailing discourse on classical rhetoric, and this rewriting provides an opportunity for the creative writing studies scholar to reimagine the role of the workshop instructor mentoring marginalised populations. Among the creative writing studies scholars who have already begun this work (Leahy 2005; Haake 2000; Bishop 1990; Donnelly 2010), the fundamental question remains: How do we facilitate writing workshop so that other voices are heard? Plato's marginalisation of rhetoric and poetics remains a unifying legacy between creative writing and rhetoric, and it is time that scholars and workshop leaders acknowledge the ways their teaching of workshop builds a potentially oppressive Socratic structure and procedure. In order to destabilise and reimagine the framework through neosophistic instruction, it is worth briefly examining the rhetorical paradox that defines magic.

In *Rhetoric, Magic, Literacy: An Eccentric History of the Composing Imagination*, William Covino (1994) departs from defining magic as an enterprise based in deception or illusion, and he argues for an alternative definition, one that sees magic as functioning to disarm power relationships rather than create them. He defines magic as 'a conceptual construct for evaluating the power of language' and as 'a liberatory alternative to established rationalism' (Covino 1994, 5). In this definition of magic, Covino distinguishes between the concepts of arresting and generative magic. Covino associates arresting magic with articulate power sources in the form of sanctioned institutions such as universities and governments. These sources of arresting magic control knowledge through discourse and other control mechanisms while, in contrast, generative magic is associated with inarticulate power sources such as the imagination.

Covino argues that academic fields and institutions may arrest discourse, and therefore it is the responsibility of generative magic (and the fields that articulate knowledge in this way) to confront institutional structures. He writes that 'magic is in another sense the practice of disrupting and recreating articulate power: a (re)sorcery spells for generating multiple perspectives [...] generative magic is a dialogical critique that seeks novelty, originating at a remove from the mass culture it would interrogate' (Covino 1994, 8). The dialogical concerns of generative magic are in the spirit and tenor of the pedagogical legacy of the sophists. This legacy is bound by the notion that the irrational (in the sophistic tradition of *antilogikê*) and the illusory (magic) can form the foundation for critiques of institutional or sanctioned knowledge.

What the Neosophistic Workshop Might Look Like Using *Antilogikê* and *Dissoi Logoi*

The workshop remains foundational to the educational structure of creative writing despite the fact that its epistemological framework has remained critically and artistically under-imagined. As a predominately Socratic and Aristotelian affair, the current workshop format lacks the discursive nature of sophistic discourse and risks arresting the qualities in discourse it seeks to support and develop, namely: voice, originality, and imagination. The neosophistic workshop might allow the workshop facilitator to displace their authority and invite more inclusive writing practices. What might this inclusivity look like though? How can facilitators encourage an artistic discursivity in workshop? Ideally, these questions may lead to more diverse workshops beyond the Socratic and Aristotelian models illustrated above. In the final section, I will outline one potential workshop model using the concept of *antilogikê* and *dissoi logoi* and my experience in Dr. Darrell Spencer's workshop. And I encourage readers to imagine others.

Greenbaum discusses *antilogikê* and *dissoi logoi* as the sophistic practice of holding more than one possibility to be true simultaneously. One reader may argue that the submission is voice-driven while another might maintain that the piece is narrative-driven. In either case, the workshop facilitator oftentimes chooses (with more or less art) which outcome the workshopping author should choose. The apprentice writer acquiesces and what is enacted is consistent with Socratic methodology whereby *possibilities* are reduced in order to establish what is *probable*. This epistemological stance is prevalent to workshopping by now, though sometimes, shadings of the sophistic emerge as an alternative. In Dr. Darrell Spencer's creative writing workshop, a course I took as a graduate student ten years ago, the critique was shifted toward the sophistic.

Spencer began the workshop by listening to student conversations about a submission piece and documenting the conversation through his handwritten notes. After we had created the corpus of feedback on a submission, he did not present his argument for the revision and instead turned his attention to our comments. In the second phase of workshop, Spencer embodied the sophist who articulates points of contradiction and indeterminacy in the discussion of the piece and he asked clarifying questions that ushered in the second phase of the conversation. The contradictions that emerged in the first phase were not revisited as points of personal (or group) conflict, but as opportunities where peers might reimagine their argument and generate options for rewriting. In many instances, Spencer parlayed questions to individual students in order to see if each might change their opinion, or adjust their position, all in way that exhibited his willingness to offer feedback that was not top-down (from him to us), but rather facilitatory and grounded in the artefact of our conversation. The conversation provided an impetus to amend our initial opinions, and it oftentimes served to generate more thoughtful, focused, and engaged responses to the workshop submissior. Spencer's workshop was reflective of the contingency of our feedback, and he allowed us the opportunity to reflect and entertain opposing arguments and suggestions for revision. His pedagogical motive was not self-motivated, or only in the interest of the workshopping author, and the dialogue highlighted the ways we questioned the craft of fiction writing more broadly.

The discursive nature of the neosophistic workshop is only accessible if and when the facilitator displaces themselves from the primary role of final judge on a workshop submission. In the neosophistic tradition, discursivity becomes possible with the availability of contradictory feedback. Rather than establishing probabilities and revision solutions for the workshopping author, the neosophistic workshop, whether facilitated by the teacher or students, should be interested in possibilities for revision and encouraging tolerance of an indeterminate outcome. The double argument (*dissoi logoi*) holds that knowledge is born of a collective and contingent argument where the dialogue travels away from rather than toward resolution. Below are questions that may be used to enact the pedagogical objectives of a neosophistic workshop.

Examples of neosophistic writing workshop questions for facilitators

- Where in our workshop conversation do we see contradictory readings and interpretation? What are the sources of these discrepancies and how might the writer act?
- Where might the writer consider our indeterminacies as productive points of action?
- What voices are under heard in the story? How might they be brought to the reader's ear?
- How does your feedback on Student Z's submission demonstrate your aesthetic perception on the relationship between realism and experimental or avant-garde writing?
  What qualities in the submission are crafted, conditioned, or inspired by the present moment? And what qualities in the submission feel more timeless and transcendent?

Although the leadership of the workshop facilitator has been the primary concern of this essay, I suggest that the neosophistic workshop also encourages the inclusion of marginalised voices among apprentice writers. Because the published author moves out of a Socratic and Aristotelian position, the instructor allows for a feedback loop that is influenced by critical pedagogy. In this pedagogical context, the workshopping author benefits from more possibilities and directions for revising their submission and creates a more productive site for developing knowledge in craft. Craft never only represents the relationship between the artist and the artefact of their creation, and in a way that differs from the solitary artisan in her studio, the writing workshop may shift the ways writers conceive of the artistic process. Apprentice writers find value in the feedback they *receive* in workshop, however, it is more essential to recognise how students' performances of authorship (as they *articulate* feedback) develop their own artistic process. As a workshop facilitator guides students to articulate their critique on a submission in workshop dialogue, they are enabling and propagating a way of thinking that becomes craft knowledge. Witnessing the irresolution, the disagreements, and entertaining opposing views is a complex enterprise, but one that yields a neosophistic education for the creative writing student.

Correspondence

Any correspondence should be directed to … Ben William Ristow, Department of Writing and Rhetoric, Hobart and William Smith Colleges, 300 Pulteney St., Geneva, NY 14456, USA, (bristow@hws.edu).

Notes

1. *Antilogikê* arrives from the sophistic tradition (notably among Protagoras and Antiphon) of argumentation, the belief that 'to every *logos* a *logos* is opposed' (Kirby 1996, 300). *Dissoi logoi* translates from the Greek as literally 'different words', though in educational practice it is the activity of arguing both sides of an argument or 'double argument'. The term also refers to the unattributed classical treatise of the same name. *The Stanford Encyclopedia of Philosophy* entry for 'Ancient

Logic' provides an explanation of the treatise *Dissoi Logoi* and the distinction between Platonic and sophistic concepts of truth. The entry reads: 'Opposed were the views (1) that truth is a – temporal – property of sentences, and that a sentence is true (when it is said), if and only if things are as the sentence says they are when it is said, and false if they aren't; and (2) that truth is an atemporal property of what is said, and that what is said is true if and only if the things are the case, false if they aren't the case' (Bobzien 2006, para. 4). I claim in this essay that temporal and context-based (the first premise above) 'truths' are more appropriate for facilitating creative writing workshop in the neosophistic rhetorical tradition.

2. Wallace Stegner refers to the pedagogical elements of workshop as 'mild Socratic guidance' in *On the Teaching of Creative Writing: Responses to a Series of Questions* (1988, 60) without expanding fully on the intention of his use of the term. It is possible that Stegner is simply referring to the ways that workshop often utilises a conversation that is similar (and somewhat different) than the Socratic dialogue. In the neosophistic rhetorical scholarship of Andrea Greenbaum (2002) and Susan Jarratt (1998), the Socratic dialogue is distinguished from the sophistic mode of logic and argumentation, and the latter provides as an alternative method for understanding knowledge and writing.

3. See Gunn, Joshua (2005). *Modern Occult Rhetoric: Mass Media and the Drama of Secrecy in the Twentieth Century.* Tuscaloosa: University of Alabama Press.

References

Bishop, Wendy. 1990. *Released into Language: Options for Teaching Creative Writing.* Urbana, IL: National Council of Teachers of English Press.

Bobzien, Susanne. 2006. "Ancient Logic." *Stanford Encyclopedia of Philosophy.* Metaphysics Research Lab. (Center for the Study of Language and Information / Stanford University). http://plato.stanford.edu/entries/logic-ancient/

Covino, William. 1994. *Magic, Rhetoric, and Literacy: An Eccentric History of the Composing Imagination.* New York: State University of New York Press.

Donnelly, Dianne. 2010. *Does the Writing Workshop Still Work?* Bristol: Multilingual Matters (New Writing Viewpoints).

Gere, Anne Ruggles. 1987. *Writing Groups: History, Theory, and Implications.* Carbondale, IL: Southern Illinois University Press.

Greenbaum, Andrea. 2002. *Emancipatory Movements in Composition: The Rhetoric of Possibilities.* Albany, NY: State University of New York Press.

Gunn, Joshua. 2005. *Modern Occult Rhetoric: Mass Media and the Drama of Secrecy in the Twentieth Century.* Tuscaloosa, AL: University of Alabama Press.

Haake, Kate. 2000. *What Our Speech Disrupts: Feminism and Creative Writing Studies.* Urbana, IL: National Council of Teachers of English Press.

Jarratt, Susan. 1998. *Rereading the Sophists: Classical Rhetoric Refigured.* Carbondale, IL: Southern Illinois University Press.

Kirby, John T. 1996. "Greek Rhetoric: Early Classical Period." In *Encyclopedia of Rhetoric and Composition: Communication from Ancient Times to the Information Age*, edited by Theresa Enos, 299. New York: Routledge.

Leahy, Anna. 2005. "The Value and Cost of Nurturing." In *Power and Identity in the Creative Writing Classroom: The Authority Project*, edited by Anna Leahy, 13–25. Bristol: Multilingual Matters (New Writing Viewpoints).

Plato, Ion. 2000. *Selected Dialogues of Plato: The Benjamin Jowett Translation.* Compiled by Hayden Pellicca. New York: Modern Library.

Stegner, Wallace. 1988. *On the Teaching of Creative Writing: Responses to a Series of Questions.* Hanover, NH: University Press of New England.

Creative writing: a Newtonian thought

Graeme Harper

An object at rest stays at rest; an object in motion stays in motion at the same speed, and in the same direction, unless an external force is applied to it. Acceleration occurs when a force is applied to a mass; the greater the mass, the greater the force needed to accelerate it. For every action, there is an equal and opposite reaction. These are Isaac Newton's laws of motion, first published in 1687 in his Philosophiæ Naturalis Principia Mathematica (Mathematical Principles of Natural Philosophy).

Newton's third law (for every action there is an equal and opposite reaction) is based on an interaction. Indeed, forces come about because of interactions: action, reaction. Newton's law suggests that the bird flapping its wings must be pushing down on an equal force of air in order for flight to occur. That is: action, reaction. Newton's law suggests that the force the ground applies to your bike tyre is equal to the force your bike tyre applies to the ground. Action and reaction. So, if creative writing is action, what then is the reaction?

Newton's first law (an object at rest stays at rest; an object in motion stays in motion at the same speed, and in the same direction, unless an external force is applied to it) suggests nothing changes unless an external, or what is sometimes referred to as 'unbalanced', force takes part. Could it be that in a pure, balanced, uninterrupted state, therefore, the action of creative writing requires an equal reaction from a readership or audience for movement to occur? I am of course stretching the Newtonian principles and their application here; and I am not defining what this 'movement' might be. Equally, Newton's first law is often referred to as the 'law of inertia', which is hardly a creative enterprise! But as a thought experiment: if the action of creative writing is matched equally by the reaction of reader/audience, is this not the most pure form of a Newtonian law? Producing, that is, an equality of forces that propels the entirety of the creative writing interaction forward? Such a suggestion would mean that:

- If the actions of creative writing could be defined according to their 'volume' or 'mass' and
- These actions could be considered comparatively so as to compare what the 'mass' would mean in a singular instance of composing (say in the composition of a single novel or poem or screenplay) and
- The individual reader's reaction was matched to the action of the mass, perhaps because of some quality or qualities in the mass, or what we might call the 'conditions of pair matching', then

- It could be determined by the creative writer what creative writing actions were needed then or in a similar circumstance to propel forward the creative writing interaction between the creative writer and their reader/audience.

Isaac Newton is responsible not only for his three physical laws, but also for the statements that 'I can calculate the motion of heavenly bodies but not the madness of people', along with the somewhat ironically tempered: 'tact is the art of making a point without making an enemy'. Newton believed the world would exist at least to 2060, which is somewhat comforting – though not entirely. As one of the world's greatest scientists, mathematicians and philosophers he also believed in, and wrote extensively about, alchemy. I am not making a point, merely offering an observation: action that is, in anticipation of reaction.

'Unconscionable Mystification'?: Rooms, spaces and the prose poem

Paul Hetherington and Cassandra Atherton

Since the 19th century, when a number of French writers – most conspicuously Charles Baudelaire and Arthur Rimbaud – introduced what we may think of as the modern prose poem into European literature, prose poetry has been part of a debate about the contemporary usefulness of existing literary modes and genres. While early French practitioners partly used the form to problematise traditional poetic prosody, once this aim was achieved prose poetry remained a significant contemporary literary form. In the context of contemporary developments in prose poetry, this article discusses John Frow's observations that texts are able to perform or modify a genre, or only partly fulfil generic expectations, or be comprised of more than one genre. It also discusses the authors' *Rooms and Spaces* project, which explores ways in which prose poetry may be considered 'poetic'; how it may be room-like and condensed; or open and highly suggestive (sometimes both at once); and how prose poetry is intertextual and polysemous. Prose poetry may be generically problematic but the authors suggest that this may make it an exemplary post-postmodern form; and that reading prose poetry may provide significant insights into how unstable genre boundaries really are.

1. The Uncertain Status of Prose Poetry

When, in a prose poem from his 'Mercian Hymns' sequence, one of Geoffrey Hill's (2009, 89) characters states 'Not strangeness, but strange likeness ... I am your staggeringly-gifted child', he might almost have been speaking about prose poetry itself. This is a form that is widely written, yet as a significant part of contemporary literature in English it exists in a kind of critical half-light – perhaps largely because it is 'strangely like' both poetry and prose without clearly being one or the other. Aware of this critical neglect, many prose poets have resorted to writing explicitly about the form, asserting in various works that '[a] prose poem should be as square as a Picasso pear' (Horvath 2009, 289); that '[p]rose-poetry is when a person behaves differently from what is considered normal' (Loydell 2009, 292); that '[w]e fill pre-existing forms and when we fill them we change them and are changed' (Bidart 2009, 296); and that '[t]he prose poem is not a real poem of course' (Jenkins 2009, 299). Such comments indicate that prose poets are often uncertain about how their works relate to established literary forms and genres.

Despite its mid-19th century origins in ground-breaking and acclaimed works by writers such as Charles Baudelaire (in a work variously referred to as *Petits Poèmes en prose* or *Le Spleen de Paris,* 1869), Arthur Rimbaud (in *Illuminations,* 1886) and the *Divagations* (1897; 'Wanderings') of Stéphane Mallarmé – not to mention the sometimes exquisite and generally nostalgic works of Aloysius Bertrand in *Gaspard de la nuit* (1842) – the prose poem has never been unequivocally accepted as a legitimate poetic form in English. In France the form has gained more widespread acceptance and Kevin Brophy (2002) discusses various reasons why English-language writers may be less enthusiastic than their French counterparts about it:

> For many English language poets free verse made room enough for the prosaic in poetry ... and at the same time drew prose closer to the poetic. Another suggestion has been that the prose poem might have been important in France where there was a more strict tradition of forms to rebel against. Anglo-American poetry was always less dominated and less restricted by rigid adherence to forms.

At a more general level there are various reasons and speculations advanced as to why prose poetry may be an oxymoronic phrase and George Barker (1985) concludes that prose poetry is no more than a kind of illusion or nonsensical creature, reports of which are to be treated with scepticism:

> Like the Loch Ness monster the prose poem is a creature of whose existence we have only very uncertain evidence. Sometimes it seems to appear, like a series of undulating coils, out of the dithyrambs of Walt Whitman; several French critics claim to have taken photographs of this extraordinary beast, and a great many American poets possess tape recordings of the rhapsodies it chants up from the depths of the liberated imagination. (1)

Yet, despite Barker's scepticism, it is not always precisely clear what makes poetry poetical – or, for that matter, prosaic – even where ancient canonical works are concerned. Andy Brown notes that '[p]rose poetry ... occurs in the early sacred texts of other cultures' and that '[a]ncient prose poetry also occurs in secular books', citing the *Pillow Book* of Sei Shonagan as an example of 'a list-like book akin to many present-day variations on the prose poem' (2012, 319). Emmylou Grosser comments that in studies of Biblical poetry there is contention about the matter, given that 'the ancient Hebrew poetic texts have been passed down to us in mostly unlineated form' (2013, 5):

> For those who view poetry as a kind of elevated style that is identifiable by the concentration of certain poetic features (most of which can also be found in prose), prose and poetry in the Bible are best viewed as the opposing ends of a continuum ... For those who argue that prose is best

contrasted with verse, which by definition is language set in lines, prose and verse are best viewed as distinct categories, whether the poetic lineation is obscure or obvious … (3)

This develops David Petersen's and Kent Harold Richards' view that 'Most contemporary interpreters of Hebrew literature agree that poetry and prose are on a continuum' (1992, 28) and provides, in analogical form, a nice summary of some key features of the contemporary debate about prose poetry. While most critics accept that prose may be 'poetic', in a general sense, only some agree that poems may be written in prose rather than in verse – even if that verse is so-called 'free verse'.

However, the more hardline position that defines poetry as clearly separable or distinct from prose begs as many questions as it appears to answer. Steven Monte (2002) sums this up as follows:

The most foolproof definition of prose poetry, 'poetry written in prose', sounds uncomfortably tautological. A glance at the French *poème en prose* clinches this reaction. The next best approach throws the question 'What is prose poetry?' back at the questioner – 'you tell me what "prose" is and what "poetry" is, and I will tell you what "prose poetry" is' – to make the point that the two terms that constitute 'prose poetry' are themselves difficult to define unambiguously. (2)

Following Monte, one may question whether what once looked like a clear distinction between two separate literary classifications holds true. In many cases when people talk of prose, they mean something like 'narrative prose fiction'. And when they talk of poetry they frequently mean something like 'condensed, highly suggestive and often imagistic writing composed of lines that do not run to the page's right hand margin' – or they mean verse rather than poetry and are invoking the notion that verse is identifiable by such characteristics as metre and rhyme, or other aspects of verse's formal patterning of language. Poetry and prose, as general terms, tend to defy precise definition if only because some prose works are indisputably 'poetic' and some poems tend to be prosaic. Indeed, in the first issue of *The Prose Poem: An International Journal*, editor Peter Johnson (1992, 6) posits, 'Just as black humor straddles the fine line between comedy and tragedy, so the prose poem plants one foot in prose, the other in poetry, both heels resting precariously on banana peels'.

To some extent, such issues may relate to how one understands genre. John Frow (2015) makes the point that genre classifications are often problematic, questioning whether:

texts in fact 'belong' to a genre, in a simple type/token relation (general form/particular instance), or should we posit some more complex relation, in which texts would 'perform' a genre, or modify it in 'using' it, or only partially realise a generic form, or would be composed of a mix of different genres? (11)

'UNCONSCIONABLE MYSTIFICATION'?: ROOMS, SPACES AND PROSE POEM

Frow also asks '[w]hat happens when genre frames change?' (2015, 11) and '[d]o texts have a definite and fixed structure?' (12). If the broad classifications we apparently summon up by the terms 'poetry' and 'prose' may not denote clearly definable literary forms – although various forms, such as narrative poetry or the novel, are usually assumed to be a category of either poetry or prose, but not both – and if the broad classifications we call 'poetry' and 'prose' are more elusive than we would often assume, then the prose poem may be a demonstration of how certain kinds of literary works are unclassifiable, or perhaps even extra-generic – in this case, both poetic and prosaic at once. To put this point another way, if prose poetry simultaneously draws on the literary techniques associated with a number of genres, does it make a claim to be a hybrid genre all of its own outside of the categories of 'poetry' and 'prose'; or, perhaps more accurately, is there a case for it to be considered a hybrid *kind* of work that is generically unstable?

Further, and more generally, prose poetry may demonstrate that prose and poetry are not to be understood as dualities, or in binary terms, even if we agree that they are different genres. Lewis Turco (2000) contends that:

> in the Western *Judeo-Christian tradition* there is ample precedent for writing any of the *genres* – song, *narrative poetry*, and *dramatic poetry*, in either of the *modes* – *prose* or *verse*; therefore, genres do not depend on the modes in which they are written. 'Verse', a mode, is not equivalent to 'poetry', a genre. To ask the question 'What is the difference between prose and poetry?' is to compare anchors with bullets. (4; emphasis original)

Prose poetry may well be a form that implicitly asserts, and reveals, significant continuities between poetry and prose that deserve further discussion, and may even suggest that poetry and prose are genres that always tend to bleed into one another. Kevin Brophy (2002) writes that:

> It is perhaps impossible to discuss the prose poem sensibly. If you move too far towards categorising the different forms it can take, you can end by defeating its defiant formlessness; and if you move down the path of pointing out its poetic strategies you re-align it with that form of poetry it is deliberately discarding.

Ali Smith (2014) extends this observation:

> Despite the fact that it is not at this time a politically-charged, inherently disruptive form, it retains its odour of paradox. Its facility for narrative play, and for play with language register, un-hierarchical patterns and unemphasised possibilities, its openness to 'unpoetic' language and language from a range of registers, are prospects that the form offers. (113)

If a hallmark of prose poetry is that it appears to encompass and amalgamate a wide variety of otherwise apparently separate forms, the prose poem's protean tendencies have been noted since its inception. For example, Marie Maclean (1988) observes that Baudelaire's prose poems 'include in perfect but minimal form the *Märchen* or wonder-tale, the *Sage* or anecdote, the fable, the allegory, the cautionary tale, the tale-telling contest, the short story, the dialogue, the novella, the narrated dream' (45). Edward Kaplan writes that 'Baudelaire ... tangles the web of dualistic categories as he formulates a confluence of opposites. Interpreters should preserve the genre's integrity by applying the chemist's notion of amalgam' (2009, 13).

It may be that when Kaplan, in discussing Baudelaire's work 'The Bad Glazier', mentions Baudelaire's 'unconscionable mystification' (2009, 45) he provides a phrase that can be applied to a consideration of the prose poem in general. And when Ali Smith writes that '[t]he prose poem provides a home of the sentence that refuses to make sense and the paragraph that refuses to progress ... continu[ing] to attach itself to the big and little mysteries of the world' (2014, 113), it is clear that she sees the form not simply as unorthodox, but as puzzling and shifting; and as defying clear categorisation. Nikki Santilli (2002), too, believes that the prose poem is impossible to pin down:

> In the paradoxical and unorthodox world of the prose poem, and despite being the literary genre most accommodating to the field of its own theorization, there can be no seminal text – of either a primary or secondary source. (18)

What, then, is prose poetry doing and is this at all clear to anyone? Why should a reader care? Is the category of prose poetry an 'unconscionable mystification' in generic terms? Does the prose poem still trouble critics because it challenges assumptions about what most of us mean when we speak of the poetic?

2. The *Rooms and Spaces* Project

Our collaborative project, *Rooms and Spaces: the Still Movement of Prose Poetry*, was designed to explore the issues outlined above, along with a variety of related matters. Here is part of the project outline:

> The *Rooms and Spaces* project investigates
> (1) ways in which the significant literary form of prose poetry may be said to be 'poetic';
> (2) ways in which new prose poems about rooms and spaces by the project collaborators may exemplify how prose poetry may act as either, or both:
> (2.1) contained and restrictive 'rooms' that enable significant effects of poetic imagery and condensation
> (2.2) 'open' spaces that enable significant effects of poetic indeterminacy and a ramifying suggestiveness;
> (3) ways in which prose poetry employs intertextual references;
> (4) ways in which prose poetry may be a self-consciously literary form;
> ...

(7) ways in which prose poetry utilises poetic imagery, particularly visual imagery; along with lyric effects that suggest a sense of timelessness or stasis;

(8) … how prose poetry makes use of narrative effects that convey a sense of movement through time and history. (Hetherington and Atherton 2014)

Our investigation of these issues centres, in the first instance, on our own creative practice, contextualised by contemporary theories and approaches to the prose poem as a form. We wrote works for the project that address ideas of actual and metaphorical rooms and spaces. These works are 'poetic' in their intent (more on this below); are condensed and employ visual and other imagery; are suggestive and to some extent indeterminate; create effects of stasis and timelessness; and frequently, and in a fragmentary way, employ narrative modes familiar to readers of prose fiction, including continuous lines with no breaks. In writing and analysing our prose poems we are not trying to resolve all of the issues and contentions associated with prose poetry, but to illuminate key issues connected to current discussions about the form. It may well be that there is nothing final to say about prose poetry, but rather a number of provisional and indicative statements about how *some* prose poetry operates and what *some* of its main features are.

3. Four Prose Poems

Cassandra Atherton's work, 'A Room of One's Own', is a useful point of departure for our discussion. This prose poem is driven by a personal and to some extent idiosyncratic engagement with Virginia Woolf's famous extended essay of 1929:

> A Room of One's Own
> You weigh me down. Like stones in a coat pocket. Until my incandescence is stifled and my 'nugget of pure truth' is stripped back to a room in my grandparents' house in the suburbs where I once wrote poetry. The white desk is still there, pushed against the bay window. If I open the top drawer, I know that my old fountain pen will still be there. Bite marks on the lid from long days at school. The garish hippopotamus curtains are still too red. The carpet is more of an electric blue than I remember. A little fish of an idea becomes a cat without a tail. How do I write the space between my heart and my pen?

The poem takes the form of a personal meditation that develops Woolf's insight that 'a woman must have money and a room of her own if she is to write fiction' (1989, 4), incorporating allusions to her observation that thought may be like 'the sort of fish that a good fisherman puts back into the water' (5), her meditation on a 'cat without a tail' (11), and her reflection on the 'incandescent' (56) nature of an 'unimpeded' artist's mind (57). It also references Woolf's suicide and quotes her famous phrase 'a nugget of pure truth' (4).

In beginning with an address to an un-named other, the poem foregrounds the centrality of the point of view of its female speaker and the polarisation between the speaker and the 'other' who is addressed. Its confident, decided voice dramatises key aspects of Woolf's concerns in personal, closely situated terms, re-encoding Woolf's essay as a series of suggestive tropes and images rather than as an extended argument (as one finds in the original essay). Atherton's poem evokes a particular room and sense of creative and intimately-charged space through presenting selected and idiosyncratic details of the room the poem remembers – a white desk and a pen with bite marks on the lid, 'garish hippopotamus curtains' and an electric blue carpet. As the poem presents this powerful sense of an actual room, it invites the reader to consider the actuality (or otherwise) of their own creative spaces and associated relationships. More generally, the poem presents the idea that time, space and location are enmeshed in intricate ways that move in and out of one another; and in and out of the desire to make creative work.

Further, in invoking Woolf's concept of a room where creative thought may flourish freely, the poem establishes its own room as emblematic of all rooms where a woman's private creative life may thrive. Indeed, the poem's rectangular shape on the page is reminiscent – as are so many prose poems – of looking from above at a room's plan and being given access to part of that room's resonant multiplicities – particularly those that involve personal histories and activities. This is a charged and metaphorical view. Yet the poem also leaves a great deal unsaid. Nikki Santilli (2002) contends that:

> The way in which the prose poem achieves a high level of intelligibility within a minimal number of sentences is, I believe, made possible by the absences it accommodates. As a fragment, the individual prose piece is an inevitably elliptical text and always stands in relation to a larger absent whole that represents the sum of its unselected contexts. I give the term 'implied context' to this active space of signification. (22)

The implied context of Atherton's poem is, most obviously, the reading of Virginia Woolf's essay on which it partly and intertextually depends, but there is also a larger implied context that is constituted of the many narrative threads and other unstated observations that the poem does not explore or make. If we knew more about this poem's 'grandparents' house' and its 'suburbs', and more about its 'you' – or, for that matter, its narrator – we might have a short story or lyric essay instead of a prose poem, and we would very likely be provided with one of the key readerly satisfactions so often provided by such works – a sense of being sufficiently 'in the know' about a subject that we can imaginatively construct almost a whole world around its utterances.

In this case, however, Atherton deprives us of this satisfaction, insisting that we attend to the strangeness of the details she presents and the fragmentary nature of the scenes that her poem fleetingly conjures. We sense that a narrative resides in the work but cannot resolve its details or direction; we sense that there are statements being made that address quotidian reality but we can hardly grasp what that 'reality' might be; we are given a sense of the past but this primarily emphasises the current and continuing importance of the issues the poem raises. More generally, the concrete details that the poem provides and precisely renders function symbolically and emblematically to conjure a world which is irretrievably and timelessly bound to its own potent suggestiveness, contributing to a timeless lyric crystallisation of ideas and feelings in unparaphraseable form.

Prose poems of this kind inhabit an open space that begins where there is no particular beginning and concludes without resolving any particular narrative. They open questions and scenarios. This work demonstrates how prose poems so often create tropes of indeterminacy and ambiguity where structure and patterning of the kind employed by many lyric poems is present but subdued, and where narrative gestures are partial and fragmentary. The linguistic space of prose poetry tempers the features of traditional poetry and prose in order to conjure ramifying and verbally suggestive tropes where unfolding narratives are present but largely implicit, and the condensations of poetry are able to fall naturally into paragraphs rather than truncations of poetic lineation. In this way, prose poems frequently open up, TARDIS-like, to reveal much more than their actual size on the page would appear to allow. They are 'rooms' in which imaginative tropes, allusions and suggestive possibilities are coaxed into unusual, sometimes reactive proximities, so that a successful prose poem's combined suggestive power may far exceed the individual suggestiveness of any of its parts.

Further, the intertextuality of 'A Room of One's Own' suggests that the brevity and condensation of many prose poems allow their intertextual references to work in a relatively unhampered way (prose poems typically have relatively little verbiage and the verbal signs they carry frequently operate in an uncluttered manner, opening up associations with great facility and speed). Julia Kristeva (1984) comments on how intertextuality of this kind constitutes 'the *passage from one sign system to another*' (59) involving

> an altering of the thetic *position* … in language, for example, the passage may be made from narrative to text … The term *inter-textuality* denotes this transposition of one (or several) sign systems into another; but … we prefer the term *transposition* because it specifies that the passage from one signifying system to another demands a new articulation of the thetic – of enunciative and denotative positionality. (59–60; emphasis original)

In Atherton's poem the thetic position shifts and eddies, at one moment invoking Virginia Woolf's text, at another moment suggesting a fragmentary but unresolved narrative; at another time explicitly addressing the issue of a woman's creativity; and all the while rendering such linguistically polyvalent associations in lyrical-poetic terms. The polysemous nature of the work – Kristeva notes that 'polysemy can … be seen as the result of a semiotic polyvalence' (1984, 60) – derives partly from this prose poem's capacity to hold its various verbal signs and intertextual associations in a kind of suspension – to the extent that, in this case, we might imagine stretching the meaning of semiosis to conjure a viscous liquid containing a saturation of intermingling linguistic signs. Such a holding-back and offering up; such an admixing to produce a strange clarity; such a looking-forwards into poetry and a looking-backwards down the passages of prose, suggests that prose poetry may belong in the interstices between what we usually mean when we say 'poetry' or 'prose'.

Hetherington's 'Reading' is another intertextual work that juxtaposes the canonical texts *Little Dorrit* and *Lady Chatterley's Lover* to metaphorically mark the shift from childhood or pre-teen friendship to adolescent sexual awakening. This prose poem is concerned with being 'on the brink', a trope that self-reflexively references the hybridity of the genre itself:

> Reading
> Under the deck rolls of chicken wire were a nascent hen yard and spiders made home there. Sophie and I brought rugs and cushions, making it our own small habitat, cuddling and talking – at twelve that seemed perfect. Sometimes her cat passed us by and once a lizard watched us from a dry stone wall. During a staring summer she read *Little Dorrit* in clear, sensuous tones, halting at words she didn't understand. I scanned the dictionary as she spelled out each one. Two years later we kissed and clamped legs. 'I do, but I don't.' We read *Lady Chatterley*, touching hands.

If prose poetry can be said to exist on the border between prose and poetry, so this poem presents two teenagers teetering on the edge of new experience. The hen yard is, significantly, 'nascent' and Sophie reads in a 'clear, sensuous … halting' manner. The journey from innocence stops just shy of fulfilment or 'understanding'; everything, including the genre, is in a state of *becoming*. It is through the shared experiences of literature that Sophie and the narrator deepen their relationship and move towards an understanding of themselves and each other. This, in turn, frames the reader's experience and their relationship with the text. It demonstrates literature's ability to introduce new perspectives and fresh readings of the world in creative contexts, both real and imagined.

Using intertextual references and allusions in prose poetry adds to the genre's economy of expression and simultaneously allows for an 'opening out' of ideas when the reader's knowledge of an intertext comes into play. Literary allusions enrich the reading experience, allowing the reader to add or contribute to the text through their prior knowledge. A link is forged between the original text, the outside text, the reader's developing textual response and what Helen Gildfind defines as the author's own 'imaginative universe' (2011). The choice and use of intertexts allows for insight into the writer's internal libraries, webs, interests and imaginations. When an intertext is used, it is placed in a new context and thus, reframed and reworked, it grows in meaning. As mentioned above, prose poetry is markedly extended by its intertexts.

In 'Reading', Sophie's and the narrator's reading place is 'under the deck', a subversive and neglected space which becomes emblematic of teenage expression. For the duration of the prose poem, the space becomes their whole world and the site of their fumbling towards ecstasy. Indeed, their 'small habitat' is an allusion to the opening chapter of *Lady Chatterley's Lover* where D.H. Lawrence grapples with the future of humanity post-war: 'The cataclysm has happened, we are among the ruins, we start to build up new little habitats, to have new little hopes' (2008, 5). There is some resilience in the hopeful rebuilding that this quotation foregrounds, just as there is some hope for the narrator with Sophie.

They build their 'small habitat' with 'rugs and cushions', a comfortable, pleasurable hideaway where the cat passes by and their only witnesses are a Dickensian lizard and the personified summer, as it stretches out before them. Significantly, the lizard 'watche[s] from a dry stone wall'. It remains still in Hetherington's poem and yet 'pass[es] swiftly over rough stone walls' (1967, 2) in *Little Dorrit*. This subtlety prioritises stasis over movement. Sophie and the narrator are stuck in a moment with only hope to propel them forward. Like Dickens' extended play on 'staring' and the 'staring habit' in Marseilles – he writes that '[t]he universal stare made the eyes ache' (1) – Hetherington's 'staring summer' voyeuristically encourages the gaze. While Sophie and the narrator try to keep 'out of the stare' by cloistering themselves away in their own sort of pleasure dome, they cannot escape the lizard watching, the intense gaze of summer nor, self-reflexively, their reader's eye.

Sophie, like Constance Reid, the female protagonist of *Lady Chatterley's Lover*, is introduced to love affairs as a teenager, but Sophie is educated by reading about Connie's exploits rather than experiencing them herself. She lives vicariously through literature. As the prose poem depicts a life lived through or with literature, it emphasises that while Sophie may have moved beyond the child-like Amy Dorrit, she is not ready to align herself wholeheartedly with the sexually progressive Lady Chatterley. While she leaves the cerebral pursuit of words in the dictionary to experience the 'clamp' of her legs with the narrator's, their liaison ends with the chaste but intimate image of 'touching hands'. There is a suggestion, here, of anxiety concerning chastity, a theme referenced in both *Little Dorrit* and *Lady Chatterley's Lover*.

The clamping gesture and anxiety is reminiscent of the form of the prose poem with its tight rectangular appearance and compression. It looks like prose on the page – a seemingly innocuous paragraph – but the anxiety comes from realising it is something else. It masquerades as prose but its poetry is *strange* to the unsuspecting reader. In this way, the prose poem is both subversive and deceptive. Margueritte S. Murphy (1992) observes that:

> even the tamest prose poems disturb or startle us to some degree as they differentiate themselves from other prose genres, for the defeat of reader expectation seems integral to the genre. While the gesture to write poetry in prose no longer has the 'shock value' it once had, the prose poem is necessarily a genre in conflict with tradition, turning constantly against the prose genres it employs, vacillating between authoritative and marginal modes of prosaic discourse. (199)

Dominique Hecq (2009) contends that:

> [t]he prose poem as a subversive form … argues for the coexistence of simultaneous and heterogeneous spaces in the mode of (re)presentation

itself and, indirectly, for the reintegration of poetry into a larger spectrum of literary and extra-literary contexts. (4)

Prose poetry turns on an anxiety of space. Indeed, the prose poem's form could be defined as an instance of the Freudian *uncanny*: 'everything that was meant to remain secret and hidden has come out into the open' ([1919] 2003), 132). In this sense, what initially appears to be a paragraph of prose is, on a first reading, ousted as a prose poem. The moment the reader realises this, the experience of reading the text becomes unsettling because the familiar is made strange. Reader's expectations are disrupted when meanings are defamiliarised and Gerald Graff (1995) argues that:

> Defamiliarization may mean exploding all perceptual categories, including those inevitably left intact by the most uncompromising realism. This formalist strategy attempts to defamiliarize not in order to expose some truer reality behind the veil of customary perception but in order to dislodge from us the expectation that we can ever locate such a reality at all. (73)

The reading of the line 'I do, but I don't' is the central ambiguity of the piece. It is these equivocations that the unique form of the prose poem celebrates. This line could be spoken by either of the characters, given that it is not directly attributed to the narrator or to Sophie, and while the retrospective narration suggests that it is probably Sophie whose says this – given that the narrator seems readier for a sexual relationship – the prose poem allows for more possibilities. Written in first person narration, its use of 'I' is more closely associated with the narrator than Sophie and so the interpretation of the line becomes entangled in pronouns. Furthermore, as no-one verbally responds, which prevents the sentiment from becoming dialogue, the reader can question whether it was said or thought. While there may not be a sexual coupling there is a textual merging. As the narrator moves from consulting the dictionary to reading *Lady Chatterley's Lover* with Sophie, the pronouns 'I' and 'she' become 'we' in the final two lines. This suggests that it is through literature that these teenagers become one, just as in the prose poem, prose and poetry become one.

The prose poem is both direct and complex. Expressed in simple language and most often written in the familiar form of a compressed paragraph, prose poetry celebrates dichotomies. In this way, prose and poetry are roomed together in the paragraph and united. As Henry Hart writes, '[t]he prose poem ... stalks the border between genres like a double agent, disguising the identities of both by blending them' (1993, 100).

In Hetherington's 'Notebooks', another poem about reading, the unexpected is foregrounded in a daughter's post-mortem encounter with her mother's journals:

Notebooks
When she found her mother's notebooks in the shed in the back garden, their pages were stuck together with age and dirt; light had yellowed

'UNCONSCIONABLE MYSTIFICATION ?: ROOMS, SPACES AND PROSE POEM

> them, insects had mottled and eaten them. She threw them in the skip, along with so much desultory-looking furniture, not even bothering to prise the pages apart. What, after all, had her mother ever done? A few committees, work, those few friends she kept to herself. Some of the notebooks landed on the top of a writing desk. It seemed almost poignant – that they might lie for a few more hours where they were written. Days later, after the skip was gone, she regretted her casualness – two notebooks lay on the grass next to where the skip had been. She took them inside and a page fell open. 'And then to love in this way – it has been completely unexpected ...' She read every page, jemmying them apart with a knife, exposing pain and ardour. Her mother was a stranger. Her words were of someone else's life.

Over the course of this work, the familiar is made strange when, after reading 'every page' of her mother's remaining notebooks, she realises that her mother is 'a stranger' to her and '[h]er words were of someone else's life'. The limited third person narrative point of view is a metaphor for the daughter's limited view of her mother's life, understood in terms of '[a] few committees, work, those few friends ...' before her mother's writing exposes experiences to which her daughter was not privy. This is obvious from the 'closed' imagery and phrasing: 'pages stuck together'; 'not even bothering to prise the pages apart'; and 'jemmying them apart' – which is juxtaposed with the moment when 'a page fell open'. The words she reads point to her mother's attempt to express what had been astonishing, and perhaps even ineffable, paralleling her daughter's inability to express her emotions at finding her mother's secret life. Hetherington is making an important point about the public and private roles of women. Publicly, the mother has led an almost stereotypical life of unspecified and perhaps undervalued 'work' and domesticity but her writing desk and notebooks suggest a life less ordinary. Interestingly, her writing desk is found in the shed, a traditionally masculine space, which indicates her subversion of the traditionally 'feminine' domain. It is through writing that she finds liberation from circumscribed roles.

Susan Sontag wrote in her journal, published as *Reborn* (2008), that it is '[s]uperficial to understand the journal as just a receptacle for one's private, secret thoughts – like a confidante who is deaf, dumb and illiterate. In the journal I do not just express myself more openly than I could to any person; I create myself' (162). In this prose poem there is 'pain and ardour' in her mother's notebooks but more importantly, Hetherington demonstrates that she is 'creating' herself. It was in her private life that she was able to write herself into being.

In general, then, the prose poem is well suited to foregrounding identity-making and associated transformations in its subversion of the genres of 'poetry' and 'prose'. In its creation of a new genre that is at least two other genres at once, it emphasises the instability of what may otherwise look fixed and known, also emphasising what is fluid and coming-into-being. Jahan Ramazani observes that a 'genre's others are often multiple' (2012, 15) and prose poetry is the literary form that perhaps most persuasively suggests that genres – or at least the prose poem as genre – may be almost all 'other'. John Frow has observed that

> it seems to me important to stress the open-endedness of genres and the irreducibility of texts to a single interpretive framework. Derrida is right to distinguish between participation and belonging, and to argue that the 'participation' of texts in genres cannot mean a subsumption of the members of a class in the closed totality to which they belong. Texts work upon genres as much as they are shaped by them.... (2015, 30)

It may be true that prose poetry is a genre so actively worked-upon by the various texts that belong to it, that it is almost an entirely open form. Just as the creative space evoked by 'Notebooks' transgresses boundaries – the notebook becomes a great deal more than its lined paper pages – so the prose poem is so very much more than its lines of justified text.

Atherton's work 'To Die For' further exemplifies the way in which creative space in a prose poem may sometimes ramify in a variety of directions at once, artfully and subversively:

To Die For
He wanted me to take flowers to the hospital. But I thought it was tactless. He didn't seem to understand that she would have to spend the next six days watching them putrefy and die. She would smell moist Death creeping up the slimy stalks, turning the water a cloudy green. And she would have to pull the bedclothes over her head. Like the grandmother in Little Red Riding Hood. Petrified. Putrefied. She would have to ask the nurse to take them away. And the nurse would think she was ungrateful and tell her how lovely they were and how they brightened the room. And she would try to tell the nurse that Death didn't brighten a room, He only made her the femme fatale in a film noir. But the nurse would already be halfway out the door. And she would be left to wither in her private room.

As this poem meditates on the act of taking flowers to someone in hospital, it deconstructs a conventional gesture of comfort and solace for the sick and dying. Cut flowers become emblematic of death and the poem powerfully contrasts the difference in point of view between the poem's speaker and the 'he' who has advocated the gesture. As with Atherton's poem discussed earlier, 'A Room of One's Own', this sharp contrast between the narrator and another not only generates the poem's point of departure but is responsible for much of the oppositional verbal energy that follows; and, as with 'A Room of One's Own' the other in this poem represents conventionality and an impediment to a woman's free sense of being-in-the-world.

In this case, it is a hospitalised woman who will suffer because of convention, obliged to confront her own mortality in the sliming and withering of flowers, knowing that if she protests the nurse, like the 'he', will not understand. Although this poem is partly about Death, capitalised and personified as it is – the poem suggests that Death inhabits the withering flowers as dangerously as the wolf from Little Red Riding Hood; another example of a potent intertextual gesture – it is, crucially, also about a kind of decorum: the freedom not to be surrounded by conventional pieties and empty gestures, but to live with genuine 'tact'. This idea of tact (or, rather, tactlessness), introduced in the poem's second sentence, is central to the work and demonstrates how the condensed and ramifying suggestiveness of a prose poem is able to powerfully activate certain words and phrases. Here, a lack of tact is not only threatening and potentially deeply oppressive, but it has the capacity to generate death and unhappiness. The lack is identified with a failure to engage critically with experience.

The preponderance of short sentences in this work, studded with words that bloom darkly – 'putrefy', 'slimy', 'cloudy' and the like – have the effect, in a lateral way, of evoking the idea of a bunch of flowers (if the sentences are like stalks, many are conspicuously brightened or darkened by particular words and phrases), so that the poem, in suggesting the claustrophobia of a hospital room, also turns that room into a space that, in metaphorical terms, seems nearly as constricted as a vase. This is partly achieved by the overall terseness of the poem, and partly a result of imagery in which everything seems to contract or decay or be enclosed. There is not only slime and putrefaction at work, but a woman pulling bedclothes over her head, and a nurse 'halfway out the door'.

The effects are poetic, driven by suggestive imagery and the small speculative narrative the poem conveys that turns back on itself at the poem's conclusion as if there can be no escape. It is not so much that the woman cannot leave the room – although we are left in doubt as to whether she will – but that the room with flowers and its obdurate difficulties represent inescapable and implicit problems connected to values, judgement and even morality – that is, how we assess and make appropriate decisions and behaviour; how we understand the implications of what we do; and how we find an authentic basis for decision-making among the many conventional mores that surround us.

4. 'Unconscionable Mystification'?

Michael Delville writes:

> [i]t should now be apparent that what is at stake in the genre's multiple negotiations with literary and utilitarian discourses is the possibility of problematizing not only the nature and boundaries of poetic language but also its relevance or nonrelevance in other discursive domains. It is largely by carrying on this critical struggle with dominant aesthetic and cultural conventions that the prose poem has continued to preserve its potential for innovation. (1998, 250)

It may be that the prose poem in the 21st century will be one of the grounds for a further re-evaluation, and even disassembling, of conventional social and cultural mores. It may also be a significant ground for the re-evaluation, and even disassembling, of current literary genres, and for a reconsideration of whether many existing distinctions between poetry and prose are really very meaningful. It may be that poetic prose will constitute much of the best of what 21st-century poets have to offer – along with a 'free verse' that, although lineated, adopts many prosaic rhythms and cadences.

If poetry is no longer very often verse, in any meaningful sense of that word, and if the best literary prose may frequently be poetic, then the prose poem may indeed be one of the most potent models for what creative writers of all kinds will explore in the future. The form is Janus-faced, looking forwards and backwards, understanding transitions, providing passages and doorways. Space opens before and behind it, sometimes like closed rooms, sometimes like expanding fields. It understands both prose and poetry, and it comfortably inhabits the space between them. Its problematising of generic distinctions may be what makes it most modern (and postmodern) and which may see it become a defining post-postmodern literary form. And, in saying this, the form may not be an 'unconscionable mystification' after all. Instead, it may be a way through the quagmire of generic classifications that, a little like a literary wormhole, takes the reader into spaces that demonstrate, to borrow Frow's words, 'the irreducibility of texts to a single interpretive framework' (2015, 30).

Disclosure statement

No potential conflict of interest was reported by the authors.

Notes on contributors

Paul Hetherington is professor of writing at the University of Canberra and has published nine full-length collections of poetry, including the verse novel, *Blood and Old Belief* and *Six Different Windows*. He won the 2014 Western Australian Premier's Book Awards (poetry); was a finalist in the 2014 international *Aesthetica* Creative Writing Competition; was shortlisted for the 2013 Newcastle Poetry Prize and shortlisted for the 2013 Montreal International Poetry prize. In 2014 he was awarded an Australia Council for the Arts Literature Board Residency at the B.R. Whiting Studio in Rome. He edited the final three volumes of the National Library of Australia's *authoritative four-volume edition of the diaries of the artist Donald Friend. With Professor Jen Webb he is a founding editor of the international online journal* Axon: Creative Explorations.

Dr Cassandra Atherton is a senior lecturer in Literary Studies and Professional and Creative Writing at Deakin University, and an award-winning writer, academic and critic. She has been awarded a Harvard Visiting Scholar's position from August 2015–September 2016 and was a Visiting Fellow at Sophia University, Tokyo in 2014. She has published eight books (with two more in progress) and over the last three years has been invited to edit six special editions of leading refereed journals. She is the successful recipient of more than 15 national and international grants and teaching awards. She was a judge of the *Australian Book Review* Elizabeth Jolley Award in 2014 and was invited to judge the Victorian Premier's Literary Awards Prize for Poetry in 2015.

Correspondence

Any correspondence should be directed to Paul Hetherington, Faculty of Arts and Design, University of Canberra, ACT 2601 Australia (paul.hetherington@canberra.edu.au).

References

Barker, George. 1985. "The Jubjub Bird, or Some Remarks on the Prose Poem." In *The Jubjub Bird, or Some Remarks on the Prose Poem & a Little Honouring of Lionel Johnson*, edited by George Barker, 1–21. Warwick: Greville Press.

Bidart, Frank. 2009. "Borges and I." In *An Introduction to the Prose Poem*, edited by Brian Clements and Jamey Dunham, 296–298. Newtown, CT: Firewheel.

Brophy, Kevin. 2002. "The Prose Poem: A Short History, a Brief Reflection and a Dose of the Real Thing." *TEXT: Journal of Writing and Writing Courses* 6 (1). Accessed January 12, 2014. http://www.textjournal.com.au/april02/brophy.htm.

Brown, Andy. 2012. "The Emergent Prose Poem." In *A Companion to Poetic Genre*, edited by Eric Martiny, 318–329. West Sussex: John Wiley & Sons.

Delville, Michel. 1998. *The American Prose Poem: Poetic Form and the Boundaries of Genre*. Gainesville: University Press of Florida.

Dickens, Charles. 1967. *Little Dorrit*. London: Oxford University Press

Freud, Sigmund. [1919] 2003. "The Uncanny." In *The Uncanny*. Translated by D. Mclintock, edited by Sigmund Freud, 123–162. London: Penguin.

Frow, John. 2015. *Genre*. 2nd ed. Oxford: Routledge.

Gildfind, Helen. 2011. "Incarnadine Words and Incarnate Worlds." *TEXT: Journal of Writing and Writing Courses* 15 (1). Accessed February 5, 2015. http://www.textjournal.com.au/april11/gildfind_rev.htm.

Graff, Gerald. 1995. *Literature against Itself*. Chicago, IL: Ivan R. Dee.

Grosser, Emmylou J. 2013. "The Poetic Line as Part and Whole: A Perception-oriented Approach to Lineation of Poems in the Hebrew Bible." PhD diss., Hebrew and Semitic Studies, University of Wisconsin-Madison. Accessed January 12, 2015. http://www.academia.edu/3731763/DISSERTATION_The_poetic_line_as_part_and_whole_A_perception-oriented_approach_to_lineation_of_poems_in_the_Hebrew_Bible.

Hart, Henry. 1993. *Seamus Heaney: Poetry of Contrary Progressions*. New York: Syracuse University Press.

Hecq, Dominique. 2009. "The Borderlines of Poetry." Margins and Mainstreams: Refereed Conference Papers of the 14th Annual AAWP conference. Accessed February 5, 2015. http://d3n8a8pro7vhmx.cloudfront.net/theaawp/pages/84/attachments/original/1385080755/Hecq.pdf?1385080755.

Hetherington, Paul, and Atherton Cassardra. 2014. "Rooms and Spaces: The Still Movement of Prose Poetry." Unpublished mss.

Hill, Geoffrey. 2009. *Selected Poems*. New Haven, CT: Yale University Press.

Horvath, Brooke. 2009 "Definition." In *An Introduction to the Prose Poem*, edited by Brian Clements and Jamey Dunham, 289. Newtown, CT: Firewheel.

Jenkins, Louis. 2009. "The Prose Poem." In *An Introduction to the Prose Poem*, edited by Brian Clements and Jamey Dunham, 299. Newtown, CT: Firewheel.

Johnson, Peter. 1992. "Introduction." *The Prose Poem: An International Journal* 1. Providence: Providence College Press. Accessed January 24, 2015. http://digitalcommons.providence.edu/prosepoem/.

Kaplan, Edward K. 2009. *Baudelaire's Prose Poems: The Esthetic, the Ethical, and the Religious in* The Parisian Prowler. Athens: University of Georgia Press.

Kristeva, Julia. 1984. *Revolution in Poetic Language*. New York: Columbia University Press.

Lawrence, D. H. 2008. *Lady Chatterley's Lover*. Camberwell, VIC: Penguin.

Loydell, Rupert. 2009. "Towards a Definition." In *An Introduction to the Prose Poem*, edited by Brian Clements and Jamey Dunham, 292. Newtown, CT: Firewheel.

Maclean, Marie. 1988. *Narrative as Performance: The Baudelairean Experiment*. London: Routledge.

Monte, Steven. 2000. *Invisible Fences: Prose Poetry as a Genre in French and American Literature*. Lincoln: University of Nebraska Press.

Murphy, Margueritte S. 1992. *A Tradition of Subversion: The Prose Poem in English from Wilde to Ashbery*. Amherst: The University of Massachusetts Press.

Petersen, David L., and Kent Harold Richards. 1992. *Interpreting Hebrew Poetry*. Minneapolis, MN: Fortress.

Ramazani, Jahan. 2012. "'To Get the News From Poems': Poetry as Genre." In *A Companion to Poetic Genre*, edited by Eric Martiny, 3–16. West Sussex: John Wiley & Sons.

Santilli, Nikki. 2002. *Such Rare Citings: The Prose Poem in English Literature*. Cranbury, NJ: Associated University Presses.

Smith, Ali Jane 2014 "The Mongrel: Australian Prose Poetry." *Australian Poetry Journal* 4 (1): 7–14.

Sontag, Susan. 2008. *Reborn: Journals and Notebooks, 1947–1963*. New York: Farrar, Strauss and Giroux.

Turco, Lewis. 2000. *The Book of Forms: A Handbook of Poetics*. 3rd ed. Hanover, NH: University Press of New England.

Woolf, Virginia. 1989. *A Room of One's Own*. Orlando, FL: Harvest.

Thoughts are creative writing

In the philosophy of the mind a propositional attitude is a belief you bear toward a proposition. Propositions have truth value. They can be true or false. A thought is made up of a proposition and your propositional attitude toward it. Thoughts are mental states with content. They are distinguishable from perception and emotion. If we accept that most perception involves the senses and that emotions are connected to bodily reactions, thought then is a mental state that is most constructed, or orchestrated, and least physically attached. Thought becomes a composition, a composition of a creative kind, existing in the mind. Creative, in that it is combinatory, and fluidly so and in that it draws on individuality while assessing truth value and attempting to make sense. Written, in that a thought is inscribed in the mind in order to be available. Creative and written; so, in essence, a thought is a work of creative writing.

We could, by deductive reasoning focusing on the validity of the application of a thought, suggest that is impossible! That is, crazy thoughts, seemingly random thoughts, poorly formed thoughts, how would they fit this creative writing model? But recall, propositions have truth value, they are not all true, and a thought is made up of a proposition and your attitude toward it. So deductively whether what you are thinking is true or false, well made or badly made, does not determine whether it is a thought, and the composition of the thought does not undermine its identity.

A thought is creative writing because while it might be influenced by perception and impacted upon by emotion it is a mental state containing a proposition and your attitude toward it and it is presented in such a way to draw your attention to it and it is made, and thus created. Not all thoughts are original, nor is all creative writing. But all thoughts involve an ability, a process, a constructing, and thoughts show an ability to be more or less strong, more or less arresting, more or less satisfying, more or less entertaining, more or less informing. A thought is not like a constructed scientifically validated experiment or a methodologically sound social science exploration. It is more art than science, but it is not the image borne thing of the imagination. It is located in language and meaning. Not necessarily words, but certainly more words than non-words. And, like creative writing, not always unambiguous or direct or unequivocal – sometimes exploratory and speculative and investigative.

Thoughts are creative writing. And if all thoughts are creative writing, then creative writing is by logical conclusion the basis on which we live in, engage with, and aim to come to understand our experiences, things, our lives.

Dare I say, now there is a suggestion that really gets you thinking!

Graeme Harper

Screenwriting studies, screenwriting practice and the screenwriting manual

Craig Batty

ABSTRACT

The important roles played by screen creators, writers, showrunners, storyliners and script editors are increasingly acknowledged and celebrated by the academy. However, most current screenwriting research is about historical contexts, theoretical readings and ethnographic studies, rather than screenwriting practice. Such research has the potential to speak to practitioners, but it falls short of really connecting with those for whom screenwriting is a practice. The 'how to' books written by 'guru' authors are usually of more value to screenwriters, yet they sit uncomfortably in the academy and are seldom considered as research. As both an academic and a screenwriting author, I understand that critical texts serve a different purpose to those driven by craft, yet I also have a desire to be relevant to and have impact on creative practice. In this article I discuss how we might expand our understanding of 'screenwriting studies' to foreground concerns of practice. Screenwriting is an activity, not an end product, and I argue that we should both understand and offer insights for practicing the discipline. I draw on my own experiences to outline approaches I have used to frame my work as research that contributes knowledge and practice-based insights to the academy and beyond.

Introduction

We have experienced in the last decade what we might call a 'screenwriting turn', moving beyond a director-centric appraisal of screen works to an acknowledgement of the important roles played by creators, writers, showrunners, storyliners and script editors of these works. This is in part related to the work undertaken by the Screenwriting Research Network (SRN), whose annual conference and *Journal of Screenwriting* have shed significant light on the world of screenwriting. The turn is also in part related to the growth of screenwriting education across colleges, universities and film schools around the world, where students and teachers alike crave content relevant to their practice and are becoming interested in the potential offered by academic research.

Key books helping to define this screenwriting turn include *Screenwriting: History, Theory, and Practice* (Maras 2009), *The Screenplay: Authorship, Theory and Criticism* (Price 2010), *Analysing the Screenplay* (Nelmes 2010), *Movies That Move Us: Screenwriting and* the Power of the Protagonist's Journey (Batty 2011), The Psychology of Screenwriting: Theory and Practice (Lee 2013), Screenwriting Poetics and the Screen Idea (Macdonald 2013), Writing and Producing Television Drama in Denmark: From The Kingdom to The Killing (Redvall 2013), A History of the Screenplay (Price 2013), Screenwriting: Creative Labour and Professional Practice (Conor 2014) and Screenwriters and Screenwriting: Putting Practice into Context (Batty 2014). Along with scholarly articles found in publications such as the Journal of Screenwriting, Journal of Media Practice, New Writing: The International Journal for the Practice and Theory of Creative Writing, Media Education Research Journal and TEXT: Journal of Writing and Writing Courses, the presence of screenwriting in the academy is rapidly gaining strength.

Hundreds more screenwriting texts have been published since the invention of film, though they are almost exclusively 'how to' in nature. Screenwriting experts such as Syd Field (2003), Seger (1994), McKee (1999), Vogler (2007), Hauge (2011) and Aronson (2010) have all written internationally successful guides to the practice of screenwriting, aimed predominantly at the emerging screenwriter but also used frequently by experienced writers and screen development agencies. Even the BBC's ex-Controller of Drama Production and now Managing Director of Company Pictures, John Yorke, has joined this group of authors with his book, Into the Woods: A Five Act Journey into Story (2013). Many of these guides often come under suspicion in the academy, viewed by some academics as restrictive, content thin and serving capitalistic models of screen production. The majority of these guides also have a one-voice approach, where scholarship is limited and the author tends to advocate their methods of working only.

As an academic and screenwriting author, I find myself in an interesting predicament here. I understand that critical texts serve a different purpose to those that are craft-driven, but for a discipline whose central concern is practice (the screenwriter writes; screenplays are written for production) it feels like we might be missing something by undervaluing work intended to assist writing practice. This is especially potent at a time when the academy speaks so frequently about creative practice research[1], whose aim is not to theorise practice per se, but rather to interrogate and intellectualise it in order to generate knowledge about new ways that we can practice.

The limitations of current screenwriting research

In her keynote address at the 2014 SRN conference, Jill Nelmes reminded delegates of the 'increasing acceptance of the study of the screenplay as a form' (Nelmes 2014, 301). In part relating to her own edited collection, Analysing the Screenplay (Nelmes 2010), but also in relation to much of the work undertaken by members of the SRN, what is of interest to me is Nelmes' emphasis on the screenplay form (the text, the artefact) as opposed to the practice of screenwriting. The fact that a screenplay is written by a screenwriter perhaps assumes that practice has taken place, but the constant fascination with the screenplay form poses a common theme or issue within current screenwriting research: it is generally not about writing, but about the product of writing; and about how screenplays are consumed, critically in the academy and commercially by the industry, which can overlook the actual practice of writing. A comparison might be made here between literary studies and creative writing, which is something I will return to later.

Citing her own study of the screenplay as text and how this influenced the undertaking of two Master's degrees and a PhD, Claudia Sternberg writes that 'by 1992 I was adamant: the screenplay had to be read, it had to be read more, read critically and analytically, and read for what it was and what it did' (Sternberg 2014, 203). Sternberg is reflecting here on how she first came to screenwriting research then abandoned it, only to be reintroduced to it more recently, inspired by the growth of scholarship as outlined. She notes that current research seems to have developed a 'more sustained and diversified theorization under various framings, such as history, authorship, culture, philosophy and poetics' (Sternberg 2014, 203). From a creative practice point of view, we might pick up on authorship (writers) and poetics (craft) as two aspects that have industry 'concerns'. Yet we might also go as far as to say that the very terms *practice* and *industry* are missing from this list, and could/should be more fully embraced. Indeed, Sternberg acknowledges the existence of practice in current screenwriting research, but also that there is a need for more:

> The conversation between practitioners and academics, although not always without prejudice and contention, has also been sought and found by way of such networks [the SRN]. Practice-led or arts-based research as well as analytical insights of screenwriters into their practice offer additional pathways for future writers and researchers. (Sternberg 2014, 204)

There are two important things to note from this: first, the focus on screenwriters and their practice; second, and crucially, recognition that research can inform ('offer additional pathways') the work of future writers. It is in this connection between research and practice that I think interesting and productive bridges can be built between screenwriting research, screenwriting practice and mainstream practice-based discourse such as the screenwriting manual.

Nelmes laments the value of the screenwriting manual, not only for assisting practice but also for offering a space within which to reflect on practice. An example here might include screenwriters using the content of manuals to ask questions such as: is the screenplay working; how might it be improved; what have I achieved over the course of its development? On her own experiences of practice and research, Nelmes reflects:

> The best manuals, while being useful for a screenwriter, offered thoughtful analysis, though some were criticized or derided for capitalizing on the public interest in writing for the movies. Books such as William Goldman's *Adventures in the Screen Trade* (1984) were entertaining and informative, while Linda Seger's manuals offered constructive advice on script writing, as did Robert McKee's *Story* (1997). (Nelmes 2014, 304)

More broadly, celebrating the role of practice in the academy can offer interesting and original avenues for research, providing work that has the potential to speak to those outside of the academy as well as those within it. Sternberg writes: 'I continue to be excited by case studies based on untapped resources which bring to light lesser-known writers, screenplays and textual or personal relationships' (Sternberg 2014, 204). This is precisely the type of material that relates to practice and industry.

In my own edited collection, *Screenwriters and Screenwriting* (Batty 2014), this is exactly the discourse I wanted to offer readers. Examples include McAulay and the tumultuous development of his short film; Nash and her creative processes for developing feature films; and Liddy and the diverse experiences of debut feature film Irish screenwriters. There are some scholars who focus on screenwriting practice such as Kathryn Millard and Jule Selbo, both well known figures in screenwriting research who have strong experiences in industry (Millard in independent and essay filmmaking, Selbo in more mainstream screenwriting), and who write about practice from a 'known', reflective perspective. However, compared to the more highly developed area of creative writing research, there is still a severe lack of research that focuses on practice and the creative/professional work undertaken by screenwriters.

So what can creative writing teach us?

As Harper tells us, creative practice research generates its own 'site of knowledge' that is concerned with process and practice, not the 'post event' speculation of what we might call a 'studies' approach (literature, screen, for example) (Harper 2006, 3). Furthermore, creative practice research is concerned with:

> linking the individual (i.e. the understanding and approach of the individual writer) with the holistic (i.e. understanding of genre, form, convention, the market, the audience). There are similarities here between the post-event analysis of literature, film, theatre and other art forms, but the difference is plain enough: the critical understanding employed is used to assist the creative writer in the construction of a work at hand, and/or of their future work. (Harper 2007, 19)

It is on this basis that we might see a tension between 'how to' screenwriting manuals and 'screenwriting studies'.[2] The word 'studies', for example, could quite easily be understood as speaking only to an academic audience, just as 'how to' guides apparently speak only to practitioners. As Brien and Williamson argue,

> many [such concerns] are magnified when dealing with newer academic discipline areas such as the creative arts [... where] emergent research practice seeks to legitimise alternative forms of knowledge production that do not always sit comfortably alongside accepted norms of research. (Brien and Williamson 2009, 1–3)

Arguably, this is happening in screenwriting research: a clash between what is accepted and not accepted as research, and in some cases a strong difference of opinion between how academics and practitioner-academics value discourse that is aimed at practice-based, industry-focussed readers.

Anecdotally, a screenwriting colleague in Australia was advised by one of her PhD supervisors that referring to screenwriting manuals was not research – despite the PhD being about industry practices and discourses. Similarly, during the peer review of one of my earlier articles I was advised that referring to screenwriting 'gurus' such as Robert McKee and Christopher Vogler was not a legitimate form of research; I should instead draw from academic writing on narrative theory. The article was about how I had worked with a writer on developing a screenplay, driven by a thematic approach to structure; McKee and Vogler provided necessary context to what was not being written about (theme) in popular screenwriting discourse.

I certainly do not to want impose a wholesale view on screenwriting research. Clearly one has to consider the intentions of a researcher and the position from which they are writing – an academic who wants to be respected by screen studies scholars for advancing theoretical knowledge about the screenplay, for example. If, however, a researcher wants their work to have a wide audience and have impact on a community of creative practitioners, this context needs to be understood and valued accordingly.

All of this is to say that in the pursuit of a research activity that is outward facing and practice-based,[3] we could benefit from reconfiguring what we mean by screenwriting studies to set it apart from 'straight' screen studies. Screenwriting studies – or *screenwriting practice research* – could be thought of as being concerned with the act of writing and with creative process. Screenwriting is an activity[4] and so it becomes important to conduct research not just *about* practice, but also *for* practice. In this way, new knowledge is generated alongside and/or to influence new methods of practice, resulting in not just an *understanding* of the topic, but also *practical insights* about the topic that the screenwriter (or industry professional) can apply.

The core theme of this paper, then, is how we can better understand creative practice through an intellectual lens. This is similar to the approach offered by Jason Lee in his book, *The Psychology of Screenwriting: Theory and Practice*. For Lee, 'screenwriting studies is combined […] with more general writing studies, philosophy, film and literary studies, enhancing reflective creative thinking and practice' (Lee 2013, 2). Having set up this premise and having outlined the historical development and future potential of screenwriting research, the remainder of this article turns to a discussion of the screenwriting manual and how it might be valued as a legitimate form of research that has an impact on creative practice and its pedagogy. By drawing on my own experiences of writing screenwriting manuals, I argue that this type of discourse can and should be valued as an important type of research that benefits communities of practice outside of the academy as well as those within it.

The screenwriting manual as a genre

Bridget Conor's work on screenwriting as professional practice and creative labour is useful here, not only for understanding the genre of the screenwriting manual but also in enabling us to recognise the genre's potential as a site of research. By providing a critical reading of a variety of contemporary industry guides, Conor offers some very helpful definitions. For example, on a practical level

> the manuals represent a site of a particularly rigid and durable set of instructions and exhortations based on individualized discourse. They legitimate themselves by highlighting their universality and insider knowledge, and the careers they offer are based on singular, elite-oriented, and commercial values. (Conor 2012, 129)

They also offer 'the opportunity to dream up and invent one's own career and [provide] blueprints for doing so' (Conor 2012, 121).

Conor compares screenwriting manuals with management 'how to' guides, a genre whose fabric includes 'the expertise of the "guru" author; the proliferation of lists, steps, and rules; the use of self-help discourse drawing on the tropes of humanist psychology; and the discussion and deployment of creative labor in particular delimited ways' (Conor 2012, 125). In the context of creative labour and the new cultural economy, 'while screenwriting manuals offer endless treats and creative possibilities for budding or more established writers, they also exemplify what Lauren Berlant (2006) terms "cruel optimism" within neoliberal capitalism' (Conor 2012, 123). On a more theoretical level, 'how-to screenwriting manuals are key sites within which screenwriting labor is made utterly knowable and "do-able," and at one level, the texts proffer a singular address to writers as autonomous individuals' (Conor 2012, 127–8). They are arguably 'a sophisticated form of self-help', and for the individual writer specifically and screenwriting practice broadly, they function as 'precarious governmental tools that shape industries, practices, and subjects but in ambiguous and chaotic ways' (Conor 2012, 121).

Drawing on Caldwell's categories of production labour, Conor also considers how the manuals facilitate intra-group, inter-group and extra-group industrial relations, in the sense that they are read and understood by writers, producers, commissioners and other development and production personnel, as well as students and '"wannabe" writers' (Conor 2012, 123). Considering screenwriting manuals and other practice-focussed texts that I have written, this analysis helps to contextualise both the content and the register deployed. For example, I have a keenness for ideas to be useful to students and other emerging screenwriters, and at the same time for these concepts to also appeal to those working in industry. If we add another reader to this list, the academic researcher, then notions of content and register become even more complex. For example, one of the defining features of published research is the ability to situate ideas in their relevant contexts and provide traceable sources for others to follow up on via systematic referencing. This clearly allows intra-group facilitation – other researchers who know the rules of academic writing – yet it also potentially alienates inter- and extra-group readers who might not know how to navigate such a referencing system, let alone understand some of the language used.

To draw these ideas closer to the premise of this article, we might consider the 'once voice' approach that permeates most screenwriting manuals as problematic in terms of research. On the whole, screenwriting authors do not refer to those who have gone before them,[5] instead favouring their own ideas and models of practice in an attempt to be known as 'the one' whose screenwriting knowledge should be followed. From a research point of view, failing to refer to other authors/researchers is antithetic to academic protocol. That said, if the author of a manual refers explicitly to their experiences in the industry, and/or their experiences of teaching screenwriting, might we argue that in fact they are engaging in research – reflective practice, or even action research? These are accepted research methods used widely in educational, healthcare and creative practice research (see, for example, Moon 2004; Nelson 2013). Again comparing screenwriting manuals with management self-help texts, Conor notes that the discourse provided 'reflects Chiapello and Fairclough's (2002, 197) observation that [they] are "embedded in an actional sequence which potentially moves from acquiring knowledge to applying knowledge, from learning to doing"' (Conor 2012, 128). To this end, let us now consider an approach to understanding the content of screenwriting manuals and other practice-focussed texts as research.

Where can we find new knowledge in a screenwriting manual?

In trying to conceptualise the screenwriting manual as a research artefact, it is useful to turn to a definition of research. Let us take this example, from the Australian Research Council (ARC):

> Research is defined as the creation of new knowledge and/or the use of existing knowledge in a new and creative way so as to generate new concepts, methodologies and understandings.

This could include synthesis and analysis of previous research to the extent that it leads to new and creative outcomes. This definition of research is consistent with a broad notion of research and experimental development (R&D) as comprising of creative work undertaken on a systematic basis in order to increase the stock of knowledge, including knowledge of humanity, culture and society, and the use of this stock of knowledge to devise new applications. (Australian Research Council 2012)

I will come back to the idea of using existing knowledge to generate new concepts and understandings. Before doing so, let us also consider this additional interpretation of research, offered by Queensland University of Technology:

This definition of research encompasses pure and strategic basic research, applied research and experimental development. Applied research is original investigation undertaken to acquire new knowledge but directed towards a specific, practical aim or objective (including a client-driven purpose). (Queensland University of Technology 2014)

The point made here about applied research is important. All screenwriting manuals are written with a practical objective in mind: the writing of a new screenplay, and/or the improvement of screenwriting practice. Therefore, can we argue that there is a clear rationale for them to be understood as research? To go back to the ARC definition and its notion of an 'original investigation undertaken to acquire new knowledge', might we suggest that analysing a screenplay on the basis of existing knowledge – for example, to uncover how an aspect of craft is working or not – is a legitimate form of research? There is clearly some further unpacking needed here, such as what constitutes existing knowledge, how it needs to be presented as research, and what is meant by 'on a systematic basis'. Nevertheless, I suggest that in some cases the screenwriting manual (and other practice-based texts) can be recognised as research, and should be valued by the academy for the contribution it makes to creative practice.

Personal reflections on writing about screenwriting

My first opportunity to write a screenwriting manual came about by chance.[6] It was at a creative writing conference that I met Zara Waldeback, a fellow screenwriter and tutor who I knew from articles we had both written for *ScriptWriter* magazine. As usual we were the only two presenting on screenwriting, the other papers about prose and poetry. We were keen to work with each other in some capacity, and decided to approach the conference convenor, Graeme Harper, about the possibility of co-editing a special issue of a journal. Graeme offered us an opportunity we had never considered – to co-write a book. He had just launched the 'Approaches to Writing' series for Palgrave Macmillan and books on fiction and poetry were in the making. The missing title was screenwriting. We were interested and excited, and within a few months developed a proposal and secured the commission.

One of the core aspects of the series is that its books provide 'integrated creative and critical approaches to creative writing', enabling students and academics 'to develop both practical writing skills and a greater critical awareness of creative possibilities' (Palgrave Macmillan 2015). From the outset, then, it was clear this would be a screenwriting manual like no other: one clearly about practice, but that would also be underpinned by theories and ideas to illuminate and appraise practice, written primarily, though not exclusively, for an academic audience. This was suitable to us as authors, not only because we worked in universities but also because we had always been interested in 'going deeper' with our writing, as evidenced by some of our previous *ScriptWriter* magazine articles.

The resulting book, *Writing for the Screen: Creative and Critical Approaches* (Batty and Waldeback 2008), covers a range of expected craft topics – character, structure, genre, dialogue, visual storytelling, and so on – yet in ways that are arguably advanced for a screenwriting manual, and worthy of being considered as research. For example, in part two of the book, 'Speculations', we specifically draw on theoretical ideas from screen studies to better understand practice. Cases include genre theory, documentary and non-fiction storytelling, and ideas on the spectacle to understand visual storytelling.[7] Importantly, all of these approaches were repositioned from the perspective of the screenwriter in order to speak directly to practice. In this way we sought to repurpose screen scholarship in order to understand it in practice; as per the ARC's definition of research, what can be understood as research-led practice (see Smth and Dean 2009) within the broad domain of creative practice research. In some ways this type of work is clearly research in that it draws from critical writing and disseminates it in ways familiar to those in the academy. But I want to argue that we can go a step further in recognising it as research, by seeing the more practice-focussed discourse contained within this and other manuals as *containing* or *embodying* research.

First is the 'case study' material that is a hallmark of this and other screenwriting manuals. While in traditional research settings case studies are not always valued as research, if put into contexts that frame them as part of an existing discourse – such as having been written about in other manuals, and/or having been put into practice by screenwriters – surely this positions the case study as research. In other words, if the case study compares its subject matter to similar texts, or discusses it in relation to existing writing – in a screenwriting manual or otherwise – how can it not be research? Furthermore, if the case study offered is new, in the sense that nobody has read its subject matter in the same way, or that it is the first time the screenplay has been discussed in this way, this seems quite clearly to be research. Though the contexts and/or apparatus for reading might be specific to creative practice, is it any different from traditional textual analysis? Examples in *Writing for the Screen* include the story structure of *Misery* (1990), read via the eight-sequence approach (with references to Howard [2004] and Gulino [2004]); and a discussion of dialogue and authorship in the television series *Coronation Street* (1960–), with particular reference to screenwriter Jonathan Harvey.

Second is the way in which screenwriting authors routinely draw on their experiences of the industry and/or teaching. As a form of reflection used in much creative practice research, this type of writing involves the author-as-practitioner thinking deeply about where they have come from and what they have experienced, in this case with the intention of informing current and future screenwriters. Not all the manuals offer deep reflection, it must be noted, but sometimes they do. In *Writing for the Screen*, I drew on my experiences of working on an online, crowd-sourced (produced) screenplay, and the implications this might have for future screenwriting practice. Similarly, Zara reflected on her experiences of working collaboratively on an interactive stage-and-multimedia show for children, and how this provided the opportunity for expanding screenwriting craft. Much in the same way that educational and medical professionals reflect on their experiences to offer insights into practice, I argue that these examples operate similarly and are thus valid forms of research.

Valuing this type of work as research

Since *Writing for the Screen* I have authored and co-authored a variety of manuals and practice-focussed texts, alongside a range of academic articles and book chapters in which I explore how ideas and theories can have real world impact on practice and the industry. There have been times when it has been difficult to convince colleagues of the research value of some of my work, but in general I have been able to evidence my claims of advancing knowledge and practice. Certainly, writing articles such as this one also helps to articulate the research in such work, which I hope will also be useful to similar authors working in the academy.

At the same time, it is also true that working in a university and being part of a system that recognises and rewards research has influenced the way I write about screenwriting practice. Specifically, I have developed an approach to writing that ensures the work is understood as research; and in actual fact, this is a register I feel comfortable with, especially as it is a more 'academic' audience (meaning not only students, educators and researcher, but also those in industry seeking new and deep ideas) that I increasingly wish to relate to. In this approach I purposely speak of the work of those who have gone before me (screenwriters, screenwriting authors, creative practice researchers, and so on), not only because this is a strategic way of validating the work as research, but *crucially* also because I strongly believe in acknowledging where my ideas and practices have come from. If we expect those studying and working in the academy to read and view widely *and cite their sources*, then my screenwriting manuals and other practice-focussed texts must do the same.

In 2012 I co-published another manual, *The Creative Screenwriter: Exercises to Expand Your Craft*, with Zara Waldeback. This, however, deliberately did not contain contexts and sources because we wanted it to be accessible to a very wide readership, and for it to be used by working and emerging screenwriters, and those working in development roles that need resources to work with their writers. In this case, then, the work was not framed as or argued to be research. It was, however, later recognised as contributing to research in a different way, as part of a portfolio.

Specifically in the context of the Australian system for assessing research performance, Excellence in Research for Australia (ERA), the portfolio approach to research is one way of gathering outputs that individually do not constitute research, but that collectively do. Examples of non-traditional research output portfolios at my university include in-depth reviews and industry articles written over a sustained period of time, and themed feature articles published in a series of journalism outlets.[8] I was able to package together a portfolio of works that explored and responded to the pedagogy of screenwriting. The portfolio contained *The Creative Screenwriter*, one book chapter and two articles from an education-focussed magazine, and a short narrative framing the ways in which I had researched and disseminated ideas about screenwriting pedagogy. Supporting evidence for these claims was also provided, including adoption of *The Creative Screenwriter* internationally and the fact that the magazine articles were invited contributions based on previous work.

Although the portfolio approach is not as cut-and-dried as arguing for the screenwriting manual as research, it demonstrates the potential for valuing the work of those who write about and for creative practice (and in this case, the pedagogy of creative practice). Such an approach can be viewed in a similar way to how Haseman (2006) describes the work of creative practice outputs, which make use of 'symbolic' data[9] to shape their form and content. In the case of *The Creative Screenwriter*, it may not be written academically but in the context of its complementary outputs that more clearly articulate research about screenwriting pedagogy, it can be seen as a work that 'performs' research through its structure, content, register and so on.

Conclusion

The academy has responded to the rise of creative practice research by valuing methodological approaches, writing styles, and the research artefacts themselves. The screenwriting manual, I argue, sits somewhere between creative practice and more traditional research; and as I have posited, it can be valued as a research artefact that offers both new knowledge and news ways of practicing. The context within which such a work sits will always determine the extent to which it is recognised as research, as will its content and the practice-based communities that it draws upon. Nevertheless, to follow the increasing recognition and celebration of creative practice in the academy, I want to advocate for the screenwriting manual.

Such recognition might appease those working in the academy writing such texts, but more importantly it might also inspire others to write about practice in a similar way, improving the quality of screenwriting manuals and advancing the status of practice-focussed texts in the academy. If, in the contemporary academy, we are open to a more diverse understanding of what research might look like, the manual has clear potential to speak to and impact on a wide audience outside of the academy.

This approach can also inform and influence the work undertaken in the research degree, where having the confidence to argue for such work to be recognised as research might yield important disciplinary developments. Research degree supervision occupies a large portion of my current academic role, and it is by unpacking and re-defining research that I have become more confident in mentoring emerging researchers to find their own research methods and methodologies. In short, if the PhD is the ultimate space for innovation and risk taking (see Cherry and Higgs 2011), then where better to push the boundaries of what we conceive as research?

Notes

1. There are far too many books and papers on this topic to mention, but key texts include *Practice-led Research, Research-led Practice in the Creative Arts* (Smith and Dean 2009); *Practice as Research: Approaches to Creative Arts Enquiry* (Bolt and Barrett 2010); *Research Methods in Creative Writing* (Kroll and Harper 2012); and *Practice as Research in the Arts: Principles, Protocols, Pedagogies* (Nelson 2013).
2. Responding to the rise in screenwriting research, in 2013 Palgrave Macmillan established the book series, 'Studies in Screenwriting', steered by key members of the SRN.
3. This is assuming that readers of this journal are creative practice researchers, are supervising creative practice research projects, or are otherwise interested in how research can underpin the activities of creative practitioners.

4. Screenwriting is also a product if we think of it in terms of 'the screenwriting work of Author X' – their body of work. However, for this article I am focussing on screenwriting as a practice – as something undertaken, and therefore requiring certain types of research in order for the activity to happen and/or improve.
5. One notable example is Aristotle, who is referenced by many screenwriting authors. For more on this, see Brenes (2011; 2014).
6. Drawing on Joseph Campbell's work, however, it might be argued that this was anything but chance: rather, it was the result of previous publishing and networking, and two passionate screenwriting tutors craving more literature to draw from in teaching and research.
7. Anecdotally, this understanding of creative practice through a critical lens is one of the reasons why many universities have recommended the book on reading lists.
8. In the case of journalism, and in the right context, we can understand the activity of writing journalistically as a research practice.
9. For example, an artist may use specific colours to evoke a sense of something, the colours being symbolic data of what the research has revealed.

Disclosure statement

No potential conflict of interest was reported by the authors.

References

Aronson, L. 2010. *The 21st Century Screenplay: A Comprehensive Guide to Writing Tomorrow's Films*. Studio City, CA: Michael Wiese Productions.
Australian Research Council. 2012. Excellence in Research for Australia: national report. Available at: http://www.arc.gov.au/pdf/era12/report_2012/ARC_ERA12_Introduction.pdf [accessed April 7 2015].
Batty, C., and Z. Waldeback. 2008. *Writing for the Screen: Creative and Critical Approaches*. Basingstoke: Palgrave Macmillan.
Batty, C. 2011. *Movies That Move Us: Screenwriting and the Power of the Protagonist's Journey*. Basingstoke: Palgrave Macmillan.
Batty, C. 2014. *Screenwriters and Screenwriting: Putting Practice into Context*. Basingstoke: Palgrave Macmillan.
Bolt, B., and E. Barrett. 2010. *Practice as Research: Approaches to Creative Arts Enquiry*. London: I.B Tauris.
Brenes, C. S. 2011. "The Practical Value of Theory: Teaching Aristotle's *Poetics* to Screenwriters." *Communication and Society / Comunicación y Sociedad* 14 (1): 101–117.
Brenes, C. S. 2014. "Quoting and Misquoting Aristotle's *Poetics* in Recent Screenwriting Bibliography." *Communication and Society / Comunicación y Sociedad* 27 (2): 55–78.
Brien, D. L., and R. Williamson. 2009. "Supervising the Creative Arts Research Higher Degree: Towards Best Practice." *TEXT: Journal of Writing and Writing Courses* (Special Issue 6). Accessed August 19. 2011 available at: http://www.textjournal.com.au/speciss/issue6/content.htm.

Cherry, N., and J. Higgs. 2011. "Researching in Wicked Practice Spaces: Artistry as a Way of Researching the Unknown in Practice." In *Creative Spaces for Qualitative Researching: Living Research*, edited by Joy Higgs, Angie Titchen, Debbie Horsfall and Donna Bridges, 13–22. Rotterdam: Sense Publishers.

Conor, B. 2012. "Gurus and Oscar Winners: How-To Screenwriting Manuals in the New Cultural Economy." *Television & New Media* 15 (2): 121–138.

Conor, B. 2014. *Screenwriting: Creative Labour and Professional Practice*. Abingdon: Routledge.

Field, S. 2003. *The Definitive Guide to Screenwriting*. London: Ebury Press.

Gulino, P. J. 2004. *Screenwriting: The Sequence Approach*. New York: Continuum.

Harper, G. 2006. "Introduction." In *Teaching Creative Writing*, edited by Graeme Harper, 1–7. London: Continuum.

Harper, G. 2007. "Creative Writing Research Today." *Writing in Education* 43: 64–66.

Haseman, B. 2006. "A Manifesto for Performative Research." *Media International Australia, Incorporating Culture & Policy* 118: 98–106.

Hauge, M. 2011. *Writing Screenplays That Sell: The Complete Guide to Turning Story Concepts into Movie and Television Deals (20th anniversary edn)*. New York: Harper Collins.

Howard, D. 2004. *How to Build a Great Screenplay*. London: Souvenir Press.

Kroll, J., and G. Harper. 2012. *Research Methods in Creative Writing*. Basingstoke: Palgrave Macmillan.

Lee, J. 2013. *The Psychology of Screenwriting: Theory and Practice*. London: Bloomsbury.

Macdonald, I. M. 2013. *Screenwriting Poetics and the Screen Idea*. Basingstoke: Palgrave Macmillan.

Maras, S. 2009. *Screenwriting: History, Theory, and Practice*. London: Wallflower Press.

McKee, R. 1999. *Story: Substance, Structure, Style and the Principles of Screenwriting*. London: Methuen.

Moon, J. 2004. *A Handbook of Reflective and Experiential Learning: Theory and Practice*. Oxford: Routledge.

Nelmes, J., ed. 2010. *Analysing the Screenplay*. Abingdon: Routledge.

Nelmes, J. 2014. "Screenwriting Research: No longer a Lost Cause: A Keynote Presentation at the SRN Conference 2013." *Journal of Screenwriting* 5 (3): 301–311.

Nelson, R. 2013. *Practice as Research in the Arts: Principles, Protocols, Pedagogies, Resistances*. Basingstoke: Palgrave Macmillan.

Palgrave Macmillan 2015. Approaches to Writing. Accessed October 6, 2015. Available at: http://www.palgrave.com/series/Approaches-to-Writing/AW/.

Price, S. 2010. *The Screenplay: Authorship, Theory and Criticism*. Basingstoke: Palgrave Macmillan.

Price, S. 2013. *A History of the Screenplay*. Basingstoke: Palgrave Macmillan.

Queensland University of Technology. 2014. Higher Education Research Data Collection: specifications for the collection of 2013 data. Accessed April 7, 2015. Available at: http://www.research.qut.edu.au/data/downloads/herdc/2014HERDCSpecifications.pdf.

Redvall, E. N. 2013. *Writing and Producing Television Drama in Denmark: From The Kingdom to The Killing*. Basingstoke: Palgrave Macmillan.

Seger, L. 1994. *How To Make A Good Script Great*. New York: Henry Holt.

Smith, H., and R. T. Dean, eds. 2009. *Practice-led Research, Research-led Practice in the Creative Arts*. Edinburgh: Edinburgh University Press.

Sternberg, C. 2014. "Written to be Read: A Personal Reflection on Screenwriting Research, Then and Now." *Journal of Screenwriting* 5 (2): 199–208.

Vogler, C. 2007. *The Writer's Journey: Mythic Structure for Writers*. 3rd ed. Studio City, CA: Michael Wiese Productions.

Waldeback, Z., and C. Batty. 2012. *The Creative Screenwriter: Exercises to Expand Your Craft*. London: Bloomsbury.

Creative writing, as it happens: the case for unpredictability

Unpredictability is one of humankind's most treasured traits. We believe unpredictability to be the lifeblood of hope, the core of belief, the substance of our psyches, the unfulfilled potential that exists in each one of us. We therefore celebrate unpredictability as predictably as we seek it out. We want unpredictability to be a personal and communal trait that always measures us favourably against machines and against nature. Elements of the predictable (the cyclical, the quantifiable, the repetitive and the habitual) simply make machines and wild nature inhuman. To be human, alternatively, is to be unpredictable. It is in unpredictability that human love is thought to dwell, and in unpredictability where it thrives. The extraordinary strength of a love, the resilience of a love, the emerging love, born where it could not be expected to be found, the love between polar opposites, the love not unsettled by onerous circumstance, the love that overcomes distance or challenges time, the love that is uniquely, individually, idiosyncratically expressed. Our attraction to each of these is evidence of our belief in the importance and power of human unpredictability.

Nevertheless, while we clearly find unpredictability of enduring value we have spent a great deal of time endeavouring to negate it. In fact, we have codified our endeavours to remove unpredictability from our lives in centuries of laws and regulations that seek to limit unpredictability's legitimacy. We have grown increasingly to expect that our journeys from one place to another will take well-established routes, and that we will arrive at scheduled times. In education, we've come to believe that certain disciplines are necessary for a well-rounded understanding of the world and, indeed, all that lies in it and beyond it. In this there is a much vaunted prediction that each individual will be equipped with knowledge that allows them to become productive members of a society, and provide for their own success and well-being. In that way they will also contribute to the success and well-being of the communities in which they dwell. We have sought to make the weather predictable, through the application of empirical science; to increase the predictability of medical interventions to the point where many are all but guaranteed; and to create discernible patterns in markets for goods and services that allow industry to look ahead and markets, whether local, national or global, to speculate in order to maintain an economic dynamism, but only within a generally agreed tolerance, so that economic forces act in measured ways and results come in systemically understood patterns.

All this and more we have done in the name of promoting predictability and negating unpredictability. Yet still we dearly want unpredictability to exist. It is in this vein that we appreciate and encourage human creativity. It is why we speak enthusiastically and often about our imaginations. It is to unpredictability we are referring when we hope to find in ourselves and in others inspired ideas, originality and ingenuity.

When teaching creative writing the nurturing of inspiration, originality and ingenuity refers directly to the encouragement of unpredictability. If not yet explored formally to any productive extent, colloquial and anecdotal references to unpredictability are nevertheless common in creative writing teaching – times when a teacher relates a story of an unexpected moment of discovery in drafting, or suggests a student do something to 'stimulate your imagination'. Yet, despite a considerable enthusiasm for unpredictability, over a great deal of time and across cultures, and a casual and causal recognition of unpredictability within creative writing practices, we have yet to ensure that our belief in unpredictability, our long and indeed persistent reference to it, and our continued desire to embrace it as a fundamental part of our humanity is formally acknowledged in creative writing teaching and learning.

Is it that we are simply incapable of approaching a condition with which we have so much affinity? Is it that we would rather dismiss actions we find difficult to approach than attempt to understand them? Or is it that we are so disempowered within the institutions where we teach that we cannot formally embrace a trait we have so long valued and so enthusiastically treated as part of what it is to be human?

Recently, during a video conference in what has now been some years of such global discussions via the International Center for Creative Writing Research (ICCWR; www.iccwr.org), a question arose about the role of oral examinations in creative writing programmes. I pondered with colleagues, Dr. Robin Michel from Oakland University and Dr. Stephanie Vanderslice of the University of Central Arkansas, how oral examinations have played a part in graduate creative writer assessment. It was at that point, with thanks to those colleagues, that I began to wonder if we in creative writing academe have somehow let something come adrift. Worse, have we been complicit in pushing something aside, claiming that by doing so we were legitimising our teaching and research practices in a way that made us stronger, comparatively at least, in a higher education environment in which meaning is sometimes reduced to exposition without much regard for the value in narration, description and argumentation? That important something we have marooned in the name of disciplinary credibility is unpredictability.

At first unpredictability seems much like randomness, a kind of dangerous presence, an arrival unruly enough to unsettle the ease by which we make our way along a path through a forest, or the confidence with which we flick a light switch and expect light to flood in. At that point, unpredictability acts not as a thing of love but as a thing of fear. We desire the certain in those cases and, not finding it, blame unpredictability. We point to it to explain our inadequacies. We are lost because of unpredictability. We cannot see our way because of unpredictability. Unpredictability stands between us and our goals, our progress is impeded, we are identified as being less capable, liable to succumb to this mysterious maleficent fluidity. Because of impending unpredictability we narrow our vision, let go our sense of possibility and focus firmly on the immediately graspable. If at the point we are the same creature as the one who yearns for the extraordinary, the challenging, the unique we nevertheless subdue this in the interests of accessible clarity and, in doing so, we are rewarded by again seeing the path before us. We relax in witnessing the dark room become lit. But what have we lost in doing this?

The fact is, we appreciate human unpredictability as ardently as we appreciate human love. Like unpredictability, love too is something very few of us can completely define. We can suggest elements of it, and offer up evidence of its results. Pushed to put more substance in a definition we might describe love as a condition with a temporal shape, recalling its beginnings perhaps, its growth and sometimes its diminishing. Love in such a description consists of a recollection of sensations and ways of responding. But we struggle to find certainty in this and therefore to ground our definition. We baulk at something that is transcendent yet commonplace, sacrosanct yet imperfect, so individual yet often shared. Finally, unable to reach a definitive sense of what we're considering we decide to acknowledge love by referring to its opposite: hate, perhaps indifference, enmity, animosity, apathy. The contrary more easily defines the proposition. The source of a definition of love, its sense, is now merely and frighteningly deemed to be its opposite. The path is clear. The light is lit. But what have we set adrift by doing this? What is it of ourselves that is now marooned?

Consider therefore a creative writing pedagogy in which unpredictability cannot be acknowledged, not least because it cannot be understood or defined. It does not exist because while we will anecdotally accept it, even celebrate it, revealing as it does the creativity of the type of writing with which we're engaged, and thus suggesting the human worth of our work, we will not formalise unpredictability for fear that because we cannot define it then *ipso facto* we cannot defend it. In our classes we ask instead for critical explorations of the textually evident. We suggest that in this enterprise there will be revealed a kind of model of behaviour that, even if not simply manifest in the text, has been organised in the mind and the emotion that produced that text. We simply define unpredictability, and all that it brings, according to its opposite. In this way we have, in a phrase, sighted the path, and merely need to share our vision of it to connect all around us to it. That is the switch we can flick. The light comes on. Unpredictability cannot exist in such a pedagogy because it cannot be explained; even if it can be shown in the personal narrative, the description, the argumentation, it is an antithetical mystery that we have no way of adequately formalising or even approaching.

At which point, in my thoughts, arrives a creative writing student's oral examination. Here we frequently find a creative writer exploring for her or his examiners how a piece of writing came about. Not in the vein of the explanation that has been manifest as written critical text, suggesting a modelling of behaviour that itself represents what some other disciplines in higher education call methodology. Rather, in the more open forum of conversation, also exploring elements of the imaginative, the creative, the fortuitous, the emotional, the personally contextual. In any written critical work that is present in the room these events could of course be hinted at. But in the fixity of the page, the discourse of the paper, the requirements of the exegesis, the comparative needs of a discipline holding its head up among other academic disciplines, these events are reduced to mere simulacra, a version of the predictable. However, what emerges in conversation, in the oral moment, is something else. It is both an exploration of unpredictability and it is unpredictability itself.

Not all creative writing assessment involves oral examinations. Globally we see variation across levels – so, oral examination sometimes at graduate level but not very often at undergraduate. Different types of examination occur also, some involving multiple conversational participants, Chairs of Committees, External Examiners, Internal Examiners, Mentors, Supervisors, some by regulation required to be silent (other than their potential subversive use of facial expressions, we could call these 'absent presences'), some part of a discussant 'team'. Here and there a student of creative writing might face an audience of their peers and in that oral experience wonder on the aural impact. That is: who is hearing what, and in what ways are they hearing it? Does the work on the page sound as it reads?

The ephemeral nature of the spoken, combined with various elements of the unscripted, makes the oral examination an active exploratory event. The student largely cannot determine what might be asked and the examiners, in whatever guise, cannot guarantee what might be offered in reply. The conversation is certainly posed but it is not predictable. This might not be a straightforward empowerment of inherent unpredictability, but it at least points toward our acknowledgement of its importance in creative writing. Ask how and when the unpredictable occurred and we get closer to the truth of what occurred in its entirety, off the page and on it. In this way oral examinations reveal much about creative writing that we will not otherwise capture, and thus not otherwise acknowledge, represent or examine in our work or the work of others.

Should we therefore not re-examine the use of oral examinations in creative writing programmes? Perhaps we should do this as a matter of urgency, if we truly seek to accurately understand what a creative writing student has achieved, what they have learnt. From there it might be this further consideration of oral examinations encourages us to consider other under-used pedagogical tools. Are there are other methods of accomplishing greater veracity in our work? In that vein, we might wonder why more use is not made of the metaphoric in the critical exploration of creative writing. By this I mean if we struggle to articulate that much vaunted existence of unpredictability, we might more successfully do so by shifting the plain of reference. In doing that we always open up the opportunity for bridging the intellectual and the imaginative, the critical and the creative. In metaphor explanation gains narrative depth, argumentation becomes multi-sided, description is imbued with the qualities of both the literal and the figurative. Metaphoric exploration potentially unearths cognitive processes that were, and are, at play but would not otherwise be unearthed.

And surely, too, this is not the end of the list of potential exploratory, investigative, communicative tools we have to use in our creative writing programmes – to inform our assessments of individual student successes, the extent of student learning. If unpredictability is so much at the heart of the human condition, there are almost certainly other actions we can take to better understand and share what is happening when we are writing creatively.

While we currently might celebrate unpredictability, while we might treat it as precious to us, while we have acknowledged that it is part of creative writing, we have not yet been brave enough to really defend it. For a discipline in which the emotional is so important how strange it is that on something as fundamental as this we cannot better express our feelings.

Graeme Harper

The writer and meta-knowledge about writing: threshold concepts in creative writing

Janelle Adsit

ABSTRACT
The threshold concept has become an important tool for scholarship on teaching and learning. This article proposes 12 threshold concepts for creative writing that emphasise aesthetic sensitivity, the diversity of the textual landscape, historical knowledge of craft traditions, and the complexities of the writing process.

Creative writing can be a transformative experience. Students leave the creative writing course with a sensitivity and critical perspective on the world of letters that they did not have before. But what provides this increased sensitivity, this new perspective? What lenses do creative writing students come to 'see through and see with'? To identify these lenses is to locate the threshold concepts that shape creative writing instruction.

The term 'threshold concept' came to prominence in Scholarship of Teaching and Learning (SoTL). Mobilised by researchers J. F. Meyer and Ray Land (2003), the term challenges disciplinary instruction to name the forms of meta-knowledge that a curriculum provides. Meyer and Land offer a set of characteristics that are definitive of threshold concepts, defining them as at once troublesome in that they are challenging to a learner's previous understandings and schemas; developmental in that they cannot be understood in a single moment, but come to be realised over a series of liminal stages; bounded in that they encapsulate and describe beliefs that are definitive of a field; integrative in that each bounded concept is linked in a web of other concepts that constitute a disciplinary framework; and irreversible once acquired – that is, they fundamentally transform a learner's practice, sense of themselves and the world, and/or way of being.

The idea of transformation is key. Learning means undergoing a change. In his book *What the Best College Teachers Do,* Ken Bain argues,

> learners must (1) face a situation in which their mental model will not work (that is, will not help them explain or do something); (2) care that it does not work strongly enough to stop and grapple with the issue at hand; and (3) be able to handle the emotional trauma that sometimes accompanies challenges to longstanding beliefs. (Bain 2004, 27–8)

How does this three-part process happen in creative writing, and what ideas or concepts prompt it?

Particularly in the last year, a range of disciplines have worked to identify the threshold concepts that are central to their curricula (Adler-Kassner and Wardle 2015; Bravender, McClure, and Schaub 2015; Clark 2015; Launius and Hassel 2015). In particular, the threshold concept is a tool that is getting considerable attention in writing studies, especially in conjunction with Writing about Writing approaches. Composition theorists Linda Adler-Kassner and Elizabeth Wardle's edited collection *Naming What We Know* was recently released in 2015, presenting a list of threshold concepts for writing studies developed by a group of 45 writing researchers from rhetoric and composition. The threshold concepts the group came up with include the following:

- Writing is a social and rhetorical activity.
- Writing is a knowledge-making activity.
- Writing addresses, invokes, and/or creates audiences.
- Writing mediates activity.
- Writing is not natural.
- Writing involves making ethical choices.
- Writing speaks to situations through recognisable forms.
- Writing is a way of enacting disciplinarity.

While many of these threshold concepts may apply to creative writing in part or in full, my purpose here is to propose a set of threshold concepts that are specific to the literary writing curriculum – to add to the conversation about what the creative writing curriculum stands for and aims to achieve. In proposing the set of concepts to follow, I offer a reframing of the Benchmark Statement for Creative Writing, developed in 2008 by the Higher Education Committee of the National Association of Writers in Education (NAWE), the national subject association for creative writing in the UK. A revision to the 2008 Benchmark Statement, a Quality Assurance Agency for Higher Education (QAA)-authorised Creative Writing Benchmark, was published last year. These 'benchmarks' are not framed in terms of threshold concepts; they instead propose learning outcomes. The threshold concepts suggested below are meant to be complementary to these benchmarks.

Threshold concepts in creative writing

The following is a list of threshold concepts that I make central to my own teaching. I list them here as a way of encouraging further conversation in creative writing about why and how the discipline offers a transformative education for a diverse body of learners. I present these concepts as at once reflective of trends in creative writing instruction and as anticipatory of what creative writing instruction is becoming. Such a list is inevitably incomplete, and I offer it here primarily as a means of prompting further conversation about the role threshold concepts might play in how we conceive our practice as writers and teachers.

Concept 1: attention

Creative writing involves specific modes of attention as writers learn to be close and critical observers of the world. Writers learn to account for the ethical considerations involved in perceiving and reinventing the world through their research and observation.

This threshold concept focuses on the place of research in creative writing. Research is about invention, about generating texts; it is also about examining the page against the world. The term 're-search', derived from a French term from the late sixteenth century, denotes the idea of looking intensively. Several books have been written on the subject of research in creative writing, including Jen Webb's *Researching Creative Writing*; Jeri Kroll and Graeme Harper's *Research Methods in Creative Writing*; the *Developing Qualitative Inquiry* series published by Routledge; and a range of books released by Sense Publishers in the Netherlands on poetic and narrative inquiry. Such texts, and the creative writing research methodologies they represent, constitute an important part of the creative writing curriculum, which stands to teach writers the importance of going outside of the self and one's received knowledges. Research can be undertaken for the purposes of gathering inspirations, authenticating details and memories, and generating unexpected connections.

Our students can sharpen their abilities to detect when a poem or story fits a predetermined expression that is problematic (e.g. reinforces a stereotype). They can learn to pay attention to these expressions – and the realities they construct or represent – in new ways. This work should permeate the curriculum – teaching students in workshop, in their readings, and in their invention exercises to address the propositions of a text, to be sceptical of 'what comes' to them. Discourses that are 'in the air' and then internalised have served to maintain interconnected forms of oppression. To perpetuate these received discourses may be to participate in injustice.

Concept 2: creativity

Writers benefit from a robust toolkit of applied theoretical frames and process heuristics for generating texts. Principles from creativity studies are useful for increasing the versatility of writers.

Learned flexibility in the composing process allows the writer to adjust to the demands of a particular text and improvise new techniques for invention when a 'block' presents itself. Students come to see the composing process as recursive and they learn to attend to the intentions they may have for a text in relation to what unintended elements emerge in the process of creation.

There are many ways this threshold concept may translate to praxis: students can keep a process journal and collect information about their own and other writers' processes along with writing prompts. This journal may be separate or integrated with a journal for collecting material for writing, inspirations, research, and information. Students may also be responsible for presenting new process ideas to the class. They can read findings from the psychology of creativity and become familiar with theories of the stages of creativity: how do the five stages of preparation, incubation, intimation, illumination, and verification translate to creative writing, for instance?

Borrowing from creativity studies and the psychology of creativity, I invite the students to run a number of experiments to see what fosters their own creative thinking. One assignment asks them to remove something that they are used to using, to figure out how to write without it. This might mean writing with their non-dominant hands, writing without a pen or pencil, or writing without the alphabet that they learned in grade school.

THE WRITER AND META-KNOWLEDGE ABOUT WRITING 51

We discuss what it means to create an environment for oneself that supports creativity, across different circumstances. We review Susan Straight's April 2014 *Los Angeles Times* article on learning to write without a room of one's own. We talk about what it takes for each of us to clear out time and space for our work, recognising how our circumstances differ. We share resources and strategies for doing this, and we talk about how we can support each other in this practice.

Concept 3: authorship

Writerly identity is constructed by a range of cultural forces. Cultural messages about the identity and lifestyle of the writer can be critically examined as we gain resources for building a writing life.

In the creative writing course, constructs of the writer and the writing life can usefully become an object of critique, analysis, and methods-based study. Students are most likely to fully engage with writing if they come to see themselves as writers, but this does not mean that they must adopt the role uncritically or without a complex understanding of what the subject position is and how it has been constructed.

To better understand the power of these constructs of the writer – and, in turn, the way they are located in networks of power – we need to ask a basic question: Just what is a writer? What assumptions have historically been embedded in the subject-position of the creative writer? How are the writer and the writerly life constructed through the discourses we've encountered in and out of the academy? What do we associate with the figure of the literary writer? What are the implications of our associations? How do these preconceptions about the writer translate to preconceptions about writing? How do our common conceptions influence us when we sit down to compose? What embodiments are associated with the figure of the writer, and who has been excluded from the subject-position? Who stands to lose and who stands to gain from the assumptions we've inherited about the writer and the writerly life? How can writers construct identities, professions, and lifestyles that support literary production across a range of material situations and positionalities, thereby challenging the ways that cultural ideas may seek to limit and exclude? The goal is to uncover presumptions that we might have, which might work against us in the writing process.

We attend to specific representations of the writer in popular culture and various media – such as films, television episodes, and books that portray writers as characters. We look at a series of Hollywood clips of films that present writer protagonists, such as *Dead Poets Society* (1989), *Poetic Justice* (1993), *Wonder Boys* (2000), *Finding Forrester* (2000), *Adaptation* (2002), *Midnight in Paris* (2011), *Ruby Sparks* (2012), *The Words* (2012), and *Perks of Being a Wallflower* (2012). What images of the writer circulate in popular media, such as films, mass-market creative writing advice books, and internet discourse? Constructs of the writer translate to messages about what it takes to belong to the literary community. Because these constructions of the writer come to signify belonging in this way, 'the writer', as a construct, is also a site of exclusion.

In exploring this threshold concept, we read Leslie Marmon Silko's 'Language and Literature from a Pueblo Indian's Perspective' (2004), and list some of the common Western assumptions about writers this essay addresses. Silko presents a picture of storytelling as 'a whole way of being'. In Silko's essay, stories are not owned by their tellers; they are co-created in a community and sustained by a community. Rather than conceiving of the author as originator and owner of a story, the storyteller in Pueblo culture has a responsibility to 'give away' and to share with the community. The storyteller gives a truth in the form of a narrative, and that story takes a life of its own, carried forward by the community. This counters colonial notions of the subject-who-knows (in this case the writer) as imparting truth to passive listeners. Silko offers a picture of storytelling as an invitation for co-creation of meaning. The ways that student-writers negotiate this reality belongs on the workshop table for discussion.

Concept 4: language

Language choices are bound to issues of power. Supporting a polylingual and multimodal literary community requires deliberate attention from writers, which manifests in each writing occasion.

Multilingualism can be an important value in a creative writing curriculum, as an intentional area of study. Creative writers should know language, as the material they work with, for the ways it is tied to identity, culture, history, and power.

With this threshold concept, student-writers can come to ask: How can we expand the possibilities of literary writing as we value multivocality? How can writers support linguistic diversity? And what are the risks and possibilities of writing in a language or vernacular that is not one's own? They can write with consciousness of colonial history - how colonialism has operated by erasing cultural languages and forcing the adoption of a dominant code.

Creative writing is a site where we can think about the words we use to talk about language-use. Anzaldúa 's 'How to Tame a Wild Tongue' provides a useful way forward in this discussion (2007). In this essay, Anzaldúa calls attention to the beliefs that surround language use: 'we speak *poor* Spanish'; 'we are told that our language is *wrong*'. I ask creative writing students to list on the board the phrases they've heard or used themselves to evaluate someone's language-use: 'her writing is *deficient*'; 'he needs to be in a *remedial* English class'; 'this writing needs to be "*cleaned up*"'; 'she is a *bad* writer'; 'his essay is *riddled* with errors – *horrible atrocities* of the language'; 'this is a *violation* of good speech'. I ask them: What do you associate with these words – 'poor', 'wrong', 'deficient', 'remedial', 'cleaned-up', etc.? In what other contexts are these words used? Do these words connect 'good speech' and 'good character'?

We note how in 'How to Tame a Wild Tongue', Anzaldúa code-switches and forces the English-speaking monolingual members of her audience to accommodate her tongue. Anzaldúa writes that 'as long as I have to accommodate the English speakers rather than having them accommodate me, my tongue will be illegitimate' (81). The essay's construction (e.g. its form, its use of language) supports her message. An analysis of this piece gives students in creative writing the opportunity to think about what it means for them to write with all the languages that create their histories and identities, and what it means to write their characters' relationships to language. The complexities of this terrain have always been present for the field of creative writing, even as many classroom conversations have skipped over this ground. It is ground that we need to honour with attention to how language moves, and how history conditions its movements.

Concept 5: genre

There are no universal standards for 'good writing'; however, there are conventions that are particular to established genres.

I often quote for my students Donald Murray's claim that in writing '[t]here are no rules, no absolutes, just alternatives' (2003, 6). Murray's claim introduces the idea of the convention - and the purposes that conventions serve in particular genres and writing situations.

The creative writing curriculum can expand the alternatives that are available to writers – and strengthen students' ability to evaluate these alternatives – by providing a window on the vast and ever-multiplying textual landscape, in all its diversity. At the same time, creative writing also teaches genre traditions and the histories that give rise to the genres we write within. The critical creative writing curriculum emphasises narratology and poetics in order to give students a sense of the lineages they join when they adopt the conventions of the minimalist short story or the lyric poem. This gives writers a better sense of what it means to adopt these conventions, what politics might be carried in the continuance of these conventions.

Concept 6: craft

Craft choices produce effects in the reading experience. While these effects cannot be entirely predicted, writers can weigh the risks and possibilities of each craft choice.

Writers can be equipped to analyse the craft choices they make and to anticipate the potential effects of these choices. Thinking in terms of what a craft choice (for example, the choice to begin a story with an alarm clock) may *risk* and what it *makes possible* shifts the conversation away from absolutist claims to what is 'right' or 'wrong' in literary craft. Thinking instead in terms of possibilities allows that a writer may find ways of making use of the risks of, for example, a cliché (as in the alarm clock example) to achieve an aesthetic intention (e.g. establishing the story as a parodic metanarrative). For example, repetition, as a craft choice, risks frustrating readers with redundancy. At the same time, repetition can be used to build motifs that accumulate layers of meaning. We look at how particular texts use repetition to create patterns and break them. When we analyse these patterns, we talk about the risks and possibilities of predictability – interrogating how established conventions may serve a story by locating it in a genre, by bringing a readership to it, by offering readers a particular type of satisfaction in being able to forecast what will occur in a plot line, etc. At the same time, predictability can bore. And predictable clichés or hackneyed language can bring with them associations that the writer would rather not have embedded in the text (for example, the poem that reminds readers of an advertising slogan that is irrelevant to its orientation). We talk about the common conventions of storytelling for instance, (e.g. inc ting incidents, dialogue attributions, consistency of point-of-view and tense, etc.) and the purposes these conventions serve for their readers. Through the framework of craft analysis, we learn that departures from convention should be purposeful – which means the writer must weigh the risks and possibilities of these choices.

Asking students to preface their work with critical and reflective writing promotes the metacognition and analysis necessary to the process of writing – the writer's evaluation of the moves a text can make, as that text comes into being. Students can be assessed for their growing abilities to identify, argue for, and enact craft choices that serve their emerging texts, aesthetic projects, and audiences. This aspect of the curriculum is significant preparation as it may provide the space for students to contribute to disciplinary knowledge about creative writing.

Concept 7: community

Writers are formed by the communities they engage. An analysis of craft must be grounded in an understanding of the varying orientations of readerships. Diverse audiences come to their texts with diverse needs.

This threshold concept is related to the craft analysis framework described above. To provide some guidelines for understanding the risks and possibilities of a text, writers think about the diverse needs of audiences.

In the process of composing a text, a writer may pose a series of questions to herself. Will this make sense? Would it help my reader to know this about the character in paragraph one? Will my audience read this passage as an allusion to the Cold War? Will my audience see this characterising detail as a racial marker? Have I assumed certain things about my characters' experiences based on their race, class, sexual orientation, etc., and how can I interrogate these assumptions? What authenticating details will members of my audience need to feel that this setting is real, given that some members of my audience live in this place? The creative writing class can refine students' ability to ask these types of questions and to think about their audience in complex ways, not allowing the literary audience to become monolithic.

In order for students to gain a broader understanding of audience and the potential use-values of imaginative texts, students can research a range of interpretive communities – to understand how various discourses and cultural forms are used and valued by diverse audiences. 'Who can access this text?' is a question I regularly pose to my students. They learn to not only question where and how the text circulates, but also to interrogate the assumptions of a text in order to answer this question.

Creative writing should exist to help students enter new readerships and interpretive communities with cultural sensitivity. Taking this as a learning outcome, the creative writing curriculum may provide space for community projects in which students interact directly with readers and fellow writers. Students can undertake service-learning projects such as helping teens at a rehabilitation facility produce zines, leading a journaling workshop, or hosting poetry slam competitions at a coffeehouse (See Coles 2011; Ann Thaxton 2014). Such projects should be undertaken with care and thorough consideration for the intended and unintended effects. Alternative assignments may be less intensive, with a reduced demand on community partners: an assignment could be as simple as writing a poem in chalk on an off-campus sidewalk and observing how people respond to it as they walk by.

This conception of writing moves away from the centrality of 'self-expression' and instead emphasises the co-constructed nature of texts, which are developed from a network of relations and intertextuality. Writers compose from what they've read and from what they understand of other writers and readers. Thus, a text cannot be divorced from the complex sociocultural and ecological communities that writing takes place within. These communities are not unified, homogeneous groups that exist prima facie for the writer to enter; rather, a writer's community may be constructed or met.

Concept 8: evaluation

Literary value is contingent. The evaluation of literature is shaped by cultural and historical forces.

Our responsibility as creative writing teachers is to help our students navigate the contingencies of literary value. Students can better understand how their writing may be used and valued in the world and that such evaluation is contingent (Herrnstein Smith 1988). The use-value of a text does not inhere in the text itself. Students in a critical creative writing classroom do not work toward meeting a universal standard of art, since any universal is but a privileging of one perspective. Rather, they uncover how literary values and expectations are produced. Features of good writing vary from one situation to another. These variations depend, for example, on where a work is located in literary history, how it calls upon certain traditions, and how readers come to the work. What is effective for one interpretive community will not necessarily work for another. Students in creative writing need tools with which to identify these variations as they pertain to the work they read and write.

Our reading and engagement with diverse aesthetics needs to be primary in creative writing pedagogy. This entails thoughtful and contextualised engagement with the Black Arts Movement, Créolité, Négritude, Kanaka Maoli, Nadaism, slam poetry, Ultraísmo, Pinoy poetics, the Misty Poets, Afro-Futurism, Chhayavaad, the Disability Poetics Movement and Crip poetry, and many other aesthetic traditions of written and oral literary forms, including postliterary poetries and micropoetries (Damon 2011). Students should work in written and oral modes, improvisational and occasional modes. Graduates of a creative writing programme should know the Dark Room Collective, El Teatro Campesino, and the Nuyorican Poets Café, as well as they know the New Formalists or the Imagists. Literary history is broad and multifaceted; it includes collectives, manifestos, and principles that emerge in different times and places. History conditions each of these emergences, and our students should write, read, and evaluate literature with a well-developed sense of this history.

Concept 9: representation

All forms of representation, including literary production, can be interrogated for assumptions, values, and ideologies.

Creative writing is a form of cultural production. It both reflects and stimulates culture. Our realities are constructed by common narratives. Narrative shapes our ways of knowing. How we represent something in narrative affects how that thing is known.

There are master narratives that dominate a social imaginary, as the ideological scripts that act upon us.[1] Master narratives tell us what is good, what is valuable, what is beautiful, what is right. They are contingent, they can be changed, but they are powerful forces that produce material effects. The fact that 'the socially dominant class has the final say in the designation of what is "real" (what "makes sense") and what is "non-real" (what is "non-sense") in a society' has everything to do with literary production and the workshop conversation, as Donald Morton and Mas'ud Zavarzadeh make clear in their essay 'The Cultural Politics of the Fiction Workshop' (1989, 157). The ideological scripts of the dominant class affect what is made legible in the workshop conversation, what is readable in a text.

Conscious of these ideological scripts and how they operate, the writer is faced with a decision: Do I write in a way that relies upon and reinforces master narratives? Or do I write to counter them? Writers are shaped by the cultures of which they are part, but they in turn can influence the culture. The creative writing class has a responsibility to take into account the effects of the cultural productions that we teach – those written by our students and those assigned on our syllabi. Student texts – along with the published texts that accompany them on the creative writing syllabus – can be analysed for the ideologies they represent. What cultural ideas does a particular text mobilise? What cultural assumptions does it call into question, and what assumptions or stereotypes does it rely upon? We can prompt our students to ask the following about their own texts and the published and peer-written texts they encounter:

- What common or established ideas does this text reinforce or destabilise?
- With every choice a writer makes, they forward an understanding of the world. How would you describe this text's understanding of the world?
- Whom or what is the text meant to speak for or about? What is centred and what is left to the margins of this text?
- How does the text represent its subjects? Are the representations potentially damaging, alienating, silencing, or oppressive?
- What are the potential ramifications of the text? Who or what stands to gain from the text? And who or what stands to lose or be lost? Whom or what does the text serve?
- What might this text do in the world? How might it change societal understandings, representations, or beliefs?
- What exigencies does the text call upon? What desires does this text seem motivated by?
- Has the text avoided oversimplification? Has the text done justice to the multivalent, complex, and diverse nature of human experience with regard to the issues it invokes?
- How might this text avoid locking down its representation, avoid allowing the text to 'stand in for' or reduce?

Students in creative writing come to understand how a literary text produces cultural meanings. Student-writers in the creative writing course learn to manage literature-as-representation with sensitivity, cultural competency, and critical awareness.

Concept 10: resistance

Literature can forward social change and the transformation of culture. Literary production is a unique means of putting the world into question.

Students can identify purposes for their work, recognising that literary texts can be a means of social change – even as their particular rhetoricity is different from explicit argumentation. Creative writing is an occasion to consider what it means to engage literature as a form of resistance. The creative writing course can explore the intersections of art and activism.

Art-as-critique can disrupt prevailing norms, can subvert knowledges of the status quo, and can produce new ways of thinking. Art gives us something to think with, as it also shapes our structures of feeling. And art indeed can intervene. Accepting that one may have a purpose for writing does not require that we surrender the value we place on uncertainty. Writing from a place of uncertainty allows us to go deeper into our purposes, to offer stories and poems that have more layers to excavate. We can invite our students into this work of delving into the political spheres that matter most to them – not to the exclusion of other forms and approaches to creative writing, but to acknowledge the significance of politicised literary production.

Concept 11: theory

Historical knowledge of aesthetic theories is important to the practice and craft of writing. Writers write within and against traditions, and thus benefit from a robust theoretical knowledgebase of cross-cultural artistic thought.

Creative writing is a discipline with a robust tradition of theory – written by writers, for writers. Students in a creative writing curriculum can become well-versed in these theories, gaining the language to describe, critically examine, and put into practice aesthetic concepts such as Langston Hughes's critical evaluations of how history and power relations shape the literary text, Nadine Gordimer's articulation of the relationship between literary production and responsibility, and many other concepts emerging from the aesthetic tradition. Examples of aesthetic theory address central questions regarding the relationship between literature and politics, between rhetoric and aesthetics.

The creative writing classroom is a place to examine how far theoretical concepts can take a writer, which forms of text-making these concepts describe or fail to describe. The creative writing classroom can be a place where the things we think we know about writing are re-evaluated and historicised.

Concept 12: revision

Writers learn to be responsive to what emerges in the process of creation, as they also bring comparative literary analysis to bear on their revision process.

A critical approach to revision dismantles assumptions about 'correcting' a text. It refuses to arrest the revision process into a list of dos and don'ts. We can put a diverse range of texts into conversation and ask what is possible.

In the workshop classes I teach, we complete a focused revision series in which students do a global revision of a single piece four or five times. With each iteration of the piece, they have to take a different approach. In the process of completing this assignment, they gain a toolkit for revision. I take a comparative approach to understanding revision. For example, when I teach story structure, the class period focuses on demonstrating that the Aristotelian plot arc is neither absolute nor neutral. I aim to help students gain a set of heuristics for thinking about how plots are constructed across varied literary works. I pair an Aristotelian theory of plot with a series of stories that in many ways defy the convention of the narrative arc: Alice Munro's 'Half a Grapefruit'; Jamaica Kincaid's 'The Letter from Home'; Lydia Davis's work; Joy Harjo 'The Deer Dancer'; and Ryunosuke Akutagawa's 'In a Grove', translated by Takashi Kojima. The class session includes an examination of Leslie Marmon Silko's theory of Pueblo storytelling as a web, and the students experiment with moving their story's central events to a diagram of a spider's web that has a pronounced internal spiral.

They can discuss the impact of different aesthetics by making revisions and back revisions across different conventions. The goal is to invite the complications and complexities of the creative process. As Davidson and Fraser note of the latter,

> Polished poems announce: 'Look at how pristine and complete I am. Just imagine what kind of genius could sit down and produce such a work of art.' ... we do well to remind our students to dwell within the messiness much longer than they might like. (2006, 24)

Conclusion

Creative writing courses can encourage metadiscursive critical thinking and self-reflexivity. Students can be asked to position themselves within theoretical debates that pertain to aesthetic production and to consider their positionality within literary spheres. Students can work to articulate the rationale behind their textual choices, accounting for the traditions they draw upon and the readerly experiences they seek to create. In identifying threshold concepts for creative writing, the curriculum can come to encourage meta-cognition that will transfer across a range of occasions for writing and perhaps help students make sense of rejection notes and the vagaries of the submission-for-publication process. These are some of the benefits of a curriculum that fosters awareness of the threshold concepts that shape its disciplinary assumptions. The threshold concept is a tool that at once brings clarity about the practice of a discipline and openness to the possibilities a discipline has yet to uncover.

Note

1. Toni Morrison, interview with Bill Moyers, *World of Ideas* television series (March of 1990). Quoted in Ileana Jiménez, *The Feminist Teacher: Educating for Equity and Justice* (April 13, 2014). https://feministteacher.com/2010/04/13/exposing-the-master-narrative-teaching-toni-morrisons-the-bluest-eye/

Disclosure statement

No potential conflict of interest was reported by the author.

References

Adler-Kassner, Linda, and Elizabeth Wardle. 2015. *Naming What We Know: Threshold Concepts of Writing Studies*. Boulder: University Press of Colorado.
Ann Thaxton, Terry. 2014. *Creative Writing in the Community: A Guide*. London: Bloomsbury.
Anzaldúa, Gloria. 2007. *Borderlands/La Frontera: The New Mestiza*. 3rd ed. San Francisco: Aunt Lute Books.
Bain, Ken. 2004. *What the Best College Teachers Do*. Cambridge, MA: Harvard University Press.

Bravender, Patricia, Hazel McClure, and Gayle Schaub. 2015. *Teaching Information Literacy Threshold Concepts: Lesson Plans for Librarians*. Washington, DC: American Library Association.

Clark, Timothy. 2015. *Ecocriticism on the Edge: The Anthropocene as a Threshold Concept*. New York: Bloomsbury Academic.

Coles, Katharine, ed. 2011. *Blueprints: Bringing Poetry Into Communities*. Salt Lake City: University of Utah Press.

Damon, Maria. 2011. *Postliterary America: From Bagel Shop Jazz to Micropoetries*. Iowa City: University of Iowa Press.

Davidson, Chad, and Gregory Fraser. 2006. "Poetry." In *Teaching Creative Writing*, edited by Graeme Harper, 21–33. New York: Continuum.

Herrnstein Smith, Barbara. 1988. *Contingencies of Value: Alternative Perspectives for Critical Theory*. Cambridge, MA: Harvard University Press.

Launius, Christie, and Holly Hassel. 2015. *Threshold Concepts in Women's and Gender Studies: Ways of Seeing, Thinking, and Knowing*. New York: Routledge.

Meyer, Jan H. F., and Ray Land. 2003. "Threshold Concepts and Troublesome Knowledge: Linkages to Ways of Thinking and Practising." ETL Project Occasional Report 4. http://www.etl.tla.ed.ac.uk/docs/ETLreport4.pdf.

Morton, Donald, and Mas'ud Zavarzadeh. 1989. "The Cultural Politics of the Fiction Workshop." *Cultural Critique* 11: 155–173.

Murray, Donald M. 2003. "Teach Writing as a Process Not Product." In *Cross-Talk in Comp Theory: A Reader*, 2nd ed., edited by Victor Villanueva, 3–7. Urbana, IL: NCTE.

Silko, Leslie Marmon. 2004. "Language and Literature from a Pueblo Indian Perspective." In *Contemporary Creative Nonfiction: I & Eye*, edited by Bich Minh Nguyen, and Porter Shreve, 179–185. New York: Pearson.

Flight

A commercial airliner lands, and is now taxiing down the runway. The voice of one of the flight attendants crackles over the public addresses:

'Welcome to … ' it announces, and then adds, 'The local time is … '

A curious moment, some of those wearing wristwatches adjusting them, some not, those without (who are in the majority) seemingly taking little notice of the announcement at all. Positioned between previous time and the announced new time, between unbounded time and the newly declared local time, there is a sudden realisation that for the entire flight we have been not only in spatial motion; we have also been in temporal motion—moving, it seems, not *with* time but *through* time.

Of course, most often we are practically fixed *in* time because of being fixed in place, or we are in forms of transportation that take long enough that our movement in time is also a movement with time. But flight, certainly modern airliner flight with its speeds commonly in the 500- and 600-mph range, effectively moves *through* time. In doing so we are temporally as well as temporarily released. For those who might one day travel in outer space, and *New Writing* readers can indeed be adventurous, that phenomenon will be further enhanced in that in Earth orbit time cannot be calibrated using the sun, so astronauts choose to use their launch location's time zone to keep track of the cycle of a day or night, not least in order to retain patterns of sleeping and eating. However, this is a choice, a conscious patterning; time, otherwise, is not fixed when you are in outer space.

A commercial airliner lands, and is now taxiing down the runway. The voice of one of the flight attendants crackles over the public addresses:

'Welcome to … ' it announces, and then adds, 'The local time is … '

At that moment, you realise we have been occupying a spatial and temporal through position. That through position is also the position your creative writing occupies. Creative writing moves across and among the structured, defined, formalised operations of written language and the fluid, metaphysical, networked operations of our imaginations. Each brings and conveys knowledge, and each provides an underpinning for our understandings. Commonsensically, other forms of writing also deal in structure and form. Because humans are naturally creative, other forms of writing are similarly not without their imaginative elements. But comparatively, it is the occupying of the through space, the through time, which is most distinctive to creative writing. Creative writing is in this sense a human practice in flight and via flight. It is certainly a flight from somewhere to somewhere, some time to some time, because our creative writing has a destination. That is, often we are seeking material outcomes, outcomes that emerge at a time and in a place. However, our creative writing—in the sense of the practice we are engaged in, not its destination—this practice exists in through time, in through space. Creative writing in that way is flight itself.

Operating between understandings, and borne on the back of a network of individual and group knowledge, creative writing requires critical methods of investigating it and discussing it that are equally comfortable and equally accurate in a temporal and spatial through position—that is, in flight. Much critical opinion has failed to engage with the through position of creative writing. Holist critical opinion has attempted to fix works of creative writing (and those creative writers who produce them) in historical periods, in social and cultural conditions. Holist here refers to methodological holism whereby analysis favours social phenomena and the influence of these macro elements on all things. Alternatively, individualist critical opinion, again largely focusing on reading back into our practice from completed and most often well-distributed final works, has endeavoured to ground the completed work or the creative writer in terms of individual actions, often attributing functional roles to those actions without acknowledging the fluidity of individual positions informed by phenomena that are evolutionary, if systemic, widely networked and connected, if also grounded in the singularity of a self. Neither methodological holism nor methodological individualism alone suffices to investigate and discuss creative writing, and certainly not to explain it. Creative writing is motion, and its through position is a network of macro and micro elements sparking off each other constantly. Effectively, in flight, flying, motion. Which is why the end results of our practices are alone not indications of this complex network of action and result, varieties of material evidence and thoughts, and feelings, facts, counter-facts, the real, the fantastical, the personal, the cultural and the social.

As we progress further in exploring creative writing as a practice, we will draw on a wider network of knowledge and understanding. We will do so because we have yet to reach adequate explanations of creative writing. We therefore seek to know more, to understand more thoroughly. We will do so in order to consider how the practice really occurs, what it produces in its entirety (both physical and metaphysical results), and how we might better understand the relationship between its through position, the ways we act in occupying that through position, and how we value the results of our undertaking creative writing. Creative writing is flight, and much as flight is remarkable, it too is comprehensible. Creative writing is flight.

Graeme Harper

Cognitive poetics and creative practice: beginning the conversation

Jeremy Scott

ABSTRACT
This article sits on the critical-creative boundary and draws upon aspects of the field of cognitive poetics – the principled study of what happens in the mind as readers read – to explore how an understanding of these processes might benefit the creative writer. The paper is pioneering in that it considers the implications of cognitive poetic approaches for the 'mechanics' of prose fiction explicitly in terms of creative practice rather than from the perspective of the stylistician or literary critic. It is in providing a principled and rigorous account of the way readers read that cognitive poetics has much to offer the writer. Indeed, the article will argue that writing and reading, rather than being separate activities, should be seen as interrelated positions along a cline.

If it can be agreed that creative practice benefits from engagement with theoretical perspectives, then one potential candidate for such a perspective is literary stylistics (Scott 2014[1]). To broaden this argument, it will be suggested here that the discipline's relatively recent 'cognitive turn' (cognitive stylistics, or *cognitive poetics*) and the resulting focus on processes of linguistic world-building and the mechanics of 'actualising' readings provide invaluable insights into what happens when readers read (Turner 1991, 1996). This assertion will be grounded first by a discussion of the interrelatedness of writing and reading processes from the cognitive perspective. Subsequently, *schema theory* and the concept of *deixis* will be used as examples of just two of the many potential intersections between cognitive poetics and creative practice. Finally, some suggestions will be provided for practical exploration of these intersections.

The cognitive linguist Keith Oatley (2003, 161–174) has coined a useful neologism which allows the critical and creative orientations of the act of writing to be viewed as interchangeable and conceptually identical. Oatley uses the term *writingandreading* to describe the way in which two activities, traditionally considered separate, are often intimately and inextricably bound together:

> 'Writingandreading' is not an English world. It should be. We tend to think of the two parts as separate. Pure writing is possible. One may just write an email, careless of syntax and spelling, then press a key, and off it goes into the ether. Pure reading is also possible: one can absorb, if that is an apt metaphor, the information in a newspaper article with almost no thought except what the writer has supplied. More usually we writeandread. As I write this chapter, I am also

COGNITIVE POETICS AND CREATIVE PRACTICE

reading it, and I will read it again, and re-write and re-read. Even in my first draft I have made four or five changes to the previous sentence, though only two (so far) to this one. ... A text is not autonomous. That is to say it does not stand alone: responsibility is distributed between writer and reader. (2003, 161)

There is more to this notion, though, than simply reading, editing and redrafting. Oatley refers here to an essential dichotomy which lies at the heart of creative writing and the worlds that it builds: between that which is *autonomous* and that which is *heteronomous* (Howarth 2012). If the former term can be used to categorise something that can be demonstrated to exist independently of perception, then the latter refers to that which is brought into existence and validated only by the presence of an observing consciousness (responsibility for the building of worlds is distributed between writer and reader).

Oatley's term 'writingandreading' highlights the essential interconnectedness of the sentences and the imaginary worlds that they build, in essence by treating the heteronomous worlds formed in the act of reading and the autonomous texts which give birth to them as equivalent and interchangeable. Creative writing as artefact, as typed or printed words on a page or screen, is autonomous. It has a physical, sensory presence as the reader turns its pages or, indeed, scrolls through it with a mouse or a fingertip. The worlds that it builds in the imagination are – at least intuitively – heteronomous. To put this as simply as possible, and at the risk of glibness: our thoughts do not just shape our world, they *are* our world. As cognitive poetics can demonstrate, this proposal is analogous to the ways in which imaginary worlds are built from linguistic prompts as well as the ways in which such worlds take on a powerful, resonant and affective existence in the imagination. It also raises various philosophical and ontological questions. In what sense is the felt experience of a story world different from the felt experience derived from the actual world? How is it that story worlds can take on an existence of their own? Most readers will have had the experience of being truly gripped, moved, gladdened or saddened by a poem or story; if the worlds that these texts create are 'unreal', then how do they both stimulate and simulate real emotional responses? (See Stockwell [2002, 171–3] and Oatley [1992, 18–20] for further discussion of this as well as some theoretical propositions in response to the question.)

So, creative practice at its most invigorating should involve becoming both writer and reader at the same time, through the processes of writingandreading, and an awareness of the needs and responsibilities of both agencies should be foregrounded. At the risk of stating the obvious: it is impossible to write without reading. Indeed, the interchangeability of writing and reading could be seen as part of a definition of *creative* writing, as opposed to what Oatley (2003, 161) characterises as 'pure' writing: when writing happens without any particular attention to style and structure, without revision, as would often (but not always) be the case in an informal and instrumental, information-imparting email. The act of creative writing is characterised, then, by the two activities being more integrated, or part and parcel of the same process. This assertion is given further strength by viewing the act of reading in terms of performance, as formulated by, among others, Iser (1980) through reception theory. Any text constructed from language is not, of course, simply 'received' in a passive sense by its reader (Jauss 1982), but is interpreted according to individual cultural contexts and lived experience. By including the element of performativity, the hybridity of the writingandreading process can be taken a step further. The heteronomous and autonomous aspects of the text come together and merge in the act of creative writingandreading, resulting in a hybrid account of creative practice that makes the heteronomous cognition of the created worlds inseparable from their creation through autonomous language.

One of the principal ways in which this element of performativity (on the 'reading' side of the cline) can be explained is through *schema theory*. Briefly: a schema (Bartlett 1932; Schank and Abelson 1977) is a cognitive framework that helps the participant in the discourse world (in the case of creative writing, the reader) to sort, organise and interpret incoming linguistic information by activating pre-existing 'mental baggage', often dependent on cultural context and background. For example, British and Irish readers will have a particular 'pub' schema which will be activated when processing that noun, calling to mind mental representations of a bar area, beer taps, glasses, customers, the smell of food, the hum of conversation and so on. Schemas allow shortcuts to be taken when interpreting the, often complex, linguistic information provided by the text. It is this facility in the mind of the reader that writers exploit through the use of linguistic cues from which readers subsequently build worlds; thus, from minimal linguistic input, a rich and complex text-world can be constructed cognitively through a combination of the 'top down' information stored in the relevant schema (say, the pub schema just mentioned) with 'bottom up' linguistic information from the text itself, which might impart more specific information building on the initial schema (the pub has a thatched roof and is next to a pond, for example). The reader's perception of the world built by a text is dependent upon the ways in which that reader's package of schemas is reinforced or challenged during the act of reading (Semino 1997, 119).

The ways in which a reader builds worlds in response to a piece of creative writing are also related to deictic function: that aspect of language which indicates the position of and relationships between objects (e.g. 'here', 'there', 'yesterday', 'now', 'up', 'down'). Cognitive approaches to discourse are based on the idea that mind and body are inextricably connected, and that the centre of perception in cognitive terms equates more or less neatly with the deictic centre, or *origo*. Evidence for this comes from language used to position the user in relation to the surrounding world, giving rise to a – often inescapable – sense of subjectivity. However, deixis is not limited to spatial descriptives, but can also refer to the position of objects and entities, and to perception, time and relation. It is the deictic aspect of language that allows readers to identify with the characters of a text, or, more specifically, to experience *empathy*. Stockwell (2002, 43) refers to this process as 'deictic projection'. In everyday discourse, language users are able to 'throw' their deictic centre (in a similar way to the way a ventriloquist throws his or her voice) to occupy an external position by saying, for example, 'Look behind you!' or 'It's to your right.' It is obviously desirable to shy away from making too many hard-and-fast pronouncements about what constitutes 'good' writing, but the creation (or simulation) of empathetic engagement might be a starting point for discussion[2] (see Keen [2010] for a principled account of its significance in the study of the novel). Obviously enough, readers are more likely to empathise with autonomous objects (such as fellow human beings) rather than heteronomous notions or concepts. Through its proposal that readers conceptually project to the contextual locus of the speaker of deictic cues in order to comprehend them, Deictic Shift Theory (e.g. Galbraith 1995) offers a model of how the deictic references determining contextual coordinates are processed by readers, how they render the deictic centre of the text autonomous (making 'concrete' the simulated actions, perceptions, experiences etc. of the narrator or character), and how this contributes to readers' conceptualisation of the world of the story. Deictic Shift Theory accounts for the psychological and physical processes whereby the reader's own deictic centre (both spatial and ontological) can be transposed to form an imaginative structure that is constructed both conceptually and orientationally. The reader's deictic centre, or origo, is then used within this imaginative structure for the purposes of orientation. Merleau-Ponty (1962, 112) called this process 'a summoning of the body's freedom from immediacy'. In creative practice, the writer should be mindful of levels of engagement, or freedom from immediacy, and where on the scale of empathetic engagement the reader will situate him- or herself in relation to the text through deictic shifting.

It is hoped, then, that this article might point the way towards a principled and rigorous reflection on creative practice based on some aspects of cognitive poetics. Given the myriad ways in which that discipline has shed revealing light on the imaginative processes involved in reading, it would be an insular writer indeed who refused to engage with critical theory that has so much to say about the target of their work. To reiterate: what is writing without reading? The summary and suggestions that follow, then, are intended to prompt further research, exploration and debate:

(1) Generally, and as an overarching ambition: setting the notion of writingandreading at the centre of the creative process (indeed, as a definition of *creative* writing), with a focus on the ways in which the autonomous features of language can transform into the heteronomous story worlds that inhabit readers' imaginations, alongside the fact that the acts of writing and reading can be viewed as interchangeable. In short, awareness of what happens when readers read should be a prominent factor in creative practice.
(2) Being mindful of the insights of schema theory, and the ways in which creative writing can reinforce, disrupt or modify schemas.
(3) Considering how Deictic Shift Theory and deictic projection (Stockwell 2002, 43) might account for the extent to which a reader empathises with characters and their situations. The appropriateness of the term 'empathy' in this context is also in need of more detailed consideration.
(4) Using schema theory to monitor the merits and contextual appropriateness of diegetically versus mimetically oriented narrative discourse ('showing' versus 'telling'), bearing in mind that the disruption and modification of schemas is one of the key processes that lends dynamism and momentum to narrative fiction.

This article could be read as an appeal to creative writers, particularly those who work in an academic context, to consider engaging with these principled critical approaches to linguistic world-building and the relationship between writing and reading. Even if the relevance of this framework is rejected, then it is hoped that some energy can be found in the disagreement. It is, of course, beyond the scope of this short article to go into sufficient depth and detail on the myriad concrete, practical applications of these concepts; in any case, as the title of this piece suggests, it is hoped that other writers and scholars will wish to formulate their own responses. However, for some more detailed discussion of these principles and suggestions for their application in the context of creative practice 'at the coalface', see Scott (2014, 2016).

To summarise the notion as far as possible, I would like to turn to Bertrand Russell:

We have a number of experiences which we call 'seeing the sun'; there is also, according to astronomy, a large lump of hot matter which is the sun. What is the relation of this lump to one of the occurrences called 'seeing the sun'? (2011, 117)

The 'lump of hot matter' is the artefact; 'seeing the sun' is its writingandreading. Both should sit firmly at the heart of the practice and meta-discourses of creative writing.

Practice

These suggestions for practice aim to stimulate creative exploration of cognitive approaches to the text, and to make awareness of these approaches an integral part of practice, rather than simply a tool to put to use in 'post-event' textual analysis. The first exercise explores the interconnectedness of writing and reading, whilst the second and third demonstrate the significance of schema theory and deixis

- Write a one-paragraph descriptive passage of prose based on one of the following prompts: a farm; a market square; a city coming to life in the morning; the take-off of a jumbo jet. Now rewrite the passage, removing *all* adjectives. What effect does this have in terms of the interaction between mimesis (or 'showing') and diegesis (or 'telling')? When you have considered this, take *one* (only one) of the adjectives previously removed, and put it back in. What changes about your piece? Why?
- Select a piece of creative work that describes something (either physical, like a landscape, or abstract, a mental state perhaps, or simply a point in time). Now identify the particular linguistic features that activate and/or rely upon particular schemas in the reader's mind. If possible, exchange the work with other readers and carry out the same approach, comparing and contrasting observations in order to highlight how different individual readings can be. In detail: which parts of the individual reader's schemas have been used to create different readings and interpretations? Which aspects of the text lead to different readings, and which to similar ones?
- Is it possible to conceive of a piece of creative writing which contains no deictic language? Try to write such a text. What is its status as fiction? What kinds of imaginary worlds does it build in the imagination?

Notes

1. See also Boulter (2007).
2. And yet: it is of course possible to envisage creative writing that draws its efficacy from a sense of *dis*-engagement and alienation.

Disclosure statement

No potential conflict of interest was reported by the author.

References

Bartlett, F. C. 1932. *Remembering: A Study in Experimental and Social Psychology*. Cambridge: Cambridge University Press.

Boulter, Amanda. 2007. *Writing Fiction: Creative and Critical Approaches*. Basingstoke: Palgrave Macmillan.

Galbraith, J. 1995. "Deictic Shift Theory and the Poetics of Involvement in Narrative." In *Deixis in Narrative: A Cognitive Science Perspective*, edited by J. F. Duchan, G. A. Bruder and L. E. Hewitt, 19–59. Hillsdale, NJ: Lawrence Erlbaum.

Howarth, P. 2012. "Autonomous and Heteronomous in Modernist Form: From Romantic Image to the New Modernist Studies." *Critical Quarterly* 54 (1): 71–80.

Iser, W. 1980. *The Act of Reading: a Theory of Aesthetic Response*. Baltimore: John Hopkins University Press.

Jauss, H.-R. 1982. *Towards an Aesthetic of Literary Reception*. Upper Saddle River, NJ: Prentice Hall.

Keen, S. 2010. *Empathy and the Novel*. New York: Oxford University Press.

Merleau-Ponty, M. 1962. *Phenomenology of Perception*. London: Routledge.

Oatley, K. 1992. *Best Laid Schemes: the Psychology of Emotions*. Cambridge: Cambridge University Press.

Oatley, K. 2003. "Writingandreading: the Future of Cognitive Poetics." In *Cognitive Poetics in Practice*, edited by J. Gavins and G. Steen, 161–174. London: Routledge.

Russell, B. 2011. *The Problems of Philosophy*. New York: Simon and Brown.

Schank, R. C., and R. P. Abelson. 1977. *Scripts, Plans, Goals, and Understanding*. Hillsdale, NJ: Lawrence Erlbaum Associates, Inc.

Scott, J. 2014. *Creative Writing and Stylistics*. Basingstoke: Palgrave Macmillan.

Scott, J. 2016. "Worlds From Words: Theories of World Building as Creative Writing Toolbox." In *World Building: Discourse in the Mind*, edited by J. Gavins and E. Lahey, 127–146. London: Bloomsbury.

Semino, E. 1997. *Language and World Creation in Poems and Other Texts*. London: Routledge.

Stockwell, P. 2002. *Cognitive Poetics: an Introduction*. London: Routledge.

Turner, M. 1991. *Reading Minds: The Study of English in the Age of Cognitive Science*. Princeton: Princeton University Press.

Turner, M. 1996. *The Literary Mind: The Origins of Thought and Language*. Oxford: Oxford University Press.

Structuring empathy

Does it come simply from understanding others or something more than this, the thing? You know, the thing? Where you read a poem or watch a film or hear the words of a song and it appears the writer of that work is speaking directly to you? Individually, specifically, to you.

Empathy is often considered to be core to successful creative writing. That is, empathy defined generally as the ability to understand the feelings, thoughts, experiences of others. But such a definition of empathy, applied to creative writing, must surely be inadequate. The idea of understanding others certainly seems valid – though works of creative do not always display understanding of their receiver. Writer and audience can at times be at odds on understanding but in tune, somehow, on the style, spectacle or mode of delivery. For example, a writer might present a political position in a creative work that is at odds with the politics of the reader but the genre of delivery may still be attractive, may still make the reader feel considered, included, referenced.

No, that thing many see as core to creative writing is not empathy. Not in the way empathy is ordinarily considered. Rather, it is a distinctive form of empathy we can call 'structured empathy'.

Structured empathy is empathy embodied in language and organised formally into a mode of communication that has dimensions. Creative writing, while clearly imaginative, is nevertheless constructed on principles of written communication. It is designed to be transferable; that is, to be made in such a way that even without the writer in the room while you are engaging with their work communication (both intellect and emotional) will take place. Empathy in the general sense will not alone function through creative writing. It is structure – or more accurately our 'structuring', as creative writers – that gives strength and depth and significance to the empathetic exchange.

What are the components, then, of structured empathy? Clearly these are: emotional revelation in transferable ways (the writer largely being absent, the writing having to communicate empathy through form as well as content); a combination of imbuement and exchange (so that the writing both represents and communicates feeling – one without the other falls flat); and the creating of a pattern of exchange, so that resonance and arrangement assist in displaying and communicating empathy.

Structured empathy, while seeming as an idea or term to say spontaneous empathic outbursts are less productive, really isn't making any claims to being superior to the general definition of empathy. Simply, structured empathy offers the possibility (and it is significant if this is *only* a possibility, though it might be much more) of empathy shared from one to many, from one time to another, from one location to another, from one instance to another. The structuring gives it transferability and, in our case, the writing (inscribing, making more permanent) creatively employs the imagination to make the empathetic exchange more complete. We thus structure empathy through creative writing in order to offer it more completely, more widely, from ourselves to sometimes an immeasurable number of other human beings.

Graeme Harper

Creative work as scholarly work

Nigel Krauth and Peter Nash

ABSTRACT

This article identifies the debate regarding differentiation between creative and exegetical (or scholarly) components in postgraduate research submissions and surveys the 2000-year history of creative-exegetical writing. It marks out a body of work where creative writers themselves explore and direct the theory and analysis of creative writing's processual activities, suggesting a hybrid form that constitutes a genre in itself – what we call the Creative-Exegetical. In conclusion, the article argues acceptance for the creative work as scholarly work in the creative writing research space. The trigger for this article was provided by Peter Nash, a student at Griffith University, Australia, who in 2018 thought to challenge the status quo by submitting a crime fiction story as a 'reflective essay' in an Honours-level research course. Pete had already published stories in *TEXT: Journal of Writing and Writing Courses* which were fictions dealing with aspects of the writing process, and he wanted to go further.

An introduction, which includes an historical survey of creative writing about creative writing recognisable as part of a creative-exegetical genre, along with examples where creative product and exegesis are indistinguishable

University creative writing schools in the United Kingdom, Australia and New Zealand recognise the requirement that a research degree submission comprises two components: a creative work and an exegesis. The creative component is submitted in a range of forms: novel, memoir, play, poetry, multimodal text, etc. The exegetical component is submitted as a scholarly commentary on the creative work to analyse the personal, social, historical, literary or industry contexts that influenced its making, or the practical and intellectual processes that informed its praxis, all of which seeks to demonstrate the value of the creative work as research in the university context.

The relationship between the creative and exegetical components in the research submission has been argued over the last 20 years (see, amongst many: Perry 1998; Kroll 1999; Brady 2000; Krauth 2002; Krauth 2011; Williams 2016; Cawood and Williams 2018), as has the perceived difference between these components and the potential that exists for them to be more closely allied by being, for example, plaited, woven or collaged together (Watkins and Krauth 2016; Williams 2016; Krauth 2018). The issue behind the debate about differentiation between creative work and exegetical work reflects the differentiation Aristotle made in the *Poetics* (c.335 BCE) and the *Rhetoric* (4th century BCE). As Wilbur Samuel Howell explained in 'Aristotle and Horace on Rhetoric and Poetics' (1968):

> so far as types of discourse are concerned, Aristotle's *Poetics* is a treatise on writings ordinarily allocated to departments of literature in the modern university, whereas his *Rhetoric* ... must be called [a treatise] on the writings studied in the modern university in departments of public address, history, philosophy, and the social and natural sciences. (Howell [1968] 2009, 328)

Howell elaborates:

> The *Poetics* ... discusses plot, character, thought, diction, melody, and spectacle. These six terms denote the six aspects of tragedy, and the first four of them are applicable as well to narrative poetry and the epic ... The doctrinal constituents of the theory of rhetorical discourse, on the other hand, are invention, arrangement, delivery, and style, as Aristotle himself specifies in the *Rhetoric*. (Howell [1968] 2009, 328–9)

Ways in which Aristotle's seemingly separate *Poetics* and *Rhetoric* in fact overlap have been analysed (see e.g. Howell [1968] 2009; Molette [1968] 2009; Hart 2018). Hart says:

> In *Poetics*, Aristotle discusses rhetorical tropes that poetry uses, and in *Rhetoric* he discusses the art of poetry in that text not only demonstrates the overlap between the worldly art of rhetoric and the otherworldly craft of poetry, but it also suggests that both rhetoric and poetics, the world and literature, can be other to each other in different contexts. In other words, rhetoric can be framed within poetry and poetry within rhetoric: rhetoric can be poetic, and poetry can be rhetoric while also being distinct and themselves. (Hart 2018, 5)

But, in the Creative Writing discipline, the creative component in the research submission has been approached almost exclusively as if it belonged to Aristotle's *Poetics* category, while the exegesis has been seen to be *Rhetoric*-oriented.

A discussion occurred recently between a supervisor and an Honours candidate in our school:

Candidate: I've been reading a lot about the non-traditional research degree submission in the Creative Writing field, and I'm wondering why I can't just hand in my creative piece as full requirement for the degree.

Supervisor: Well, there's a lot of history here. You should go back and read—

Candidate: Yes, but, I mean, what I want to do is a creative piece that includes all the exegetical stuff inside it. I want to write a detective story that performs the research I'm doing. I'm going to write creatively while at the same time writing exegetically ...

As you may guess, the conversation was between the authors of this article. Pete was determined to try his hand at calling the discipline's bluff, to see if a creative piece of writing could be at the same time a scholarly research essay. Nigel agreed to ride pillion.

Nigel has to confess, however, that in his article 'The Preface as Exegesis' (2002) he said:

> ... exegetical activity is a framing device positioned between the world created in the fiction (or play or poem) and the world the reader inhabits ... it involves a narrative voice obviously different from that employed in the creative text ... It is *a part* of the main work, but *apart* from it. (Krauth 2002)

Nigel asks his current Honours students to read his 2002 article. They say they find it helpful. Yet also, they question it; and he couldn't be happier. They query the need for

CREATIVE WORK AS SCHOLARLY WORK 71

two voices, especially if those two voices can be woven together in a blended submission. His answer currently is: Many features of the academic research landscape have changed since 2002, a key one being that we now *know* that writing creative products is authentic research as acknowledged by the Australian Research Council in the ERA 2009–2012 decision-making process,[1] albeit with the mandatory inclusion of the Research Statement which may be regarded as an academic footnote to the creative work (Australian Research Council 2017, 64). We have been free under ERA to check back and see just where over centuries legitimate research into creative writing practice was carried out.

Creative writing in English has had many innovators and analysts of practice who carried the field forward. Some analysed practice in *separate* critical works with voices different from their creative works (including Sir Philip Sidney, Ben Jonson, Samuel Taylor Coleridge, Edgar Allan Poe, EM Forster, TS Eliot, Virginia Woolf) while others provided equally significant exegetical analysis *inside* creative works couched in the voice and language of the creative work itself (including William Shakespeare, John Dryden, Alexander Pope, Lord Byron and Karl Shapiro). But something happened in the last 70 years to change the way we identify progress in understanding the nature of creative writing practice.

In the *Norton Anthology of Theory and Criticism* (2001), the editors say:

The enclosure of post-World War II theory in the university and its increased professionalization have meant that contemporary non-academic critics, literary journalists, *and writers* have been largely excluded from the theory canon – a trend slowly being reversed, we hope. (Leitch 2001, xxxvi, emphasis added)

They quote Jonathan Culler who wrote:

[F]ormerly the history of criticism was part of the history of literature (the story of changing conceptions of literature *advanced by great writers*), but ... now the history of literature is part of the history of criticism. (Culler 1988, 40, emphasis added)

The idea that the exegesis is a return to the profound history of creative writers *themselves* advancing the research and development agenda for literature is not often conceptualised in creative writing studies. A significant exception to this is Brian Dibble and Julienne van Loon's 'Writing Theory and/or Literary Theory' (2000):

The theory/practice schism is a relatively new development which has been most heavily underlined in the latter half of the twentieth century. Originally the two activities were conjoined: in addition to being a wide-ranging philosopher, Plato was a literary critic who also wrote dialogues, and Aristotle was the same ... An instructive quiz would be to ask people to define the following as literary critics or creative writers: Horace, Dante, Boccaccio, Ronsard, Sidney, Jonson, Dryden, Campion, Milton, Pope, Wordsworth, Coleridge, Shelley, Poe, Sainte-Beuve, Arnold, Hugo, Flaubert, Zola, James, Tolstoi, Conrad, Eliot, Pound, Ransom ... No one should fail the quiz, because all of those people were both writers and critics. (Dibble and van Loon 2000)

Thinking and writing exegetically and creatively *together* is not an upstart phenomenon recently manufactured in Creative Writing schools. It has been around since, at least, Plato's writings on writing (390–370 BCE) and those of the Roman poet Horace (65–68 BCE). Here follows a brief examination of creative-exegetical writing from the past. In these examples, the writers write in established creative forms while also writing about their creative practice and interrogating the forms and genres they write in.

Examples of poetry where creative product and exegesis are indistinguishable

Horace's *Ars Poetica* (c.19–10 BCE) is a 476-line poem written in Latin. It is couched in the form of a letter of advice to Roman senator Lucius Calpurnius Piso and his sons who were interested in writing poetry. Translations today typically reproduce this poem in prose, made to *look like* an essay, and editors talk about it as if it was intended only as a critique of others' poetry, and not as the poet's exegetical analysis of his own practice. Here is a section from early in the poem (translated into prose, unfortunately):

> Maxima pars vatum, pater et iuvenes patre digni,
> decipimur specie recti. brevis esse laboro,   25
> obscurus fio; sectantem levia nervi
> deficiunt animique; professus grandia turget;
> serpit humi tutus nimium timidusque procellae:
> qui variare cupit rem prodigialiter unam,
> delphinum silvis appingit, fluctibus aprum   30
> in vitium ducit culpae fuga …
>   Sumite materiam vestris, qui scribitis, aequam
> viribus et versate diu, quid ferre recusent,
> quid valeant umeri …   40
> (Horace 1936, 452)

Most of us poets – father and sons [i.e. addressed to Piso and his boys] – are deceived by appearances of correctness. I try to be concise, but I become obscure; my aim is smoothness, but sinews and spirit fail; professions of grandeur end in bombast; the over-cautious who fear the storm creep along the ground …

You writers must choose material equal to your powers. (Horace 2001, 124–5)

This is both good advice and very good exegetical self-scrutiny. Horace questions the poetic fashions of his times, but queries also his own ability to avoid obscurity, inelegance, and melodrama. He suggests that while a writer should take risks, they should also know their own limits. Later in the poem, he says:

> … non alius faceret meliora poemata: verum
> nil tanti est. ergo fungar vice cotis, acutum
> reddere quae ferrum valet, exsor ipsa secandi;   305
> munus et officium, nil scribens ipse, docebo,
> unde parentur opes, quid alat formetque poetam,
> quid deceat, quid non, quo virtus, quo ferat error.
>   Scribendi recte sapere est et principium et fons.
> (Horace 1936, 474, 476)

I could write as good poetry as any; but nothing is worth that price, and so I'll play the part of the whetstone, that can sharpen the knife though it can't itself cut. In other words, without writing myself, I will teach function and duty – where the poet's resources come from,

CREATIVE WORK AS SCHOLARLY WORK

73

what nurtures and forms him, what is proper and what not, in what directions excellence and error lead.

Wisdom is the starting-point and source of correct writing. (Horace 2001, 131)

Apart from expressing an admirable modesty, Horace here indicates the ultimate importance of conveying the results of analysing his practice – even to the point where teaching how to write, on the basis of his own insights, is potentially more important to him than writing itself. By couching his *Ars Poetica* Master Class in Creative Writing in the form of creative writing itself, he drew attention to the whole concept of the exegetical: the obvious choice of mode with which to deliver writerly wisdom gained from self-examination was the creative mode itself.

Horace's endorsement of the creative-exegetical form produced a significant line of influence. Subtending from him, in Shakespeare's time and after, when the dynamics of English creative writing began to be investigated and understood, writers interested in the creative-exegetical deferred to Horace particularly. John Dryden, Alexander Pope and Lord Byron are notable, as too more recently Archibald MacLeish (his 'Ars Poetica' published in 1926), Karl Shapiro (his 'Essay on Rime' in 1945), and Czeslaw Milosz (his 'Ars Poetica?' in 1968) (Shapiro 1945; MacLeish [1926] 2018; Milosz [1968] 2018). (For a detailed consideration of the many works in English which owed a debt to Horace, see Golden 2010. His account excludes many other exegetical poems which don't acknowledge Horace so explicitly.)

Alexander Pope's *An Essay on Criticism* (1711) is a 750-word poem entirely devoted to the crafts of writing and interpreting writing. As is mentioned in popular lore, the poem is the original source for several oft-repeated English language phrases: 'A little learning is a dangerous thing', 'Fools rush in where angels fear to tread', and 'To err is human, to forgive divine', among others. The point never made, however, is that these pieces of advice were originally delivered *specifically to writers*, in a poem which was specifically exegetical. For example, here is the original context for 'A little learning is a dangerous thing':

> A *little learning* is a dangerous thing;
> Drink deep, or taste not the Pierian spring:
> There shallow draughts intoxicate the brain,
> And drinking largely sobers us again.
> Fired at first sight with what the Muse imparts,
> In fearless youth we tempt the heights of arts,
> While from the bounded level of our mind,
> Short views we take, nor see the lengths behind,
> But, more advanced, behold with strange surprise
> New distant scenes of endless science rise! (Pope 2008, ll.215–24)

As Horace did, Pope warns immature writers against superficiality and the danger of not engaging fully – in perception and understanding – in pursuing one's practice. A writer should work to get beyond the idea of passionately whipping something off in order to further and deepen their vision, to achieve greater insight.

But also, Pope addresses critics and writers together, in the understanding that the exegetical is a process shared by both types of writing. That is, the writer needs to self-criticise, as too the critic. *An Essay on Criticism* starts:

> 'Tis hard to say, if greater want of skill
> Appear in writing or in judging ill;
> But, of the two, less dangerous is th' offence
> To tire our patience, than mislead our sense. (Pope 2008, ll.1–4)

Pope says that creative writers might bore us with bad writing – not such a dangerous thing. But critics can mislead us with dishonest or inauthentic interpretation of creative work – a greater ethical issue. Pope here undertakes an insightful analysis of the exegetical: he says that things that are wrong about how critics operate are also things that are wrong about how writers operate. When writers don't analyse their own practice personally, honestly and authentically, they replicate what critics do in misrepresenting them. The exegetical, according to Pope, draws together writing inspiration, writing output and writing self-analysis. Pope particularly draws attention to the idea that literary critics likely operate out of misunderstanding of the writing process as opposed to being representative of it.

From the 19th and 20th centuries, we can consider examples provided by British poet Lord Byron and American poet Karl Shapiro. These writers indicate the power of the creative-exegetical form Horace established, as too the longevity of problems faced in writing. Here is Byron's take on the *Ars Poetica* lines we considered above:

> The greater portion of the rhyming tribe
> (Give ear, my friend, for thou hast been a scribe)
> Are led astray by some peculiar lure.
> I labour to be brief – become obscure;
> One falls while following Elegance too fast;
> Another soars, inflated with Bombast;
> Too low a third crawls on, afraid to fly,
> He spins his subject to Satiety ...
>
> Dear Authors! suit your topics to your strength,
> And ponder well your subject, and its length;
> Nor lift your load, before you're quite aware
> What weight your shoulders will, or will not, bear. (Byron [1811] 2006)

Byron's poem, called 'Hints from Horace' (1811), performs more than 'hints': it tracks and translates Horace. But in the process, it nails more firmly the exegetical intention into the developing history of English writing. It repeatedly addresses contemporary authors, repeatedly provides insights gained by the poet in his own practice, and repeatedly it updates the poet's writerly insight into his literary world.

Karl Shapiro's 72-page long 'Essay on Rime' (1945) addresses a panoply of twentieth-century writing issues. It opens with these lines:

> This is a tract on the treble confusion
> In modern rime. The premise that our verse

CREATIVE WORK AS SCHOLARLY WORK   75

Is in decline has not, I am convinced,
Been honestly attacked or well defended.
Critics in particular have minced matters
By acquiring all the authority to talk ...
I think it is high time that everybody
With a true love of rime assert his views.

(Shapiro 1945, ll.1–6, 10–11, emphasis added)

Shapiro immediately points out the key issue addressed in this article: that critics and commentators have appropriated the authority to talk about writing theory thus disenfranchising writers themselves and separating the concept of writing about creative writing away from the genres of creative writing itself. Shapiro goes on to consider prosody, language and writerly commitment not only in poetry but also in prose, James Joyce being among his most admired practitioners:

Ulysses is a polyhedron, a thousand
Faces, and some of these the scholar's, and one
The prosodist's. No single work in English
Debates and illustrates so many forms
Of prose and rime, or so concerns itself
With craft and method, running the lexicon
Of metric. It is a textbook and a guide ...

(Shapiro 1945, ll.458–464)

While Shapiro considers writers and writing styles from Horace and Shakespeare to Whitman and Eliot, he confirms that his own work is under scrutiny here too:

For the most part, the poets I have discussed
Are those who seem the best to illustrate
Our errors; covertly, I have employed
My own poems freely as examples. Thus
What I have published elsewhere in the trend
Of modern rime, I criticize herein ...

(Shapiro 1945, ll.2037–2042)

Shapiro's beautiful poem rounds off this selection of works which demonstrate just how exacting, edifying and entertaining the creative-exegetical form can be.

Examples of drama and prose where creative product and exegesis are indistinguishable

Tracing the Horatian impulse, where one writes about one's creative practice while performing it, we can cite William Shakespeare's verse drama. In *Henry V* (c.1599), Shakespeare included in his Prologue a performed exegesis focused on the effects of dramatic writing upon audience perception and thinking. His insightful analysis still stands as central to understanding how writing for the theatre works. In Prologue speeches made by the character Chorus throughout the play (220 lines in total, a significant component of the piece) Shakespeare analysed a range of audience-response activities which included the now-recognised staple of theatre studies: 'willing suspension of disbelief', i.e. why we 'believe in' fictions presented on stage.[2] Chorus asks:

> Can this cockpit hold
> The vasty fields of France? or may we cram
> Within this wooden O the very casques
> That did affright the air at Agincourt?
> > (Shakespeare 2003–2018, Act 1, Prologue: ll.12–15)

Here Chorus challenges the basic practicalities of theatre and the principles of writing for it. How does the writer produce the expansive 'real' on the reduced dimensions of the stage – the 'wooden O' being the Globe theatre, of course, but also a sort of nothing in itself? How can the broad scale of the vision in the writer's mind be transferred to an audience via this unprepossessing, restricted structure? Well, by appeal to and contract with the mind of each individual in that audience:

> O, pardon! since a crooked figure may
> Attest in little place a million;
> And let us, ciphers to this great accompt,
> On your imaginary forces work.
> > (Shakespeare 2003–2018, Act 1, Prologue: ll.16–19)

A zero (or nothing) turns 10 into 100. And adding more zeros (more nothings) in short space easily gets to a million. The audience does the multiplication by nothings in their minds. This ridiculous formula is what almost every writer for the theatre relies upon: it was an essential aspect of Shakespeare's writing process for him to think through; it was brilliant of him to put it so eloquently on stage. He summed up the process with Chorus saying to the audience: 'Still be kind, / And eke out our performance with your mind' (Shakespeare 2003–2018, Act III, Prologue: ll.1086–7).

Horace's verse piece was not the only classical prototype for creative writing about writing. Another was provided by Plato who regularly used dramatic dialogue to express his philosophy: in *Phaedrus* (c.360 BCE) he used it to talk about writing speeches. In this scene, Phaedrus holds in his hand the script of a speech written by Lysias:

Socrates: Shall I propose that we look for examples of art and want of art, according to our notion of them, in the speech of Lysias which you have in your hand, and in my own speech?

Phaedrus: Nothing could be better; and indeed I think that our previous argument has been too abstract and – wanting in illustrations.

Socrates: Yes; and the two speeches happen to afford a very good example of the way in which the speaker who knows the truth may, without any serious purpose, steal away the hearts of his hearers. This piece of good-fortune I attribute to the local deities; and perhaps, the prophets of the Muses who are singing over our heads may have imparted their inspiration to me. For I do not imagine that I have any rhetorical art of my own.

Phaedrus: Granted; if you will only please to get on.

Socrates:	Suppose that you read me the first words of Lysias' speech.
Phaedrus:	"You know how matters stand with me, and how, as I conceive, they might be arranged for our common interest; and I maintain that I ought not to fail in my suit, because I am not your lover. For lovers repent – "
Socrates:	Enough: – Now, shall I point out the rhetorical error of those words?
Phaedrus:	Yes.
Socrates:	Everyone is aware that about some things we are agreed, whereas about other things we differ.
Phaedrus:	I think that I understand you; but will you explain yourself?
Socrates:	When anyone speaks of iron and silver, is not the same thing present in the minds of all?
Phaedrus:	Certainly.
Socrates:	But when any one speaks of justice and goodness we part company and are at odds with one another and with ourselves?
Phaedrus:	Precisely. ... (Plato 1994–2009)

The dialogue goes on, but the key point is that Plato was writing about writing speeches while writing in speech. His dramatic dialogues are creative-exegetical in nature: even when he wrote philosophy, he made a script of it.

Following Plato's lead, Dryden's *Essay of Dramatick Poesie* (1668) was written mainly in dialogic prose, but with an overall story structure. The plot involves a meeting between four characters: Eugenius, Crites, Lisideius and Neander – English gentlemen all who are, it seems, writers, critics and consumers of theatre. They have taken a barge on the Thames on the same day the English and Dutch navies are locked in battle further down-river. The noise and drama of the battle provides a background to their discussion about the writing process. The dynamic of the piece, as with Plato's dramatic dialogues, is that of a somewhat static playscript rather than an event-driven story, but it nevertheless teases out aspects of the requirements of a creative-exegetical work written as fiction. It suggests that the performance of the metatextual exegetical in prose will likely depend on the subject matter being contained in dialogue, and that the setting will work metaphorically to suggest the greater discourse context, e.g. to indicate there is conflict current in the literary field.

Dryden's *Essay* starts just like a work of fiction would:

It was that memorable day, in the first Summer of the late War, when our Navy ingag'd the Dutch ... While these vast floating bodies, on either side, mov'd against each other in parallel lines ... it was the fortune of Eugenius, Crites, Lisideius and Neander, to be in company together ... Taking then a Barge which a servant of Lisideius had provided for them, they made haste to shoot the Bridge, and ... it was not long ere they perceiv'd the Air break about them like the noise of distant Thunder ... (Dryden [1668] 2017)

With the battle as backdrop, the characters discuss the nature of writing for the theatre. The elaborate debate concerns comparisons between what the ancients said about plays and what the contemporary 17th-century theatre industry was doing. Subjects such as: adhering to the ancients' unities; the viability of the tragicomic form; and the use of rhyme, are discussed. Dryden wrote plays in five acts as did many of his Restoration contemporaries – see e.g. *All for Love* (1677) (Dryden [1677] 1966) – and here in the *Essay* his character Eugenius argues the question of whether to structure a play in four acts or five, since Horace and Aristotle had disagreed on that matter:

Crites had no sooner left speaking, but *Eugenius* who waited with some impatience for it, thus began:

> ... *Aristotle* indeed divides the integral parts of a Play into four ... Thus this great man deliver'd to us the image of a Play, and I must confess it is so lively that from thence much light has been deriv'd to the forming it more perfectly into Acts and Scenes; but what Poet first limited to five the number of the Acts I know not; onely we see it so firmly establish'd in the time of *Horace*, that he gives it for a rule in Comedy; *Neu brevior quinto, neu sit productior actu* [*And not less than five and not actually extended*]: So that you see the Grecians cannot be said to have consummated this Art; writing rather by Entrances then by Acts, and having rather a general indigested notion of a Play, then knowing how and where to bestow the particular graces of it. (Dryden [1668] 2017, translation in brackets added)

Dryden's essay doesn't look, sound or feel like an essay. And even though its content concerns issues in writing poetry and drama, it is written as a 26,000-word story, something we would today call a novella.

Plato's exegetical dialogues lie behind metatheatrical plays written from Greek times onwards. Nicole Boireau says, in the context of modern British theatre:

> ... drama as discourse on and about itself within the play, has always been a major feature of the art of theatre ... [y]et, self-examination traditionally stands in danger of being treated like the bathwater of narcissism and decadence ... Far from being marginal, the ... self-conscious mechanism of reflexivity has become the subject-matter and the organizing principle of many contemporary British plays and productions. (Boireau 1988, xii, xiii, xiv)

Boireau's analysis of the creative-exegetical impulse in writers such as Samuel Beckett, Harold Pinter, Tom Stoppard and Caryl Churchill leads her to pose questions (which her edited book goes on to examine):

> Is this compelling self-examination mere posturing? Can this ambiguous and playful interplay of texts, this proliferation of images-within-images support the exploration of serious issues? Or is drama in the process of locking itself up in the prison-house of its own conventions in order to evade important commitments? Is contemporary "drama on drama" just one more form of art for art's sake? (Boireau 1988, xiv)

The same questions are perpetually asked of the creative-exegetical and, we suggest, tend to be asked by critics rather than by writers themselves. While writers see the exegetical as part of their metier, and part of the discourse they have with their audience, critics wish to claim it as readerly territory exclusively (the old elephants teaching zoology syndrome).

In an example from European theatre, Luigi Pirandello's *Six Characters in Search of an Author* (1921) is a play about the making of plays in general, and specifically about the playwright making his own plays:

LEADING MAN [*to the* DIRECTOR]:	Excuse me, do I really have to wear this chef's hat?
DIRECTOR [*annoyed by the comment*]:	I would think so [*pointing to the script*], since it's written there.
LEADING MAN:	Forgive me, but it's silly.
DIRECTOR [*jumping up in a rage*]:	Silly? Silly? What can I do if France can't produce any good theatre and we are reduced to putting on Pirandello plays which you have to be lucky to understand and which are written in a way never to please either critics or actors or public. (Pirandello [1921] 1995, 8)

CREATIVE WORK AS SCHOLARLY WORK

79

Pirandello engages with playwrights' issues throughout the play and turns his writerly look-behind-the-scenes into highly entertaining theatre. Of interest, we feel, is the fact that Pirandello relies significantly on irony and amusement in his analysis, because by sharing exposure of the writing process with the audience, he brings two sets of values into relief: the expectations of the audience on their side of the 'fourth wall' and his own, the writer's, on the other. The performance convention Shakespeare analysed in *Henry V* is based, of course, in tricks, stunts, and put-ons. Fictions rely on the reader/viewer/audience going along with and contributing to the deception which is, after all, merely a way of getting ideas to travel from one mind (the writer's) to another (the viewer's). When observed with utter clarity, as Pirandello does, the exegetical is a scenario imbued with deep ironies and humour.

The above provides a selected analysis of writing in the creative-exegetical vein and indicates that the parameters of a Creative-Exegetical genre are identifiable through a long history of practice and a significant body of work not yet fully drawn together and studied. Now we move to testing the recognition of this genre in the current academic context …

Middle section, where Pete Nash calls the creative writing discipline's bluff, to see if a short story can at the same time be a scholarly research essay

Pete submitted the following to an Honours-level course called Advanced Research in Creative Writing at Griffith University in 2018. His aim was to test how well a crime story might correlate with an academic essay submission. He had published creative-exegetical stories previously in *TEXT* (Nash 2017a, 2017b, 2018), had thought through the implications of the form, and was convinced all his scholarly research was contained in his story. His submission was accepted in the assignment category of 'Reflective Essay'. Here it is:

Cold Case Critique: Writers, Murder, and Theory

By Peter Nash

One thing Detective Jon Byrd (JB) Bowers did know was, that the person responsible for copying Vincent Van Gogh's *Head of a Girl, Bareheaded, and Head of a Man with Beard and Cap* in pencil, on the inside cover of a nondescript notebook, definitely knew what the hell they were doing.

However, there were quite a few other things JB did not understand. The first thing JB asked himself was: Was the hand responsible for sketching the Van Gogh the hand behind the writing? The second thing was: Why? Thirdly he could not understand why academia required so many disparate referencing styles. In JB's world, things were relatively simple: a crime occurred, an investigation launched, the perpetrator/s were apprehended, and justice was served. Simple, clean, clear. Do not pass go.

At first glance the notebook didn't seem to be anything out of the ordinary, nonetheless it had found its way to JB's desk under curious circumstances. From what the detective knew, its previous owner was a writer, sans beneficiaries, who mysteriously disappeared. Thus, after the requisite amount of time, the individual's house became state property.

As circumstance ordained it, if the successful bidder had shared the previous owner's proclivity for antique furniture the journal might have remained where it was, between the lowest draw and the base of a cedar writing desk. However, the new owner had no use for such Georgian frivolity, summarily dispatching all relics and remnants to an auction house, replacing the desk at auction with a Jean de Merry glass credenza.

The Georgian was purchased at the same auction by an enthusiast who discovered the journal while in the process of dismantling the desk in readiness for restoration. Inside this notebook, in neat cursive hand below what appeared to be a pencil drawing of a classic image, the collector read the following:

'"Strangled writers die: you understand."'

After reading the above, the new owner forgot about the restoration process, poured a fresh coffee brewed in a Belle Époque Origine, and proceeded to investigate further. On page five, another reference to foul play emerged:

'"You knocked: and I killed you."'

Nothing more came to light until the reader reached the final page on which the attendant message was inscribed:

'"I will keep on killing: until no readers remain."'

At this point the owner forthwith contacted the police who *tout de suite* passed the notebook along to Detective Jon Byrd (JB) Bowers.

Detective JB Bowers was much perturbed. Eighteen years busting crime, and this damn thing had to come along. Possibly the strangest case he'd encountered so far, apart from that weird episode involving a stolen giraffe and a naked person; however, that was another story. A notebook had been found under the lower drawer of an old desk by a person dismantling the item in readiness for restoration.

What worried JB most was the fact that whoever had originally owned the journal (assuming they were responsible for the writing in it) appeared to be a deranged killer. A secondary concern for JB was the academic implication present in the text. It was the marks left by the apparent criminal – the quote marks – got him thinking. Thus, after a short deliberation, JB decided that it was time he went back to school.

♠

A certain investigation produced a certain name, hence JB materialised on the campus of a certain university on a certain day in a certain room at a certain time. The lecture proved more engaging than JB had anticipated. So much so that when JB asked the lecturer if she would mind him attending the tutorial she said: 'Fine with me. Although I'm not at all sure how much two hours of Bourdieu et al will benefit you.'

JB said, '*Boor-doo*, huh, by the way, here's my card.'

The lecturer took the card, scrutinised it, turned it over, read it twice slowly, then gave it back.

'My name's Roxanne. Roxanne Hardt.'

'Pleased to meet you, Roxanne,' JB said.

'Likewise. Is everything alright?'

'I usually go by JB. Is it Roxanne or ... '

CREATIVE WORK AS SCHOLARLY WORK

'Roxanne's fine.'

'All good,' JB said. 'Reason I'm here is, I was wondering if you could help me get my head around some writing I'm investigating. So I thought I might attend one of your lectures and introduce myself that way.'

'What writing, exactly?' Roxanne said.

'Kind of a long story,' JB said. 'Possible to set up a meeting sometime later today?'

'Unless it is urgent, it's completely out … '

'Cold investigation,' JB said. 'Not urgent right now, but the subject is disturbing.'

'Today won't happen, I have a meeting with a PhD student in ten minutes, the tute, a meeting after that, and possibly another one after that … '

'In that case,' JB said, 'I'll talk with you briefly after the tutorial and work out a time that suits.'

Roxanne gave JB details on how to find Room G8.88 and went to keep her appointment with the PhD student, telling JB she would catch him at the tute.

♣

JB found the tutorial even more intriguing than the lecture. As he said to a colleague later, he couldn't deduce if it was because he was surrounded by folk seemingly thirty years his junior; or, due to the fact that people were obviously so intelligent they managed to engage in the discourse while skilfully Facebooking, Instagraming, twittering, tweeting, eating, and conversing, as well as comprehending every nuanced facet of the material under discussion.

After the tutorial, while he was waiting for the last of the students to finish speaking with Roxanne, JB walked across to a large aluminium-framed whiteboard with green writing on it. He retrieved an Art of Manliness detective's wallet from the pocket of his two-piece striped charcoal-coloured suit and, using a pen he found in the carpark on the way to the lecture, JB copied the following down exactly as it appeared on the board.

'Pierre Bourdieu: (Field)

'A field is a field of forces within which the agents occupy positions that statistically determine the positions they take with respect to the field, these position-takings being aimed at either conserving or transforming the structure of relations of forces that is constitutive of the field.'

'Pierre Bourdieu: (Practice)

'The agent engaged in practice knows the world but with a knowledge which, as Merleau-Ponty showed, is not set up in the relation of externality of a knowing consciousness. He knows it, in a sense, too well, without objectifying distance, takes it for granted, precisely because he is caught up in it, bound up with it; he inhabits it like a garment or a familiar habitat. He feels at home in the world because the world is also in him, in the form of the habitus.'

'Pierre Bourdieu: (Habitus)

'Once one has accepted the viewpoint that is constitutive of a field, one can no longer take an external viewpoint on it. The 'nomos', a 'thesis' which, because it is never put forward as such, cannot be contradicted, has no antithesis. As a legitimate principle of division which can be applied to all the fundamental aspects of experience, defining the thinkable and the unthinkable, the prescribed and the proscribed, it must remain unthought.'

By the time the last student had finished discussing the tutorial with Roxanne, JB assumed there wouldn't be sufficient time to pursue the matter he was actually there for. He went over to the desk where Roxanne was gathering up her laptop and notes, waited a few more minutes, and then, when the last student exited the room, he said:

'They stayed longer than I thought.'

'You get that,' Roxanne said.

'Anyways,' JB said. 'When would be a suit … '

'What is this about?' Roxanne said. She moved away from him to another desk where her bag was. 'I don't see how I can be of any help, and it isn't like I haven't got anything else to do.'

'Let me ask you a question,' JB said. 'The handwriting on the board, is it yours?'

'It's from a previous class, what about it?'

'I presume those are quotes or something,' JB said. 'Correct me if I'm wrong, but the name up there – Boor-doo, Bood-whar, whatever – sounds like the name you mentioned before.'

'Bourdieu. Try saying the word *boar* as in pig first, then add the word *dew*, and couple that with an *err* sound like the first part of error.'

Roxanne stowed her laptop computer quietly and looked at JB. She checked the time on her mobile telephone then picked up her oval leather bag with two rectangular brass buckles and walked over to where JB sat on the edge of the desk, legs out in front, with his left boot resting on top of the right.

'Bourdieu,' Roxanne said. 'Pierre Felix Bourdieu. French sociologist interested in the oscillation of power across societal structures.'

'What I'm interested in,' JB said, 'is answering the questions I have regarding a journal I'm investigating, and, as one of those seems related to academic referencing, I'm curious as to why the writing on the … '

Roxanne said, 'If that material was included in an academic essay or refereed journal, it would, of course, follow academic convention.'

JB placed his wallet on the desk, leaned forwards, raised his left trouser leg, rolled a green sock flecked with gold and red fleur-de-lis down slightly, and scratched his ankle.

'What's a refereed journal?' he said. 'Assuming it isn't a publication for folks adjudicating sporting events.'

Roxanne looked at her mobile telephone.

'Get to the point, Detective.'

'I'll keep it simple,' JB said. 'I am researching a notebook found in a desk which has in turn become my responsibility. I say *responsibility* because there are sections of the text that clearly indicate an intent to commit serious criminal offense.'

'Like what?'

'Murder,' JB said.

CREATIVE WORK AS SCHOLARLY WORK

Roxanne's telephone rang, and after a brief conversation she closed the device and put it back into a side pocket.

'Meeting's cancelled,' Roxanne said. 'So how is this particular situation different from any other case?'

'Two reasons,' JB said. 'Usually the investigation is less abstract and by that I mean ... '

'I get it,' Roxanne said. 'Concrete.'

'Concrete,' JB said. 'Concrete. I don't see what the hell con ... '

'Forget about it,' Roxanne said. 'What kind of research are you engaged in?'

'As far as the research goes,' JB said, 'I suppose it's plain old-fashioned detective model mark one research. Why, how many different kinds are there?'

'It can get complicated,' Roxanne said. 'From an academic standpoint, there are two types of practice-related research. Practice-led and practice based.'

'What's the difference, and which type am I involved with?'

'I'm not at all sure you'd understand.'

'I'm a detective,' JB said. 'Try me.'

Her mobile phone cut the conversation short. After she hung up, Roxanne gave JB the option of waiting in her office while she sorted the problem out or re-scheduling for later that week.

●

The window behind Roxanne, facing north toward the ocean, framed early evening light and half of the shadowed library wall. The first thing JB noticed was the pervasive amount of reading material lining the shelves and the copious amount of printed material crammed and jammed into every unoccupied space. Roxanne walked over to the window closed it, drew the shade, and selected some paperwork from the shelf nearest the window. She settled into a black and white Chromcraft office chair and shuffled the material into two piles before placing the top article from each stack in front of JB.

'There are a few things you need to understand first, Detective.'

'Tell me about it,' JB said.

'Read the highlighted sections closely and copy them down word for word while I attend to the problem I came here to deal with.'

'Why do I need to write them out?' JB said. 'I'll remember most of it, at least anything of relevance to my investigation.'

'For a couple of very good reasons,' Roxanne said. 'Firstly, because numerous studies have clearly demonstrated that the act of writing something down facilitates both cognizance and memory; and secondly, due to the fact that this is my office and as you came here seeking my assistance, please do as I ask.'

JB bent the staples up at 45 degrees and separated the paperwork into single sheets, then spread them neatly on Roxanne's classic Action Office Desk by George Nelson for Herman Miller. The blue pen he'd picked up in the carpark registered the following before running out of ink:

The Oxford English Dictionary lists two basic definitions, one with a little r and one with a big R, and within these, many many subsidiary ones. Research with a little r – meaning the "the act of searching, closely or carefully, *for* or *after* a specified thing or person" – was first used of royal genealogy in 1577, then in one of the earliest detective stories William Godwin's *Caleb Williams* in 1794 (where it concerned clues and evidence). (Oxford English Dictionary cited in Frayling 1993, 1.1)

Roxanne lent Detective Jon Byrd (JB) Bowers a sharp pencil and the detective continued to write:

Practice-led research is concerned with the nature of practice and leads to new knowledge that has operational significance for that practice. In a doctoral thesis, the results of practice-led research may be fully described in text form without the inclusion of a creative work. The primary focus of the research is to advance knowledge about practice, or to —

Roxanne finished her telephone call and looked over to see how much JB had written. At which point, JB immediately stopped writing and looked up to see Roxanne leaning over him.

'This has to be it,' JB said. 'Has to be. I'm not sure how much it will help, but clearly this is the kind of research I'm involved with here. Must be. *Practise-led research*. It does not require a creative work and the main idea is to further knowledge about … '

'Are you sure?' Roxanne said. 'Go ahead and copy the other definition out – don't worry about the italics – and then we will discuss it.'

Practice-based research is an original investigation undertaken in order to gain new knowledge partly by means of practice and the outcomes of that practice. In a doctoral thesis, claims of originality and contribution to knowledge may be demonstrated through creative —

JB stopped writing and stared intensely at the words he had just copied down.

'Are you alright, Detective?' Roxanne said. 'You haven't finished that quote and I expressly asked … '

'Yeah, I'm fine,' Detective JB Bowers said, still staring at the words. 'The thing is, though, now I understand there is a creative component, in as much as the writing in the notebook was creatively written. I mean, not formally like in a text book, but at the same time it now occurs to me that, by default the investigation itself falls squarely within the parameters of the first explanation I wrote out … '

'That being?' Roxanne asked.

'Practice-led research. New knowledge containing practical significance for that practice.'

Roxanne said, 'Detective Bowers … As we have discussed, there is material in the notebook alleging criminal activity along with some other form of underlying implication. As you can see, both types of research contain idiosyncrasies some of which will help your investigation and some of which may not.'

JB said, 'Okay, so in what direction do I take the investigation now?'

'If you want my advice,' Roxanne said, 'I'd look to the dark side.'

'The dark side,' JB said. 'Where the hell is that?'

'Creative writing,' Roxanne said.

♠

CREATIVE WORK AS SCHOLARLY WORK   85

The work, submitted as a 'Reflective Essay' at Honours level, was intended to challenge a key barrier currently in force in the Creative Writing discipline: that a creative work couched entirely within a popular genre's expectation cannot also be an academic exegetical work. One might say that, as a 'reflective essay', it was neither an 'essay' nor was it overtly 'reflective' – unless, of course, one at least considers the original meaning of *essay* (i.e. an *attempt* at something) and deeper meanings of *reflective* (i.e. looking at *oneself*). A perfectly legitimate interpretation of 'reflective essay' might be *an attempt at profoundly thinking about the writing I am doing*. This is exactly what Pete did.

Pete's challenge, admittedly, brings into account the expectation that a creative writing academic assessor will happily sit down to analyse a short story (or poem or playscript) and in the process actually assess an exegesis as well. This thought is not about interweaving, plaiting or blending the exegesis and the creative product. It focuses on the creative work and the exegesis being the one thing. It focuses on a reading that *reverse engineers* the frameworks, processes, structures and materials employed in the production of the work. It also requires that *the product itself* reveal the quality of the plans employed, the testing of materials that has gone on, the nature of the dynamics of the moving parts of the work – at least to the eye of a qualified inspector. There are readers capable only of reading Pete's submission as a fun crime jaunt. Others, such as scholar-assessors, are qualified to read it in an informed, inspectorial way.

Pete's assessor comments (reprinted with permission) included the following:

> You have provided a clever, thoughtful and accessible example of performative, conceptually engaged, ficto-critical writing. Please may I use it in future, to inspire, for other students? [3]

The same assessor, in response to a further creative work the inspired Pete submitted for the course, gave the feedback:

> What convinces me *most* about your submission … is that the creative work itself is … an artfully reflexive and deeply informed work of creative inquiry which works through story in an active, vivid, literate, witty and compelling way.

Clearly the assessor, during her readings, agreed to be convinced by the challenge of the submission. She read the work not merely as crime story, but as 'performative, conceptually engaged, ficto-critical writing'. Here the key factor in the examination of creative writing as research comes into focus: the assessor reads the piece as *a work of enquiry* into the creative writing process, not just as a story, poem or play. And s/he assesses it in agreement that the context allows for *innovative* research being done. This is in line with the traditions traced above dating back to the ancients, where creative writers wrote about writing and the writing process while using a variety of literary forms and genres.

Concluding section, where we discuss further how the creative-exegetical is read in the university research context, and we consider Todorov's concepts for genre evolution: inversion, displacement and combination

Earlier in literary history, an 'essay' could be undertaken in any written format – as shown by Dryden's *Essay of Dramatick Poesie* (1668) written as prose fiction, Pope's *Essay on Criticism* (1711) written in poetry, and Shapiro's *Essay on Rime* (1945) also written as a poem.

These hybrid works, in their titles, evoke the conflict current today in the creative writing discipline where it is predominantly thought that the exegesis *must* be performed in academic prose exclusively. As shown by the survey we have made above, seminal works of English literature demonstrate that an exegesis – a critical piece examining the writing process from the writer's own point of view – need not be written in prose, nor indeed, academic prose.

Our survey suggests it is easier to write exegetically in poetry or playscript than in prose fiction. In poetry, the performance of the exegetical and the poetic together do not conflict. The layout on the page in lines that don't go from margin to margin, the consequent rhythm, voice etc, and the subject matter, identify that exegesis and poem are simultaneous efforts – even an exegesis in appalling doggerel is possible. Similarly, exegetical theatre reveals its hybrid nature in the performance script format, or the fact of it being performed on stage: a play can be clearly about play writing. We think a PhD exegesis in verse or drama format would raise eyebrows and might ultimately be accepted by examiners, but it would not be accepted by the Australian Research Council as hybrid research work: it would require a Research Statement.

In the Australian doctoral submission context, prose-written alternatives to the apparently-traditional essay format for the exegesis involve greater complications. The prose of the expected exegesis is closer to the regular prose of fiction, so the work is harder to identify as a hybrid. A story intended to be exegetical has a hard time proving it is not forever fiction. How to carry the exegetical in a creative prose work, a story or novel – such that it is accepted as equivalent to a research essay – has not yet been fully tested in the academic context, as far as we know. In the ERA context, it would need a Research Statement, but we suggest it would also create significant trouble among examiners as an acceptable exegesis component in a research award submission. 'Hey, a candidate submitted a short story as exegesis for their PhD novel! What am I supposed to do with that?' an examiner will ask.

There are significant features in creative-exegetical poems, plays and fiction narratives. They are expository in the sense that they directly address discussion points which are part of the discourse related to the writing process in their time. They use symbolic and allegorical devices, e.g. climbing the mountain to indicate the strenuousness of the writing process, evoking the whetstone to portray the sharpening of focus involved in the exegetical process, or raising the backdrop on stage to indicate glimpses of behind-the-scenes writerly activity. Overall, these works indicate that academic knowledge will not only be pursued, investigated and discussed in writing that is devoid of literary intent and artistic merit.

So, how far is the creative writing discipline willing to go in its support for the idea that creative writing can itself be research? Practice-led and practice-based theory informed the argument that pushed Creative Writing across the line with the Australian Research Council and succeeded in having arts products in universities recognised as research. This led to a *separate-genre* notion where the academy recognises two identifiable elements in a creative writing research submission: the work in a creative genre; and its accompaniment in an academic genre. Pete's submissions challenged this, in line with the stories he contributed to the creative works section of *TEXT* where over the years the requirement has been that the matter of the creative work concerns exploration of creativity, or the nature and processes of writing, or the nature and processes of the teaching of writing, or investigation of writers. ('Information for Contributors' 2018)

In their introduction to *Bending Genre: Essays on Creative Nonfiction* (2013), Margot Singer and Nicole Walker describe the situation in universities as thus:

> We organize our textbooks and courses into tidy generic categories ... We think of genres as fixed and clearly bounded when in fact transgression is the norm ... ultimately narration and exposition and lyricism and dramatization are rhetorical modes employed by every genre. (Singer and Walker [2013] 2017, 3)

Singer and Walker's argument provides an opening for the creative-exegetical genre to state its credentials. When they ask a question about expository, fact-based prose as opposed to conventionally regarded non-fact-based poetry – 'What do we make of essays that take on structures typically found in poetry?' (2017, 2) – they answer with:

> Too often we confuse form with substance ... Genres, in sum, are not fixed categories with clear-cut boundaries, but constellations of rhetorical modes and formal structures grounded in varying degrees of fact. Genres are rooted in convention. They are also shape-shifters, in a continual state of flux. (Singer and Walker [2013] 2017, 4)

Genre is not to be equated with subject matter. Genre is the package, no more than that. And the package is decreed by social, or in our case, academic context. Tzvetan Todorov summed it up 30 years ago:

> Where do genres come from? Quite simply from other genres. A new genre is always the transformation of one or several old genres: by inversion, by displacement, by combination. (Todorov [1990] 1995, 15)

We can use Todorov's terms – *combination, displacement* and *inversion* – to describe what goes on when the creative-exegetical combines previously separated genres – i.e. where novel, poetry or drama intersect with the expository academic essay:

Combination: The explanation, contextualisation and analysis undertaken in the exegesis combine with the lyricism, imagery, dramatization, scene and dialogue of the creative product. In terms of new genre-building, this involves a process of the reader dealing with two sorts of language expectation at once – the anticipated tightly-controlled academic vocabulary, argument structure and diction, combined with the greater freedom of creative expression.

Displacement: Not confusing subject matter with form, the creative-exegetical genre displaces the dominance of academic language with currently suppressed creative language, allowing it to contribute to the thesis rather than being merely the 'other' used in the research process. The examples traced above, stretching back to the ancients, show that this way of non-discriminatory reading and writing has been done for a long time previously.

Inversion: The creative-exegetical genre turns upside-down several established language hierarchies: academic language is put to use in creative situations such as story, poetry or theatre, and creative language is employed in strategies to make argument by academic means. This type of reversal and transposal is hard to stomach for the conventionally-inclined. The creative-exegetical requires radical re-ordering of comfortable genre preferences and standard reading methods from academic assessors, and those outside universities too.

Todorov saw that 'the evolution of modern literature consists precisely in making each work an interrogation of the very essence of literature', and added: 'It is even considered a sign of authentic modernity in a writer if he ceases to respect the separation of genres' (Todorov [1990] 1995, 13). Our current context demands that we take Todorov's advice – that we question the impact of the current appetite for genre separation in the academic context – and that we forge for the creative writing discipline a better way forward based on how creative writing has been exegetically discussed for centuries in the past.

Notes

1. The Australian Research Council's equivalent in the United Kingdom is United Kingdom Research and Innovation (UKRI). Australia's ERA (Excellence in Research for Australia) is equivalent to the UK's REF (Research Excellence Framework).
2. Shakespeare's character Chorus takes his/her name from Ancient Greek theatre where the chorus was the major exegetical element in a play. Amongst other duties, the chorus interpreted action and character thinking for the audience, and regularly provided insight into the dramatist's intended purposes for the work. The authors of this article acknowledge that the subject of the Greek chorus as exegesis is a fascinating one, but a topic well beyond their expertise.
3. The authors wish to thank Dr Stephanie Green for permission to print her feedback responses.

Disclosure statement

No potential conflict of interest was reported by the authors.

References

Australian Research Council. 2017. *ERA 2018 Submission Guidelines*. Canberra: Commonwealth of Australia. Accessed July 16, 2018. http://www.arc.gov.au/sites/default/files/filedepot/Public/ERA/ERA%202018/ERA%202018%20Submission%20Guidelines.pdf.

Boireau, Nicole. 1988. "Preface." In *Drama on Drama: Dimensions of Theatricality on the Contemporary British Stage*, edited by N. Boireau, xii–xiv. Basingstoke: Palgrave.

Brady, Tess. 2000. "A Question of Genre: De-Mystifying the Exegesis." *TEXT: Journal of Writing and Writing Courses* 4 (1) (April). Accessed August 11, 2018. http://www.textjournal.com.au/april00/brady.htm.

Byron, Lord George. (1811) 2006. "Hints from Horace: The Works of Lord Byron: in Six Volumes." *English Poetry 1579-1830: Spenser and the Tradition*. Accessed June 14, 2018. http://spenserians.cath.vt.edu/TextRecord.php?textsid = 35766.

Cawood, Michael, and Tony Williams. 2018. "On Reflection: The Role, Mode and Medium of the Reflective Component in Practice as Research." *TEXT: Journal of Writing and Writing Courses* 22 (1) (April). Accessed August 11, 2018. http://www.textjournal.com.au/april18/green_williams.htm.

Culler, Jonathan. 1988. *Framing the Sign: Criticism and its Institutions*. Norman, OK: University of Oakland Press.

Dibble, Brian, and Julienne van Loon. 2000. "Writing Theory and/or Literary Theory." Accessed May 22, 2018). http://www.textjournal.com.au/april00/vanloon.htm.

Dryden, John. (1668) 2017. *An Essay of Dramatick Poesie*. Edited by J. Lynch. Accessed June 14, 2018. http://andromeda.rutgers.edu/~jlynch/Texts/drampoet.html.

Dryden, John. (1677) 1966. "All for Love." In *Restoration Plays*, edited by E. Gosse, 1–80. London: Dent.

Golden, Leon. 2010. "Reception of Horace's *Ars Poetica*." In *A Companion to Horace*, edited by G. Davis, 391–413. London: Blackwell Publishing. doi:10.1002/9781444319187.ch19

Hart, Jonathan Locke. 2018. *Making and Seeing Modern Texts*. New York: Routledge.

Horace. (19-10 BCE) 1936. "De Arte Poetica." In *Horace: Satires, Epistles and Ars Poetica*, Translated by H. R. Fairclough, 452–489. Cambridge, MA: Harvard University Press.

Horace. (19-10 BCE) 2001. "Ars Poetica." In *The Norton Anthology of Theory and Criticism*, Translated by D. A. Russell, edited by V. B. Leitch, 124–135. New York: WW Norton.

Howell, Wilbur Samuel. (1968) 2009. "Aristotle and Horace on Rhetoric and Poetics." *Quarterly Journal of Speech* 54 (4): 325–339. doi:10.1080/00335636809382908.

"Information for Contributors." 2018. *TEXT: Journal of Writing and Writing Courses* 22 (1) (April). Accessed 17 July 17, 2018. http://www.textjournal.com.au/send.htm.

Krauth, Nigel. 2002. "The Preface as Exegesis." *TEXT: The Journal of the Australian Association of Writing Programs* 6 (1) (April). Accessed May 20, 2018. http://www.textjournal.com.au/april02/krauth.htm.

Krauth, Nigel. 2011. "Evolution of the Exegesis: The Radical Trajectory of the Creative Writing Doctorate in Australia." *TEXT: Journal of Writing and Writing Courses* 14 (1) (April). http://www.textjournal.com.au/april11/krauth.htm.

Krauth, Nigel. 2018. "Exegesis and Artefact as a Woven Work: Problems of Examination." *TEXT: Journal of Writing and Writing Courses* 22 (1) (April). Accessed August 11, 2018. http://www.textjournal.com.au/april18/krauth.htm.

Kroll, Jeri. 1999. "Uneasy Bedfellows: Assessing the Creative Thesis and its Exegesis." *TEXT: Journal of Writing and Writing Courses* 3 (2) (October). http://www.textjournal.com.au/oct99/kroll.htm.

Leitch, Vincent B., ed. 2001. *The Norton Anthology of Theory and Criticism*. New York: W.W. Norton.

MacLeish, Archibald. (1926) 2018. "Ars Poetica." *Foetry Foundation*. Accessed July 17, 2018. https://www.poetryfoundation.org/poetrymagazine/poems/17168/ars-poetica.

Milosz, Czeslaw. (1968) 2018. "Ars Poetica?" In *Foetry Foundation*. Translated by C. Milosz and L. Vallee. Accessed July 17, 2018. https://www.poetryfoundation.org/poems/49455/ars-poetica-56d22b8f31558.

Molette, Carlton. (1968) 2009. "Aristotle's Union of Rhetoric and Dramatic Theory." *Southern Journal of Communication* 34 (1): 47–54. doi:10.1080/10417946809371974.

Nash, Peter. 2017a. "You Get What You Dress for." *TEXT: Journal of Writing and Writing Courses* 21 (1) (April). Accessed August 6, 2018. http://www.textjournal.com.au/april17/nash_prose.htm.

Nash, Peter. 2017b. "Murder in the Office of Final Editing." *TEXT: Journal of Writing and Writing Courses* 21 (2) (October). Accessed August 6, 2018. http//www.textjournal.com.au/oct17/nash_prose.htm.

Nash, Peter. 2018. "Hard Copy." *TEXT: Journal of Writing and Writing Courses* 22 (1) (April). Accessed August 6, 2018. http://www.textjournal.com.au/april18/nash_prose.htm.

Perry, Gaylene. 1998. "Writing in the Dark: Exorcising the Exegesis." *TEXT: Journal of Writing and Writing Courses* 2 (2) (October). Accessed August 16, 2018. www.griffith.edu.au/school/art/text/oct98/perry.

Pirandello, Luigi. (1921) 1995. *Six Characters in Search of an Author and Other Plays*. London: Penguin.

Plato. (c.360 BCE) 1994–2009. *Phaedrus (trans B. Jowett), The Internet Classics Archive*. Accessed August 1, 2018. http://classics.mit.edu/Plato/phaedrus.html.

Pope, A. (1711) 2008. "An Essay on Criticism." In *The Major Works*, 17–39. Oxford: Oxford University Press.

Shakespeare, William. (c.1599) 2003–2018. "Speeches (Lines) for Chorus in 'Henry V'." *History of Henry V, Open Source Shakespeare.* Accessed July 17, 2018. https://www.opensourceshakespeare.org/views/plays/characters/charlines.php?CharID=Chorus-h5&WorkID=henry5.

Shapiro, Karl. 1945. *Essay on Rime.* New York: Reynal & Hitchcock.

Singer, Margot and Nicole Walker, eds. (2013) 2017. *Bending Genre: Essays on Creative Nonfiction.* New York: Bloomsbury.

Todorov, Tzvetan. (1990) 1995. *Genres in Discourse.* Cambridge: Cambridge University Press.

Watkins, Ross, and Nigel Krauth. 2016. "Radicalising the Scholarly Paper: New Forms for the Traditional Journal Article." *TEXT: Journal of Writing and Writing Courses* 20 (1) (April). Accessed August 11, 2018. http://www.textjournal.com.au/april16/watkins&krauth.htm.

Williams, Paul. 2016. "The Performative Exegesis." *TEXT: Journal of Writing and Writing Courses* 20 (1) (April). Accessed August 11, 2018. http://www.textjournal.com.au/april16/williams.htm.

Why our responses matter

Responding through creative writing and to creative writing is largely what creative writers do. Let me repeat that, with a little more explanation. A creative writer responds to the world, to things from their imaginations, to their experiences, to ideas, to emotions, and so on, *through* the actions of doing creative writing. A creative writer also frequently shows an interest in both their own creative writing and in the creative writing of others, the actions and the results, and in that sense responds *to* creative writing. It is important to clearly acknowledge both these facts, because it is in this that is located much of what is meant by actively engaging in creative writing.

Others can, of course, respond *to* creative writing – literary scholars, sociologists, cultural historians, economists, geographers, other artists, readers, general interested frequent or infrequent readers – a wide variety of readers can respond to creative writing, and of course often do. But it is the creative writer who responds to creative writing from the point of view of how it is done and with the knowledge, in the case of our own work, of what we expected to have accomplished, and in the case of the work of other creative writers, how the doing (actions and results) relate to our own ways of doing, and to our results.

As creative writers, if we do not attempt to fully understand the nature of our human response but, instead, perhaps suggest that coming to any conclusions about how, why and in what ways we write is just a little beyond our critical comprehension (for reasons, say, that our imaginations are said to be mysterious or our actions difficult to fully describe) then we surely discharge any obligation for anyone else to accurately engage with how and why we respond through creative writing.

Similarly, if we largely relinquish the critical responses to creative writing to others – so, for example, to literary scholars, to cultural historians, creativity researchers, linguists, teachers of language – then we also relinquish significant critical franchise when it comes to creative writing. In the past – indeed, significantly in the West since around the end of the nineteenth century – we have appeared to do this as if it is required of us.

No one has ever suggested we creative writers should not respond to the world, to the things in our imaginations, to our ideas, to our emotions *through* creative writing. Such a suggestion would clearly be ridiculous. But equally, no one has ever suggested with any clear, sustainable argument that we, as creative writers, should not respond to creative writing critically and, indeed, that we should not be the primary source of informed understanding concerning the actions and the results of creative writing. It is for these reasons that our critical responses matter as much as our creative responses – and today this key fact needs much wider dissemination.

Graeme Harper

Shifting the power dynamics in the creative writing workshop: assessing an instructor as participant model

Donovan McAbee

ABSTRACT
This article addresses the 'instructor as participant' model of the Creative Writing workshop. Though versions of this model have been addressed in Creative Writing theory, the model itself remains under-theorised. In seeking to remedy this elision, the article articulates a pedagogical underpinning for the model, based on Paolo Freire's 'problem-posing' concept of education. The article then assesses an iteration of the instructor as participant model in practice. 'Shifting the Power Dynamics' grows out of the experience of teaching an upper level Creative Writing module entitled 'Writing for Spirituality'. In this mixed-genre Creative Writing module, students are asked to explore the ways that their own Creative Writing might help them understand and develop their personal theology or spirituality. Taking its bearings also from Katharine Haake's work, the article identifies the structural changes required in module development that help nurture a decentred workshop. The article then identifies the shifts in practice that result from the instructor as participant model, including: (1) the instructor sharing works-in-progress; (2) class participation in developing workshop ground rules; and (3) modifying the 'gag rule' on the workshop participant who is sharing their work in order to nurture dialogue.

In a Creative Writing workshop setting, students are asked to share their creative work publicly, with both their colleagues and also with their instructor. In many ways, the intimacy and vulnerability asked of students in a Creative Writing workshop exist in tension with the context of the contemporary university and its culture of constant assessment. To complicate the tensions of the broader university setting, additional tensions exist at the level of each class, the interpersonal dynamics among students, as well as the dynamics created by the instructor.

Several years ago, I began to develop an upper level undergraduate module entitled 'Writing for Spirituality' for use at Belmont University in Nashville, Tennessee. Belmont is a historically Christian university, which identifies as ecumenical in nature and enrols students from a variety of religious backgrounds. This module was initially designed for our College of Theology majors and minors. Therefore, most students in the module would have had an academic understanding of the Christian theological tradition and oftentimes a broad knowledge of other world traditions of faith. The idea behind the module was to utilise Creative Writing as a method by which students might approach their own spirituality, regardless of their faith tradition. Through developing their craft as writers, and writing alongside one another, class members would spend the semester considering the question – How might Creative Writing become a significant part of my spiritual journey? Sometimes the class would reflect on and address this question head-on, but most often, students would address the question indirectly, by simply writing stories, poems, personal narratives, and then by reflecting on where their stories have come from and where they have led them in their understanding of their own spirituality.

As I developed the class, I asked a lot of questions about my role as the instructor. To be sure, when any instructor steps into a classroom, their presence brings with it a complex set of tensions based on the perceptions of gender, race, and a variety of other forms of power (Lim 2010, 85; Petty 2005, 81, 97). These factors are at work in both the instructor's self, as well as in the perceptions students bring into the classroom (Lim 2010, 85). In seeking to develop a workshop setting that nurtures openness and vulnerability, key components which encourage risk-taking and growth in students' writing (Leahy 2010, 65), I felt that I must, insofar as possible in a university setting, decentre power in the classroom, away from the person of the instructor.

This article offers the narrative of how I negotiated the power dynamics in the Creative Writing workshop as they pertain to the instructor and determined that the best model of the workshop for this setting was the instructor as participant model. This article describes the pedagogical considerations concerning the model, as well as the outcomes of this process, and addresses the following questions: How does the role of the instructor impact the Creative Writing classroom? What would it feel like for me, as the instructor, to shift the power dynamics of the Creative Writing workshop in such a way? In conclusion, the essay begins to consider the how this shift to the instructor as participant model might impact the students' own sense of engagement with the class's content. In developing this module with a heightened attentiveness to the power dynamics at work in the person of the instructor, I surmised that by decentring power, the instructor as participant workshop model might help to nurture a richer classroom environment for students to explore their spirituality through Creative Writing. While I would argue that my hypothesis proved correct, the experience also engendered a deeper appreciation of the interpersonal aspects of decentring the power from the instructor and the tensions that arose within me in utilising the instructor as participant model of the Creative Writing workshop.

Re-assessing the workshop model

Recent scholarship confirms that the workshop is still by far the most commonly used model for teaching Creative Writing (Leahy 2010, 63; Vandermuelen 2011, 23). Because this is the case, we must remain critically reflective on the value and potential pitfalls of this model (Stukenberg 2017, 277–278; Kearns 2009, 790–791). In seeking to determine the proper role of the instructor in the workshop model, Anna Leahy insists that we must develop an 'authority-conscious' pedagogy, which responsibly negotiates the role of the instructor in the workshop model (2005, ix–x). Leahy and others who take a similar view do not suggest that the instructor should have no authority but rather a considered authority. As Mary Cantrell points out, 'The fact that students receive three hours of college credit [from our classes] and move toward a degree with that credit compels us to establish authority in the classroom' (2005, 66). Therefore, we must establish an appropriate, fitting role for authority within this context. For Cantrell, this authority must exist in productive tension with developing a pedagogy, which also 'promotes creativity and imagination' (2005, 65–68). Like Leahy and Cantrell, I recognise that a responsible 'authority-conscious' pedagogy needs to be developed.

Pedagogical considerations

If instructors need to be particularly attuned to the interpersonal aspects of our teaching and of the power dynamics centred on the person of the instructor (Elbow 1990, 207; Bizzaro 2015, 97), then a class which explicitly asks students to consider questions of spirituality and Creative Writing must proceed with an even more heightened awareness of the power dynamics at play in the classroom, particularly as they pertain to the relationship of power and the instructor. In order to develop a responsible pedagogical underpinning for this course, one which negotiated power dynamics and authority, I initially engaged with the work of two thinkers in particular. The first is Paolo Freire and his concept of a 'problem-posing' model of education in which the 'teacher-student' and the 'students-teachers' dialogically participate. The second key influence is Pat Schneider (2003), whose groundbreaking work in developing the Amherst Writers Association and its methodology has impacted many workshop leaders' approaches to the writing workshop.

Freire's work *Pedagogy of the Oppressed* identifies ways that models of education sometimes inculcate oppression, rather than promote liberation. Freire articulates how liberation might be achieved in the educational setting. In chapter two of his book, Freire critiques what he refers to as the 'banking' model of education. In this model, one which is still prevalent in many schools, 'education … becomes an act of depositing, in which the students are the depositories and the teacher is the depositor' (1993, 72). This model justifies the teacher's existence, yet it disempowers learners. To correct this model and its oppressive tendencies, Freire proposes a shift in practice and also a shift in the dynamics between teachers and students. He contends that 'the solution of the teacher-student contradiction [is to] reconcil[e] the poles of the contradiction so that both are simultaneously teachers and students' (72). Thus, he uses the terminology of the 'teacher-student' and the 'students-teachers'. In the problem-posing model, dialogue functions to form community between teachers and students (80). To further highlight the shifts that this must require, Freire insists that 'in this process, arguments based on "authority" are no longer valid' (80). For Freire, this new dynamic possesses a liberating effect on both teachers and students – and by extension, the broader society. For the context of a Creative Writing class, particularly one which chooses the workshop as its primary mode, Freire's insights can be helpful in determining how to best shape the workshop so that it more closely mirrors the 'problem-posing' model with its dialogic character, rather than a banking model. I will return to these considerations later.

While Freire's work provides the philosophical underpinning for my changing approach to the workshop setting, Pat Schneider's work provides some of the concrete changes needed to enact a liberating pedagogy. Schneider's influence on my thinking grows from her groundbreaking book *Writing Alone and with Others*. In the section of the book that addresses the workshop setting, Schneider outlines practices that nurture fruitful workshop experiences.

SHIFTING THE POWER DYNAMICS IN THE CREATIVE WRITING WORKSHOP 95

'The Five Essential Practices' that she outlines include:

(1) A nonhierarchical spirit (how we treat writing) in the workshop is maintained while at the same time an appropriate discipline (how we interact as a group) keeps writers safe.
(2) Confidentiality about what is written in the workshop is maintained, and the privacy of the writer is protected ....
(3) Absolutely no criticism, suggestion, or question is directed toward the writer in response to first-draft, just-written work ....
(4) The teaching of craft is taken seriously ....
(5) The leader writes along with the participants and reads that work aloud at least once in each writing session. The practice is absolutely necessary, for only in this way is there equality of risk taking and mutuality of trust. (Schneider 2003, 186–187)

Schneider's approach to the workshop setting coheres nicely with Freire's problem-posing model of education. Her insistence on 'a nonhierarchical spirit' runs throughout these suggestions and aligns with the notion of the 'teacher-student' and the 'students-teachers'. Her aim in each of these practices, as is true throughout the book, honours the creativity and voice of each member of the workshop. In the final practice she lists above, that the instructor must share at least some of their work with the class, Schneider makes a suggestion, that if not radical, is at least an atypical departure from the ways that most Creative Writing workshops function in academic settings.

Taken together, Freire's and Schneider's ideas caused me to develop the class in such a way as to nurture dialogue and mutuality in the workshop setting. To do so, I was forced to confront the necessity of vulnerability for the instructor in order to decentre power in the classroom. My hypothesis, or more accurately as it feels in practice, my hunch and my hope, was that by divesting myself of the 'expert' status and giving away more power in the classroom, I could help nurture an environment, where students would be encouraged to experiment and embrace their own vulnerabilities in sharing work with the class. In doing so, I was forced to assess the traditional workshop model itself and make changes in order to nurture the kind of environment I hoped to create with students.

One of the real problems with the traditional workshop model is that it can, in Freirean terms, operate in a way that appears to be a problem-posing model but that is insidiously a banking model of education. The difference between a banking model and a problem-posing model workshop hinges on the role of the workshop leader, or instructor. If the workshop becomes simply another opportunity for the instructor to hold court with their insights, while the students parrot what they think the instructor wants them to say, then the workshop has become merely an example of banking model pedagogy, shaped like a circle rather than a lecture hall. It is the instructor's responsibility to ensure that the workshop not only appears to be problem-posing but that it actually is. My suggestion to achieve this end is to decentre the power within the class by shifting much of the locus of power away from the instructor. While there are certainly a number of ways to do this, my suggestion is to move the instructor into the role of workshop participant.

Instructor as participant in the workshop

In her essay 'Dismantling Authority: Teaching What We Do Not Know', Katharine Haake offers both an insight and a suggestion regarding how instructors might shift the power dynamics in the creative writing classroom. She contends that:

> One possible role for authority in the creative writing classroom is to dismantle itself. For if we believe that alternative models for teaching should redistribute power in such a way that students may come into authentic writing of their own, we must probably begin by allowing that at least some of the time it is not the content, but the structure of how we teach that makes this possible .... One possible way of testing ourselves to see if we mean what we say is simply to teach what we do not know. (2005, 99)

Following Haake's insights, it became clear that in order to develop the instructor as participant workshop model in a way that more fully decentres power, changes must occur at both the level of the structure of the module (Haake 2005, 99), as well as in the ways that the students and instructor interact in the actual workshop setting. Only then might the workshop become a community of 'teacher-student' and 'students-teachers'.

Haake's remedy, 'to teach what we do not know', initially sounds radical, if somewhat opaque. One wonders, is she suggesting that a creative writer teach a module on neurosurgery? In her exposition, however, it becomes clear that more accurately, she means that instructors should pursue, alongside their students, questions within their discipline for which the instructor has not yet formulated answers. In Haake's model, the instructor still chooses the focusing question, as well as the reading list for the module (2005, 102–103). By exploring new material as a fellow student with her class, Haake's pedagogical practice honours the liberating dynamic of Freire's problem-posing model and provides a template for developing a workshop based on the instructor as participant model.

In order to address this structural aspect of module-design for my own context, I shaped the semester into three separate units, each of which had a thematic, as well as a craft focus, which was presented as an open-ended question. The first unit was themed, '"Where the spirit meets the bone": Spirituality and the Body'; its craft focus question was: 'What shapes your "voice"?' The second unit was themed, 'The words and the "Word"'; its craft focus question was, 'Where might words lead you?' The third theme was 'Pentimento: Turnings', and its craft focus question was 'How do you tend to tensions in your writing?' By posing open-ended thematic questions, for which no single, authoritative answer exists, the module possessed the structural aspects of a decentred classroom, similar to that suggested by Haake's work. Rather than serving as the wise sage, I became a fellow traveller with the students in seeking answers to the questions we confronted. In a sense, I was teaching and learning what I could not definitively know.

In addition to the structural elements of a decentred module, I also implemented three shifts in the ways that I interacted with the students, in order to nurture a problem-posing educational model. The first shift, which was also in line with the practices that Schneider recommends, is that I shared my works-in-progress to be critiqued by the students. While Schneider contends that an instructor must share their work from generative workshop experiences, in the context of the module, I felt it necessary to share more developed works-in-progress as well. In sharing my work, I felt a great sense of vulnerability, particularly in those times when I was not happy with where the work was. I feared that seeing how poorly written a first draft of one of my poems or of a personal essay might be, students would no longer respect me as their instructor. The vulnerability this required centred around insecurities regarding my creative work, as well as insecurities regarding my role as an instructor. One outcome of this vulnerability was to make me more aware of how often I implicitly participate in resting on my title to justify my role in the classroom. To nurture the kind of community I had hoped for, one that mirrors the liberating model Freire describes, I feel as though I must face my own vulnerabilities and not allow them to keep me from risking authenticity in the classroom. In order to nurture a pedagogy that is problem-posing, as the instructor, I need to keep my insecurities in check, so that I do not hide behind credentials in a way that causes me to lean on my authority for its own sake in the classroom. The healthy use of authority by an instructor should nurture the dialogic character of the workshop.

The second shift is that I engaged students in self-consciously determining the ground rules for our workshops. During the first session of the semester, I offered to the class the principles outlined by Schneider. We discussed each one of them, as well as the logic behind them, and considered how they might be helpful for us in our workshops together. In discussing these each semester that I have taught the module, I witnessed students catch a vision for the class and take ownership as a community for how we work together. The students chose to commit to these, and we reviewed them again throughout the semester to assess how the principles impact our time together and how students experience these. The goal of discussing and assessing our ground rules is to disperse power in the class in such a way that all workshop participants, the teacher-student and students-teachers, take ownership of the practices by which we function communally, thereby nurturing a dialogic character to our interactions. In shifting to an instructor as participant model for the workshop, student buy-in becomes an even more important way to ensure ownership of the semester by all participants in the class.

The third shift grows out of the proceeding one in that our workshops do not simply ask that the person whose work is under review remain silent the entire time. In other words, the 'gag rule', which Rosalie Morales Kearns critiques in her essay 'Voice of Authority: Theorizing Creative Writing Pedagogy' has been lifted (2009, 792–794). Kearns seeks in the workshop setting to mitigate against what she sees as the traditional model's default mode towards 'fault-finding' (795). In our classes, we too have been concerned with dialogue as our primary mode of interacting with one another, as well as developing a supportive group that does not overly-criticize works-in-progress, both concerns that Kearns addresses (795). While Kearns offers a revised model of the workshop that allows the author to guide discussion (805), our classes have chosen a hybrid model that exists somewhere between the traditional 'gag rule' and the one offered by Kearns. In our version with the instructor as participant, we have sought to honour both listening to one another, as well as asking our own questions. As Stukenberg points out, the workshop activity of receiving feedback is important for the student author in developing their 'awareness of how readers interpret, and even co-create texts' (2017, 278). Receiving feedback empowers students to listen with patience to one another and to resist responding in a merely reactive or defensive way. The author listens to everyone's comments and then is given the opportunity to not merely ask for clarification, as in a traditional workshop model, but rather to introduce new questions to the conversation. This way of approaching the workshop reinforces the dialogic nature of a problem-posing model of education and keeps the instructor from usurping the direction of a workshop.

While I argue that the instructor becoming a participant in the workshop is an effective way to build community and nurture a more effective educational model, I would not argue that it is without problematic tensions, both intra-personally for the instructor and interpersonally between the instructor and the students. Carl Vandermeulen, in his book *Negotiating the Personal in Creative Writing*, finds in his survey of Creative Writing instructors that while some agree that writing with their students might impact classes in positive ways (2011, 124–125), others articulate potential problems that come in writing with students: (1) Anxiety of instructors sharing their work; (2) Fear of losing their authority once students critique the instructor's work; and (3) A consideration that some students might find it uncomfortable to critique a instructor's work (121–123).

The first potential problem deals with internal tensions for the instructor and sharing his or her work. To feel anxiety sharing one's work seems a common experience for creative writers; at least, it has been a constant concern with my own writing in the past. To share that work with one's students adds an additional layer of potential anxiety, as seen by the second potential problem Vandermeulen identifies, the fear of losing authority when one's work is critiqued by students. In my experience, the rewards of the sharing of one's work with students far outweigh the risk of yielding to these fears. In order to nurture a liberating pedagogy, one in sync with Freire's vision and Schneider's, the instructor must live with the tensions of these risks. To hold onto authority for its own sake ultimately proves detrimental to a liberating pedagogy.

In order for students to feel comfortable critiquing an instructor's work, a genuine trust must be nurtured between the instructor and the students. Students must be assured that a critical comment regarding an instructor's work will not negatively impact their grade for the course. In order to address this potential issue, the grading rubrics for the class weighted heavily on attendance and participation, as well as risk-taking in students' drafts of the major pieces of writing. In terms of student comments on their colleagues' and on my work, students simply received full-credit for completing these aspects of the class. In my experience, this issue has proven to be the most difficult to effectively address. Oftentimes, in students' critiques of my work, I found a dearth of comments that might sound critical. In our class discussions of how to critique one another's work, we stress the importance of emphasising a piece's strengths, but we also address the importance of honest, meaningful critique. For instance, in one set of responses to my work, of the seventeen students in the module that semester, only one offered what might be called a negative critique. To one of my poems, the student responds, 'I didn't engage with it as much as I did with the others. The only thought I have as to why is that it presented a somewhat commonplace perspective on the mind. Perhaps there's more ground left to till?' And then, to ensure that I did not perceive this as a completely negative comment, the student offers, 'Or perhaps I simply didn't connect to it and that's that'. Perhaps my desire for critique and my years of receiving feedback in workshop settings and from friends has conditioned me to desire nearly brutal treatment of my work. Or perhaps, and more likely the case, students remain uncomfortable criticising their instructor's work, out of fear of retribution to their grade, or simply due to their conditioning in other educational settings. One possible solution would be to have students critique the instructor's work anonymously. The primary drawback, however, is that this too might hinder honest conversation in the workshop setting during the session when the instructor's work is being discussed. To my mind, this issue remains a hurdle to address for a more complete form of problem-posing education to occur in the Creative Writing workshop.

With any pedagogical model, there are potential benefits and risks involved. In my experience of now teaching this class for multiple semesters, the potential positive outcomes far outweigh these risks. In shifting the power dynamic in the workshop and making the model more of a problem-posing dialogic model with the instructor as participant, I believe we have achieved a richer educational experience, one that has empowered students in their writing.

Conclusion

While this article has focused on the pedagogical underpinnings of shifting the power in the Creative Writing workshop and on the internal negotiations of the instructor in that process, I would like to close by considering briefly the students' experience of having the instructor as participant. Thus far, this shift of dynamics has felt like a success. That is not to say that the classes have not had problems, but at least, in my experience, students have commented on feeling empowered by this model of the workshop. In anonymous evaluations, one student assesses that the instructor sharing his own work was 'inspiring'; another comments they were able to do their 'best work' because the class had 'creat[ed] a truly helpful, communal group' where students were 'for each other'. Another observes that the instructor 'took part in our workshops, offered and received comments on writings. This was never done in a superior way, [rather] I felt as much a writer as he is because of his encouragement and excitement about my writing'. These comments speak positively to this model of the workshop, and more than the comments that I feel as personal praise, I am encouraged by the moments when students articulate the ways that they feel empowered in their writing. In the final reflective essay of the semester, one student assesses the experience positively and identifies a desire for a similar community going forward, when they assert:

> The community that this class provided fostered mutual respect and celebration of other people's words .... There are a few of us who plan to continue this kind of writing family through the next year as we continue in our respective writing pursuits.

As I continue to teach this module and reflect on the possibilities of the instructor as participant model of the workshop, I am also increasingly interested in considering the rhetorical strategies of the workshop's dialogue. My hope is that this article elicits more research on how an instructor might ensure that a workshop's week-to-week conversation fulfils the dialogic character of Freire's problem-posing model. While I think the instructor as participant model of the workshop is a step in this direction, more work needs to be done on how the workshop operates and how the instructor's shifted authority functions in practice.

Disclosure statement

No potential conflict of interest was reported by the author.

References

Bizzaro, Patrick. "Mutuality and the Teaching of the Introductory Creative Writing Course." In *Creative Writing Pedagogies for the Twenty-First Century*, edited by Alexandria Peary, and Tom C. Hunley, 94–138. Carbondale, IL: Southern Illinois University Press.

Cantrell, Mary. 2005. "Teaching and Evaluation: Why Bother?" In *Power and Identity in the Creative Writing Classroom: The Authority Project*, edited by Anna Leahy, 65–76. Clevedon: Multilingual Matters.

Elbow, Peter. 1990. *What Is English?* New York: Modern Language Association.

Freire, Paolo. 1993. *Pedagogy of the Oppressed*. New York: Continuum.

Haake, Katharine. 2005. "Dismantling Authority: Teaching What We Do Not Know." In *Power and Identity in the Creative Writing Classroom: The Authority Project*, edited by Anna Leahy, 98–105. Clevedon: Multilingual Matters.

Kearns, Rosalie Morales. 2009. "Voice of Authority: Theorizing Creative Writing Pedagogy." *College Composition and Communication* 60 (4): 790–807.

Leahy, Anna. 2005. *Power and Identity in the Creative Writing Classroom: The Authority Project*. Clevedon: Multilingual Matters.

Leahy, Anna. 2010. "Teaching as a Creative Act: Why the Workshop Works in Creative Writing." In *Does the Writing Workshop Still Work*, edited by Dianne Donnelly, 63–77. Clevedon: Multilingual Matters.

Lim, Shirley Geok-lin. 2010. "Lore, Practice, and Social Identity in Creative Writing Pedagogy: Speaking with a Yellow Voice?" *Pedagogy: Critical Approaches to Teaching Literature, Language, Composition, and Culture* 10 (1): 79–93.

Petty, Audrey. 2005. "Whose the Teacher? From Student to Mentor." In *Power and Identity in the Creative Writing Classroom: The Authority Project*, edited by Anna Leahy, 77–86. Clevedon: Multilingual Matters.

Schneider, Pat. 2003. *Writing Alone and with Others*. Oxford: Oxford University Press.

Stukenberg, Jill. 2017. "Deep Habits: Workshop as Critique in Creative Writing." *Arts and Humanities in Higher Education* 16 (3): 277–292.

Vandermuelen, Carl. 2011. *Negotiating the Personal in Creative Writing*. Clevedon: Multilingual Matters.

Creative writing on other planets

A sure sign of life on other planets would be if someone from one of those planets finally got their act together and started writing a poem. Say, for example, someone from the planet Thermador, where (we would then discover) poetry is composed in the trillions of small nuclei of a poet's hypothalamus and transmitted to the individual mind of a reader in an instant, taking the characteristics of what on Earth is called an emotion, a feeling or a thought. Alternatively, we might be lucky enough to go to our local pub one night and find there a reading by a creative writer from Circa, in the Circinus Galaxy, which was originally created by a supernova (the writer seems a little haughty simply because of that – after all, it is quite a thing). Of course, she also is not reading alone, because creative writers from Circa go about composing their work on the skin of their peers, so that each Circadian is (like our two readers) on average 15 feet in height and 9 feet in width, and is both the blank sheet and also the walking books of those around them. To us, such Circadian creative writing is called tattooing, or a medical skin condition known here on Earth as *dermatographic urticaria*, or it refers to the dark history of skin writing that has accompanied some of the horrific human acts of war and prejudice. But, of course, these Circadians we are currently watching are not from around here, so such comparisons are laboured.

Creative writers not from immediately around us make up the majority of creative writers in the universe. But a sure sign of life on other planets would be if one of them would just finally hurry up and start writing something. Someone, say, from IllopY, where novels are composed from the larval scum found in the many IllopYian ponds of hydrogen and liquid titanium and the results consumed entirely by dedicated novel aficionados in what many there consider a fringe hedonist group. 'IYiipYT!!' as the IllopYians say – meaning, roughly, 'Most in moderation!'

Yes, it's a real disappointment that someone from another planet has not yet seen fit to start spending the time and energy, because that would be so very helpful, and it sure is a shame not a single one of them can be bothered. Someone from Wysinc 9 in the Triangulum Galaxy, say, which is some 2.73 million light years away; or someone from Andromeda XI or from WISE J224607.57-052635.0, which has 10,000 times more energy than the Milky Way but cannot even produce someone to write a short story or a 10-minute script about a girl and a grey squirrel becoming solid friends.

The fact is, creative writing is not just one of the most human acts, it is also one of the most human *comparative* acts. We use creative writing to reveal and explore how we are both similar and different. And it is in this comparative similarity and difference that we define the significance of creative writing. While it is interesting to wonder if there are other planets in the universe that are inhabitable, and even to attempt to discover these planets, we know for sure that this one is. What we need to do more often is discuss our comparative acts of creative writing so that in comparison we explore life and in that exploration of this aspect of many lives we further define what it is to be human.

Graeme Harper

Different ways of descending into the crypt: methodologies and methods for researching creative writing

Francis Gilbert and Vicky Macleroy

ABSTRACT

This article argues that we need to 'descend into the crypt' of creative writing, and use rigorous, academic research methods and methodologies to examine it. The communities that writing arises from, processes of writing, the unique psychologies of writers, the ways in which writing is used in different settings and eras all need to be researched using well-established modes of research. The article argues that while quantitative research – the use of numbers and statistics – can offer insights into creative writing, it is qualitative research which affords the richest and most meaningful avenues. It shows that auto-ethnography with its focus upon the lived experiences of authors can provide illuminating insights. But it also demonstrates that Action Research, where writers use this research method to actively improve their writing and/or teaching of it, has many affordances. Multi-modal research with its perceptions into all the different modes – pictures, moving images, embodied learning – of writing provides the researcher with cutting edge research tools. Many writer-researchers also find using psycho-analytical frameworks can nurture therapeutic insights into writers' processes. This article is aimed at all creative writers who wish to explore writing processes further using established research.

Introduction: the clash of cultures as creative writing meets academia

There are real tensions between creative writing and academic research. Framing creative writing practices in academic language could be viewed as a fundamental mismatch, a clash of cultures (Bailey and Bizzaro 2017, 81; Hesse 2010, 32). The creative writer often needs to feel free to write without having to obsessively check their work for its factual accuracy, its rigour or even its coherence. However, accuracy, rigour and coherence are all hallmarks of effective research, which seeks to communicate its findings clearly and cor-rectly (Cohen, Manion, and Morrison 2007). So, in this sense, these two ways of writing can be at odds with one another: the tortoise trying to understand the hare.

This said the rise of creative writing courses in universities has meant that a consider-able amount of research into creative writing has been conducted over the last two decades, particularly by post-graduates conducting doctoral research in Creative

Writing. It should be noted that the vast majority of these PhD students are primarily creative writers and not researchers (Harper 2008). Most of these Creative Writing PhDs have critical components which necessitated research. Furthermore, PhDs of this sort are growing in popularity.

The programme the authors of this paper teach, the MA in Creative Writing and Education, also has a module in which creative writers are educated in research methodologies and methods. Many of the authors' students find conducting research into their own writing – usually, the focus of their assignments though not always – to be a deeply nurturing experience. For example, one student, Matilda Rostant, looked at how and why they loved to write fantasy fiction despite being ashamed of doing so and concluded by saying:

> Conducting this autoethnography has taught me to not belittle genre fiction, and that the amount of work that is put in to create a fantasy novel requires, not only great imagination, but also a deep understanding of reality.

Postgraduate Tanya Royer used her research to look at the role of the unconscious in her writing life. She explained her rationale as:

> Using reflective enquiry and data-driven analysis, I made my descent into the crypt, to investigate these mysterious elements of my psyche, with the aim of finding the truest possible version of myself and, within it, my fiercest, most honest writing voice.

Keen to learn what strategies might inspire him to write, James Ward set up a series of experiments using 'free-writing' and he concluded by saying:

> Over the course of this study freewriting proved to be a highly effective means to mining personal experience and engaging with self-reflection in terms of the creative writing process. And while the emerging data caused me a degree of anxiety and psychological disconcertion, I was also like entering a space rich new creative possibilities. And with this achievement came a sense of empowerment and liberation.

Janel Pineda examined her work in the Salvadoran community in Los Angeles, conducting ethnographic interviews with various participants in poetry workshops. She concluded by saying:

> Conducting this research, and particularly, the interviews with fellow Salvadoran community organizers in Los Angeles was ultimately a transformative process that in itself was a testament to the healing work of poetry-centered practice in activism. Broadly, this project revealed to me the importance of reflecting on how poetry has continued to play an instrumental role in Salvadoran community organizing. I was personally stunned by the depth at which each participant identified with the power of poetry, regardless of their own background and relationship to poetry.

What's important to perceive here is the sheer diversity of the assignments: the inspirations, processes and affordances of fantasy fiction, the investigation of the 'mysterious elements' of the psyche, the use of free writing to unlock creativity, and the power of poetry within the Salvadoran community in LA. Different ways of writing, different conceptions of our psychology, different communities, literary traditions and cultures were all explored in these assignments, and yet the research methods and methodologies which underpinned them were similar and offered a rigorous and meaningful lens through which they could view various writing processes and practices. Tanya Royer's metaphor of 'descending into the crypt' is an apt image for what often happens when creative writing is researched because, as the metaphor suggests, this can be done in different ways: you can take a torch to illuminate the darkness, you can choose to grope your way down the steps in the dark, you can ask people about their descents into the crypt, you could look at floor plan before hand and so on. There many ways of doing it. In this article, we focus upon the ones that our students have found the most fruitful: auto-ethnography, action research, multi-modal research and the use of psycho-analytic frameworks. The aim here is to give a general outline of the approach which should trigger further reading and research.

Why research creative writing?

What happens when creative writing is linked with education and researchers start to focus on how people learn to write creatively? It is still contested, in some literary quarters, whether creative writing is a suitable process for the researcher to investigate. There are several arguments against this form of research including:

> The mystique of writers' processes is destroyed by analysis. (Light 1996, 3)

> Creative writing is essentially a 'recreational' activity and of little importance in the 'real' world. (Childress and Gerber 2015; Hesse 2010, 32)

> Creative writing processes resist research because they are ultimately different for every writer, and therefore no 'generalisable' knowledge can be drawn from examining them. (Hesse 2010, 32)

In addressing these arguments, it is worth raising the question of how creative writing processes are defined. Creative writing has been researched in the form of literary criticism for centuries. However, analysing a piece of creative writing is, in some ways, quite different from investigating the creative writing process, which is the act of a person either preparing to write or writing something. Therefore, exploring creative writing involves first looking at a writer's processes and, then latterly, the finished product. The focus can be different from the literary critic who tends to look at the finished product of a writer or writers.

Research into creative writing processes involves looking in-depth at the experiences of writers and emerging writers and seeing creative writing itself as part of the research data. Creative writing researchers who are also creative writers 'are in the world and of the world that they research. They bring their own biographies and values to the research situation' (Cohen, Manion, and Morrison 2007, 304). Research into creative writing processes also involves developing a particular theoretical lens through which to frame the creative writing within culture and society. The central argument is that researching creative writing processes can provide insights and new ideas into how creative writing can be approached and how creative writers can extend and develop their own writing and the writing of others.

For the purpose of this article, creative writing is viewed primarily as a social process, even when it is carried out alone; our language is a common language and our words only mean something because they are shared between people. Even the loneliest of writers is working with this shared language in their heads and their bodies (Vygotsky and Kozulin 2012). In this article, it is contended that creative writing involves authors becoming part of what Etienne Wenger terms a 'community of practice' (1999). He writes:

> Practice is a shared history of learning that requires some catching up for joining. It is not an object to be handed down from one generation to the next. Practice is an ongoing, social, interactional process, and the introduction of newcomers is merely a version of what practice already is. That members interact, do things together, negotiate new meanings, and learn from each other is already inherent in practice – that is how practice evolves. In other words, communities of practice reproduce their membership in the same way that they come about in the first place. They share their competence with new generations through a version of the same process by which they develop. (1999, 102)

Writers learn from each other, either by reading other writer's books, being part of a writing group or by seeking to write in the style or genre of other authors: they are writing to communicate either something to themselves or other people. They carry out their practice by writing, by speaking on the page. This is an important starting point for any researcher to consider because it has implications for how and why writing might be researched – as we will see. Having established this key concept, it is now worth considering the problems people have with the idea of researching creative writing practices.

The mystique of the writers' processes

Many Romantic writers wrote about the almost magical process of writing. Wordsworth's famous definition of poetry as 'the spontaneous overflow of powerful feelings' which 'takes its origin from emotion recollected in tranquillity' (1800, xxxiii) still holds a powerful sway over the popular imagination regarding the writing process. The argument goes: if writing is a 'spontaneous' activity then clearly there's little craft involved; masterpieces are either born fully formed or not. The process is basically opaque, and simply not visible for analysis.

There are a number of arguments to counter this. First, we know that many writers complete many different drafts before arriving at their so-called 'works of genius': so we can look at this drafting process. Second, even if a piece of writing arrives fully formed in a first draft, it might be worth looking at the overall conditions which enabled this piece to be produced: the writer's psychological state, their biography, the time, location of their writing, etc. The argument that creative writing cannot be taught comes from the same root as this argument; writers are either born or not. Again, much evidence suggests that this is not the case. Recently, Carol Dweck and a number of other researchers have shown that it is not so much a person's innate ability that contributes towards their success in the world, but their willingness to learn and grow, their 'Growth Mindset' as Dweck terms it (Dweck and Yeager 2019). Dweck's research has important implications for writers and for the research into writing processes.

Creative writing is a 'recreational' activity

Unlike the scientist, who is involved in devising important experiments which will impact potentially on people's health, their environment, new technology, etc. the creative writer produces nothing of worth to society. This is the utilitarian argument: what is the point of art? We intend to contest these arguments and, drawing on research in the field of aesthetics, will show how stories and the imagination are fundamental to the shaping of human culture: they bring people together, give them a shared sense of meaning, help bring purpose and hope to society (Harari 2015).

Philosophers since Plato have argued about the value of art; figures such as Aristotle, Kant, Nietzsche, Heidegger and de Beauvoir have all forcefully put the case that art is a fundamental human practice, and that without it, no person or culture can be fully formed (Nahm 1975).

Creative writing processes resist research

Every writer's way of working is different. This may be the case, but there are still commonalities between writers: similarities in what they read, their backgrounds, their drafting processes, and their engagement with society. In the last thirty years, technology has changed the way many writers work both in terms of how they write (using for example computers), how they engage with and respond to their readers (the internet, social media, etc), and how they live. The researcher can offer valuable insights into these points. Increasingly, there is a debate about what exactly creative writing is, with writers from diverse communities using technologies such as video, audio, photographs, computer games to address new audiences and create new forms of creative writing. Media educator Mark Reid writes: 'All poetry is cinematic, and that all cinema should be poetic' (2005, 66).

Ethical issues in researching creative writing

All researchers are made aware of the ethical issues of conducting research with other people and acquiring consent from research participants regarding privacy, confidentiality, anonymity and their responsibility to the community (Cohen, Manion, and Morrison 2007, Chapter 5). However, researchers into creative writing may decide to make different decisions relating to anonymity. Research participants may choose to be named in the research and acknowledged for their creative writing and particular creative outputs. Hill (2014), in writing about community-based projects considers the 'politics of doing good' and the 'need for an ethical approach to story sharing' (Hill 2014, 35). Researchers need to ask these questions around the notion of ownership and creative writing and whether the creative writing of others will be acknowledged and celebrated within their research study. Researchers need to think about the purpose of their research into creative writing processes and ask the question: who benefits from their research?

Methods and methodologies

This article seeks to address the challenges of finding suitable ways of studying creative writing. It explores what particular research methodologies, research methods and research questions could be employed to investigate creative writing. It takes the view that a method is a series of actions which assist research, while a methodology is a conceptual framework within which the method is situated (Bell 2014, 101). As Cohen et al. note:

By methods, we mean that range of approaches used in educational research to gather data which are to be used as a basis for inference and interpretation, for explanation and prediction ... If methods refer to techniques and procedures used in the process of data-gathering, the aim of methodology then is to describe approaches to, kinds and paradigms of research. (2007, 27)

The article perceives therefore that methods and methodologies are inextricably intertwined; a particular way of looking at the world (the methodology) informs the way data is collected and the research conducted (the method). It seeks to answer key questions about methods and methodologies by asking:

- Are there particular research methodologies that are suited to researching creative writing?
- Which research methods open up opportunities for exploring creative writing?
- What sorts of research questions might particular research methodologies generate?

In the next part of the article, we discuss both quantitative and qualitative research approaches.

Quantitative research methodology and research methods with creative writing

The idea of representing the research into creative writing processes as numbers, which quantitative research seeks to do, may enrage many creative writers. As we will see, there is very little quantitative research in this area and this is possibly the reason why: representing creative writing practices as statistics and percentages is not appealing to many practitioners. Furthermore, many researchers may not be conversant with quantitative research methods. One of the findings of this article though is that there is still plenty of scope for research into this area, not least whether quantitative methods are suitable for researching creative writing.

Surveys and questionnaires

Surveys and questionnaires often include a qualitative element, such as written responses to open-ended questions, but they are often used in quantitative research too to generate statistics. This approach involves 'gathering large scale data in order to make generalisations' (Cohen, Manion, and Morrison 2007, 128). Tymms (2017, 223–240) highlights four reasons why educational researchers might want to use questionnaires:

1. Exploratory work: finding out the best way to proceed with some research.
2. Describing a population. Looking for patterns across a large group of people.
3. Outcomes or controls in studies. Questionnaires can be used to measure the effect of a particular intervention.
4. Feedback about particular classes/courses etc.

Researchers into creative writing processes could theoretically use questionnaires for all of these reasons, but it could be argued that certain types of questions are antithetical to the spirit of the creative writer. So, for example, is it appropriate to research this subject using things like like-type questions (e.g. strongly agree, agree, not sure, disagree, strongly disagree); multiple choice; ranking ordering; semantic differentials. E.g. how do you feel about free writing? Put a mark on this continuum: hate it … love it.

This said these sorts of questions can be helpful if researchers are dealing with large classes and want to get a rough sense of how people are thinking or feeling about a particular way of writing.

However, questionnaires can be used to ask more open-ended questions. There are common pitfalls to be aware of when designing questionnaires: leading questions which produce pre-determined answers; questions which are too general and produce no interesting specific data.

Possible research areas and question using surveys and questionnaires

A large group of writers could be surveyed about the technology they use to write with, or what motivates them to write based upon a set of criteria.

Possible research questions: What technologies do writers use: why, how?

Statistical techniques: testing and assessment

The aim here is to measure 'achievement and potential' (Cohen, Manion, and Morrison 2007, 129). A set of materials need to be drawn up to provide scores that can be added up, and then groups/individuals can be compared. Gorard writes:

> Generally, researchers using numeric data want to know how strong their finding is, where that finding could be expressed as a difference, trend or pattern. This estimate of the strength of finding is computed as an 'effect' size. (2017, 139)

He adds this important caveat:

> … the approach is very limited in only being concerned with generalisability to a population. It does not help analysts decide the really important point, which is whether the result is substantively important. (138)

At the time of writing, little statistical research has been carried out into creative writing 'interventions': for example, Cremin and Oliver could only find four quantitative studies into teachers' attitudes towards creative writing (2017, 5). However, this may be a growing field. Research organisations such as the Educational Endowment Foundation, focused upon helping pupils from poor backgrounds, appear to fund only statistic research into educational interventions and may decide to sponsor research into issues such as whether creative writing can raise the achievement of children on free school meals, a key indicator of poverty. Gorard's warning that this whole approach is 'unrealistic' is worth heeding. Such research often relies on what is known as 'randomised controlled trials' (RCTs) where a strategy such as say, free writing, is compared with a class that uses it (the intervention group) and a class that is very similar in make-up but isn't subjected to the intervention (the control group). Test scores are compared before and after the intervention and an 'effect' size is produced to see whether the intervention is statistically significant. Such research often is presented very confidently as a statistic, e.g X% of students improved their creative writing by using free writing. However, Gorard and other statisticians would contest the validity and reliability of results like these. In the field of health, Pennebaker (2000) and other researchers have used RCTs to look at the health benefits of getting patients to write expressively about their traumas. Pennebaker writes:

> Writing or talking about emotional experiences relative to writing about superficial control topics has been found to be associated with significant drops in physician visits from before to after writing among relatively healthy samples. (Pennebaker 2000, 7)

However, it's important to note that Pennebaker's research is often very modest in its statistical claims, and it tends to favour an interview-based, qualitative approach to a statistical one.

Possible research areas and questions using statistical techniques

There are many ways in which creative writing is scored and assessed in schools and universities. Research could focus upon who is achieving highly/poorly and why.

Possible research questions: How is creative writing assessed formally in UK schools? Who performs well and who does not?

Qualitative research methodology and research methods with creative writing

Researching creative writing tends to fit more closely with qualitative research methodology with its focus on interpreting experience and understanding the voices and stories of participants. Researchers are able to focus on creative writing processes as well as the creative writing itself and this research approach is seen as being guided by, quite often, messy and unstructured data that researchers need to make sense of to answer probing research questions. Qualitative research methodology tends to emphasise 'the essential role of subjectivity in the research process, to study a number of naturally occurring cases in detail, and to use verbal rather than statistical forms of approach' (Hammersley 2013, 12). In the next sections, we will consider qualitative research methodologies and research methods that have proven particularly useful to students researching creative writing.

Autoethnography methodology and methods

Creative writing researchers have become increasingly interested in using autoethnography as a methodological approach to asking questions about their own creative writing processes and looking at ways to learn new ways of doing things. Writers can profitably explore their own writing processes and products by using the tools of ethnography: 'the study of people in naturally occurring settings or "fields" by methods of data collection which capture their social meanings and ordinary activities' (Brewer 2000, 6). Researchers argue that carrying out an ethnography allows deep insights into the meanings and patterns of everyday life (Hymes 1996) and ethnographies 'allow us to tell a story; not someone else's story exactly, but our own story of some slice of experience, a story which illuminates social processes and generates explanations for why people do and think the things they do' (Heller 2008, 250). Autoethnography is about making sense of individual experience and connecting the personal to the cultural. An auto-ethnography requires the researcher to examine themselves as creative writers in their 'naturally occurring settings', looking at the 'social meanings' of their writing practices.

> Auto-ethnography is a research approach that privileges the individual. It is an artistically constructed piece of prose, poetry, music or piece of artwork that attempts to portray an individual experience in a way that evokes the imagination of the reader, viewer or listener. (Freshwater et al. 2010, 504)

Freshwater et al. are at pains to distinguish auto-ethnography from a description of an individual's experiences; while auto-ethnography focuses upon the lived experiences of an individual, it aims to situate the self within a wider social, historical, geographical and psychological context. Freshwater et al. note: 'Auto-ethnography privileges the self in the research nexus between art and science'. Auto-ethnographers are nearly always seeking to illustrate wider social points within their narratives:

> An individual story presents as a fiction in a world that reveres facts. It appears to sidetrack the serious world of research rather than supplement it. However, if we are really intent on understanding the blighted lives of people who are excluded from the hegemonic control of the dominant voice we have to listen carefully to how well the stories of individuals resonate with us no matter how uncomfortable this might be. (505)

The form is particularly suited to creative writers because it is a form of creative writing. Here the boundaries between research and creative writing begin to blur.

Autoethnographic research methods are suited to creative writers as researchers. However, using autoethnography does mean the researcher needs to write well:

> Most social scientists don't write well enough to carry it off. Or they're not sufficiently introspective about their feelings or motives or the contradictions they experience. Ironically, many aren't observant enough of the world around them. The self-questioning autoethnography demands is extremely difficult. So is confronting things about yourself that are less than flattering. Believe me, honest autoethnographic exploration generates a lot of fears and self-doubts – and emotional pain. (Muncey 2010, Chapter 3, 10–11)

Creative writers use autoethnographic research methods to confront obstacles. They also open up new opportunities in their own creative writing processes. Researchers explore why and how they write creatively. Their creative writing becomes their most important data source and they also use research journals to chart changes and new ways of working (Bolton 2010, 130).

Possible research areas and questions using autoethnography

Writers can look at their habitual writing practices, gathering together data from all of their ordinary activities, taking field notes about what they have noticed about their writing over a specified period of time. They can retrospectively examine writing practices at a particular time of their life for which they have suitable data. On the MA in Creative Writing and Education, students have explored a huge diversity of topics using auto-ethnography. Nearly all of them have involved delving into challenging lived experiences. For example, in *Holding Difficulty Lightly* (2019) Eve Ellis re-imagined her experiences as a mother and poet using auto-ethnography sharpened by a feminist lens to situate herself. She delved deeply into her writing practices when her child was very young. Using note-books, diaries, and poetry written at the time, she was able to reimagine that period of her life when writing felt a transgressive act, something that mothers of babies were not encouraged or possibly permitted to do. She writes here about dreaming of signing up for a poetry evening course:

> By disregarding conventions for mothers, I created a window of time when my imagination could wander far from the armchair and my child, when I could engage fully with my identity as a writer. I was assisted in this process by the technology of the iPad, which functioned as a portal through which I could sign up for the writing course, do the research required for my poem, and draft the piece. (42)

The auto-ethnographic research enabled her to perceive that a 'trickster' archetype, that of a creative risk-taker, shaped her impulse to write, freeing her from the shackles of stereotypical motherhood; she perceived that 'mother and trickster may be more closely related than one might think' (46).

Ioney Smallhorne in *Why I Write: Using Writing to Push Back Against Oppression* (2019) used auto-ethnography to explore her lived experiences of poverty, racism, trauma and dyslexia, investigating how she found a voice as a writer in a society which was both overtly and covertly oppressive. She loathed primary school because she struggled to read and had a stammer. However, she found a form of liberation when reading with and listening to her father. She writes:

> I would have to take the Pirate books home for extra homework. My parents would spend around 20 minutes after dinner reading with me. My Dad is Jamaican (and my Mum is of Jamaican heritage) so would often tell me his version of pirate stories, edited for a young child how they were bad people, who stole land and did horrible things to the Taino, Arawaks and other indigenous peoples of the Caribbean as well as African and Indian people. This time, with my parents, set the foundations for a discerning reader who later would investigate and oppose oppression, using writing for mobilisation. It was through these sessions that I learned that books didn't always tell the truth or at least didn't tell the whole story. That the truth and stories of black and brown people had to be excavated from the memory of elders, sieved through the words that appeared on 'their' page, and translated from 'their' dominant culture and language into ours, Jamaican Patois. (95–96)

This extract illustrates the power of auto-ethnographic research. We can see that it is more than autobiography; it is the researcher situating themselves in the field, looking at relevant wider social, psychological and cultural issues such as Smallhorne does here: cultural heritage, colonialisation, oral cultures and storytelling. By 'zooming in' on this moment, Smallhorne is able to draw out the richness of her lived experiences.

Topics of successful research in this area have included mothers exploring their writing practices while looking after a baby; writers examining their formative teenage years; and the literary, psychological, social and geographical factors that nurture creative writing.

Possible research questions: what factors and practices caused me to write creatively?

Action research methodology and methods

Here a writer 'plans, implements, reviews and evaluates an intervention designed to improve' (Cohen, Manion, and Morrison 2007, 129) some aspect of their writing or possibly the creative writing practices of their students. If participants are involved, then they contribute to the research process; this is sometimes known as participatory action research.

> The premise underlying action research in education is that practitioners are in the best position to engage in inquiry about their practice. Action research is typically conducted in natural settings (schools, communities, and organisations) where a researcher is concerned about a particular issue of practice. (Klein 2012, 3)

The cycles of Action Research shown above are possibly the simplest and clearest representation of how it can be conducted; the idea is that the researcher is on a cycle of improvement continuously. Koshy notes on several occasions that Action Research is a methodology in that it has embedded within it a clear theoretical framework; it is a collaborative form of research which is all about improving real-life situations, and provides 'rigour' in terms of collecting, analysing and interpreting data (2009, 15). It could be particularly useful for writers/researchers seeking to improve their own practice either as writers or teachers.

A number of our students use Action Research because it affords a rigorous and relatively straight-forward methodology for improving one's own practice and reflecting upon it. Its focus upon the learners' 'attitudes and values' (Cohen, Manion, and Morrison 2007) offers particularly rich ways of looking at the processes of creative writing. Katherine McMahon used Action Research, to help them develop and run a tarot and creative writing workshop for LGBTQ+ people. One of the conclusions of her research was this:

> Tarot, with its rich symbolism and big themes, can be a useful prompt to support participants in exploring their identities and experiences in their writing. Combining tarot with writing amplifies the possibilities for reflection and expression inherent in both. This kind of reflective practice is essential to the formation of identity as an active process which is empowering rather than limiting. (2019, 74)

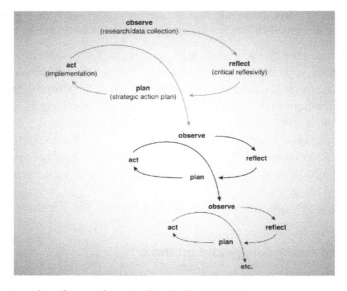

Figure 1. O'Leary's cycles of research as cited in Koshy (2009, 7).

In other words, there was a strong realisation that the methodology of Action Research which offers 'possibilities for reflection', 'reflective practice' and collaboration between workshop leader and participants was liberating for everyone. McMahon's research involved utilising the Action Research cycle of listening to herself and her participants' responses in order to bring out the full potential of using Tarot to get LGBTQ+ people to think about their 'identities and experiences in their writing'. Action Research particularly lends itself to these sorts of projects where issues connected with social justice and personal growth are central. As Pike perceives the power of Action Research lies in the fact that it is 'fundamentally ethical' because it seeks to have:

> a transformative social role, not simply because it facilitates the development and implementation of appropriate pedagogy, but because it has the potential to transform the professional culture. (2002, 36)

Action Research has played a vital role in other students' research already cited. Tanya Royer deployed 'a Buddhist-informed action research process' which involved 'a structured mix of mindfulness practice, free writing and an investigation of my spatial identity' (14). Here we can see how Action Research provided her with both structure and flexibility: she was able to infuse it with elements of Buddhism and mindfulness. This happened because both her practice of meditating in order to generate writing, and her reflective practice, where she evaluated her work and learning, involved being mindful and compassionate to herself.

Possible research areas and questions using Action Research

Looking back at many other students' research we can perceive that the Action Research cycle was unconsciously at play in much of what they did, and a major point of learning for us as tutors is that it could be utilised more often and more explicitly. Its value is that it brings clarity, honesty and a strong ethical dimension to the research because its key questions are:

- Can I improve my practice so that it is more effective on the terms laid out by myself and my participants?
- Can I improve my understanding of this practice so as to make it more just?
- Can I use my knowledge and influence to improve the situation? (Lomax quoted in Bell 2014, 17)

Action Research is particularly useful for teachers of creative writing because its central purpose is to generate a positive feedback loop whereby practice is being continually reflected upon and developed. In this sense, it is generally highly motivating, and if it isn't, then reflecting upon why the research is demoralising becomes part of the cycle of reflection. It's very helpful for any researchers who may want to explore how certain approaches can lead to better results in educational settings. The Action Research approach shares much in common with the 'Teachers as Writers' movement (Cremin and Oliver 2017; Smith and Wrigley 2012) in that it encourages teachers and pupils to work together on jointly planning a creative project. The Teachers as Writer movement encourages teachers to write alongside their students, and to dialogue with students about what is working for them.

Possible research questions: How can I improve my own creative writing and/or my teaching of creative writing?

Multimodal research methodology and methods

Researchers into creative writing have also begun to recognise the importance of multimodal research approaches to understand and make sense of experience. Theories of literacy research have shifted after the 'digital turn' (Mills 2016) with a particular focus on multimodal theory. This research approach allows creative writers to explore creative writing processes across different design modes: linguistic, visual, spatial, audio and gestural. Researchers using a multimodal research approach to interrogate creative writing processes can look at the possibilities given 'by a mode of representation to make [my] meaning' (Kress 2003, 2).

Researching creative writing processes using multimodal research methods allows creative writers to explore different design modes and, for instance, how music or visual art is part of their creative writing. It also enables researchers to look at how we learn to acquire different types of literacies depending upon the unique ecologies we grow up in (Barton 2007). This concept of ecology embraces the whole world we live in – nature, home, school, air, water, diet, etc. – and these all, in different ways influence what we say, read and write. Creative writers can collect research data to interrogate how we learn across modes and in a range of settings.

Researching and working with objects (Pahl and Rowsell 2010) has also become a significant research method for investigating creative writing processes. This approach builds on Pahl and Rowsell's theory of artifactual literacies (2010) and their notion of 'felt connections' where every object tells a story and objects remain powerful in our memories.

Possible research areas and questions using multimodality

Sara Hirsch, a poet on the Spoken Word Education and MA Creative Writing and Education programmes at Goldsmiths, researched what happened when poetry was combined with multimodal research and filmmaking. Sara's research was part of a larger multilingual digital storytelling project (Anderson and Macleroy 2016) and a pre-production stage of the filmmaking process was working with personal and cultural objects. Sara researched what happened to the students' poetry when they started working multimodally to create images and metaphors of belonging:

> Another turning point in the process was a session involving personal and cultural objects. The students were asked to bring in an item that mattered to them, particularly something that represented their culture. The students brought in flags, photos, scarves, jewellery and other items of significance, and the majority of the final poem was written in response to these objects. The prompts that the students were given ranged from free writes that were sparked by a memory of the object to exercises with more specific parameters. An example of a successful exercise was using the objects and photographs as physical metaphors for the students' sense of identity (My country is an artist, it paints the turquoise of my blood). Here the students were invited to use visual elements of the objects to represent their own emotions. By breaking down the object or photograph into a list of 'what we see' or 'what we feel', they became less like precious belongings and more like artefacts, with physical features to offer a piece of writing. (Macleroy and Hirsch 2019, 11)

This research project enabled Sara to examine some of the challenges and issues of bringing together different art forms in creative work. Her research is useful to other creative writers as it shows how these projects often take time (a school year) to set up and implement and it takes time for students to understand how they can belong to the process. The students reflected that when they understood the purpose of the project they felt connected to each other and to poetry. Their film can be seen here: *Belonging – A Spoken Word Poetry Film*: https://vimeo.com/219976715/

Possible research question: What multimodal ways of working nurture meaningful creative writing practices?

Psycho-analytic frameworks as research methodology

Psycho-analysis and creative writing are increasingly explored together. In his essay 'Creative Writers and Day-Dreaming' (1908) Freud posited the idea that creative writing itself was a form of therapy, an extension of childhood day-dreaming, wish-fulfilment and fantasising. Since then many other psycho-analysts and others working in the field of mental health have investigated the ways in which creative writing can be used to improve well-being. Some key concepts appear to be common in much of this work. These include:

- Catharsis and repression
- Identification and imitation
- Projection
- Dream imagery and archetypes

Catharsis and repression

These two concepts are intertwined. The ancient Greek philosopher, Aristotle, argued in contradiction of his teacher Plato that stories could have positive effects because the best of them allowed their audience to chance to 'purge' their extreme or dangerous emotions (2013). He put the case that a kind of purification process happens: audiences feel moments of sadness, grief, anger, depression which enables them to rid themselves of these feelings after experiencing these stories. This is what Aristotle calls 'catharsis' (2013). Subsequent theorising about the benefits of art, stories and creative writing builds upon the concept of catharsis in multiple ways. For example, Rainer argues in *The New Diary* (2004, 38–41) that diary writers should write down all their difficult feelings in their diaries in order to find a form of cathartic healing. Rainer uses Freud's psycho-analytical concept of repression to explain why this form of writing can be cathartic: feelings which have been unconsciously ignored, blocked, forbidden come to the fore and then can be 'let go' of. Much theorisation about creative writing takes these ideas as starting points. One of our students, Anna Degenaar, used a series of scheduled free writing sessions to explore challenging feelings about being female. Her research, entitled *Writing Myself Better: How Can Focused Freewriting Unlock the Female Character?* was simultaneously socio-cultural and therapeutic: she perceived how patriarchal, capitalist society nurtures strong feelings of self-hatred in women. The free writing and the research appeared to be healing for her. She wrote in her conclusion:

My research allowed me to refine my writing process by teaching me about idea generation and the way I can access difficult memories. The freewriting and reflection allowed me access to rich emotions and complex feelings that in most cases I had pushed aside or had trouble engaging with in the past. In the process I was able to hold these experience at a distance, which made them easier to learn from. By studying myself in this way, I gained a better handle on my personal history, which enabled me to better communicate my experience as a woman navigating the world. (2019, 35)

Possible research questions: To what extent are our emotions socially constructed and how can creative writing explore these social constructions? To what extent are creative writing practices cathartic?

Identification and imitation

The idea that both readers and writers strongly identify with certain characters and situations has its origins with Plato (Smith 2018), but again has been subsequently developed by many other thinkers, particularly psycho-analytic theorists such as Freud. Plato argued that art is dangerous precisely because people strongly identify with fictional, immoral characters and then imitate their actions (Smith 2018). Much research by our students examines the constricting fictions of everyday life. For example, Ioney Smallhorne (cited previously) examined the suffocating narratives which many people foisted upon her as a young girl at primary school, writing her story for her because she was of colour, female and dyslexic. Her research showed how she managed to re-write this narrative for herself.

Possible research questions: To what extent does the world write your story and to what extent can you write your own? To what extent do creative writers identify with the characters they are writing about?

Projection

Initially proposed by Freud, 'projection refers to protecting oneself from anxiety by repressing a feeling and misperceiving another person as having that feeling' (Kahn 2002, 128). A person might be described as horrible or disgusting when in actual fact it is the subject's projection of their own feelings and insecurities; a representation of how they are feeling. Much creative writing can be understood as forms of projection. A writer's description of a dystopian landscape could be a projection of their own feelings of disgust at themselves; a romantic story is a form of project or wish-fulfilment on behalf of the writer and so on. Anna Degenaar's research examined this issue when investigating the ways in which she had internalised feelings of shame about her body: she perceived this deeply by writing about her first period, first sexual encounter, feelings of discomfort, body hair, shame, initiating sex, and a one-night stand. Her analysis of her free writing showed how much projection was involved. Her research and writing enabled her to see through the patriarchal assumptions she had internalised and projected outwards into the world.

Possible research questions: To what extent do we project our fantasies and nightmares onto other people and situations? How can researching creative writing help us see through the projections? To what extent are creative writing practices a form of wish-fulfilment?

Dream imagery and archetypes

The process of writing stories could be linked to a form of conscious dreaming, with the writer using archetypes drawn from their unconscious to people their stories. Both Sigmund Freud and Carl Gustav Jung argued this process happens (Kahn 2002). Freud believed that many of the images that we produce in dreams and stories are a representation of repressed sexual desire, while Jung believed that many images are drawn from a collective unconscious that is shared by all of humankind (Kahn 2002, 169). Jungian archetypes have been of particular interest for our students because they are both creatively suggestive and also offer an imaginative lens through which to perceive creative practice. Eve Ellis (2019) was particularly drawn to Jung's analysis of the trickster archetype, a figure that is inherently playful, mischievous and transgressive, and wanted to claim it for her own. Making it part of her identity gave her the psychic space and time to be a writer. She wrote:

> My tricksterism also means continuing to set aside social conventions and inherited beliefs about what mothers are supposed to do– a fact I remind myself of on Saturday mornings when I send my partner and child off to playgroup while I head to my desk to write. (2019, 45–46)

Here we can see the power of the archetype: it appears to set Ellis free to write for herself. Tanya Royer used the archetype of the 'shadow self' in order to explicate her repressed unconscious desires. She wrote:

> Guided by the insights of Carl Jung, and by philosophers, essayists and novelists who had themselves explored the psyche's darker corners, I set out to engage this presence, what Jung termed the 'shadow self'.

In a similar way to Ellis, she set out on a psychic quest to discover this archetype. Again we can perceive the immense pull of these psycho-analytic concepts. These writers/researchers may not be using them in a strictly orthodox psycho-analytical fashion, but they are utilising them to explore socially taboo and difficult topics, which are connected with identity and the lived experiences of being a writer.

Possible research questions: What are the archetypes which are liberating or empowering for you as a writer? How might you research these archetypes and their emancipatory powers? To what extent are a writer's dreams and writing connected?

Conclusion and future implications for researching creative writing

There are a number of important findings in this article.

First, it mounts a strong case for 'descending into the crypt'. Creative writing is a worthy subject of rigorous, academic research. It debunks the idea that writing processes are opaque, utterly unique and/or irrelevant, and therefore either impossible to research or not worthy of research.

Second, it shows how there is a place for quantitative research, but that it can only go so far: analysing test data of creative writing pieces written in high-stakes examinations, getting people to numerically rate certain creative writing teaching strategies and so on has a value, but it is just a beginning. It scratches the surface.

Third, qualitative research offers the richest and most meaningful research avenue into creative writing. Its possibilities are almost infinite but we suggest that there are three main forms which have worked with our students time and again.

Fourth, auto-ethnography is possibly the most natural research method for research into creative writing because it utilises so many of the tools, values, ideas and concepts of the creative writer. It does so by situating creative writing within a more rigorous, socially contextual framework than much autobiography. This is its power: the researcher views creative writing within the relevant ethnographic 'field'.

Fifth, Action Research has many affordances for researchers because it is inherently ethical and motivational, providing many creative writers with a clear framework for improving their practice and reflecting deeply upon it.

Sixth, multi-modal research offers huge attractions for researchers because it pulls them into the richness of the worlds they inhabit, engaging them with new technologies, artefacts, pictures, photographs, videos, and perceiving the complex interconnections between creative writing and other modes, as well as making them see how the writing on the page can be transformed and enriched in other modes.

Seventh, psycho-analytical frameworks can illuminate the creative process in unexpected and emancipatory ways. Well-worn tropes and archetypes such as the 'trickster' and the 'shadow self' can have new life breathed into them when used to investigate the lived experiences of creative writing.

We strongly believe that researching creative writing in these ways opens up profound and probing questions about why and how we write. These methods and methodologies offer many ways for writers to 'descend into the crypt' of creativity.

Notes on contributors

Francis Gilbert was a teacher for 25 years in various UK state schools. He is the author of many books, including *I'm A Teacher, Get Me Out Of Here* (2004), *Analysis and Study Guide: Dr Jekyll and Mr Hyde* (2015), *The Mindful English Teacher* (2018) and *Snow on the Danube* (2019). He is now a senior lecturer in education at Goldsmiths, University of London, where he is the course leader for PGCE English and the head of the MA in Creative Writing and Education. He is a member of the Higher Education Committee of the National Association of Writers in Education (NAWE) and a Senior Fellow of the Higher Education Academy. http://www.francisgilbert.co.uk/; https://www.gold.ac.uk/educational-studies/staff/gilbert/; Twitter: @wonderfrancis

Vicky Macleroy is a Reader in Education and Head of the Research Centre for Language, Culture and Learning at Goldsmiths, University of London and co-ordinates the MA Children's Literature: Creative Writing Pathway programme. Vicky's research focuses on language development; creative writing practices; poetry; multiliteracies; and transformative pedagogy. Vicky has led research projects in the field of multilingualism and literacy. Vicky was principal investigator with Jim Anderson of a global literacy project funded by the Paul Hamlyn Foundation, 'Critical Connections Multilingual Digital Storytelling' (2012–2017), that uses digital storytelling to support engagement with language learning and digital literacy. Vicky continues to lead multilingual digital storytelling projects funded by the Language Acts and Worldmaking AHRC project and a public engagement grant from Goldsmiths (2018–2021).

Disclosure statement

No potential conflict of interest was reported by the authors.

References

Anderson, J., and V. Macleroy. 2016. *Multilingual Digital Storytelling: Engaging Creatively and Critically with Literacy*. Oxford: Routledge.

Aristotle. 2013. *Poetics (Oxford World's Classics)*, trans. A. Kenny. Oxford: Oxford University Press.

Bailey, C., and P. Bizzaro. 2017. "Research in Creative Writing: Theory Into Practice." *Research in the Teaching of English* 52 (1): 77–97.

Barton, D. 2007. *Literacy: An Introduction to the Ecology of Written Language*. 2nd ed. Malden, MA: Blackwell.

Bell, J. 2014. *Doing Your Research Project: A Guide for First-time Researchers in Education, Health and Social Science*. 6th ed. Maidenhead: McGraw-Hill Education.

Bolton, G. 2010. *Reflective Practice: Writing & Professional Development*. London: Sage.

Brewer, J. D. 2000. *Ethnography*. Buckingham: Open University Press.

Childress, C., and A. Gerber. 2015. "The MFA in Creative Writing: The Uses of a 'Useless' Credential." *Professions and Professionalism* 5. doi:10.7577/pp.868.

Cohen, L., L. Manion, and K. Morrison. 2007. *Research Methods in Education* (6th ed., Vol. 1). London: Routledge.

Cremin, T., and L. Oliver. 2017. "Teachers as Writers: A Systematic Review." *Research Papers in Education* 32 (3): 269–295.

Dweck, C., and D. Yeager. 2019. "Mindsets: A View From Two Eras." *Perspectives on Psychological Science* 14 (3): 481–496.

Ellis, E. 2019. "Holding Difficulty Lightly." In *Story Makers Dialogues* [Goldsmiths' edition], Carnegie School of Education, Leeds Beckett University, 39–48. https://www.leedsbeckett.ac.uk/-/media/files/schools/school-of-education/smd-creating-possibilities-issue-2/story-makers-dialogues-the-benefits-of-creative-writing-issue-3.pdf?la=en (accessed 30 April 2020).

Freshwater, D., J. Cahill, E. Walsh, and T. Muncey. 2010. "Qualitative Research as Evidence: Criteria for Rigour and Relevance." *Journal of Research in Nursing* 15 (6): 497–508.

Freud, S. 1908. *Creative Writers and Daydreaming*. Originally published as a translation, "'The Relation of the Poet to Daydreaming," *Clinical Psychologist* 4: 172–183, translated by I.F. Grant Duff. https://www.evergreen.edu/sites/default/files/alumni/images/Freud_Creative_Writers_Daydreaming.pdf (accessed 24 July 2020).

Gorard, S. 2017. "Statistical and Correlational Techniques." In *Research Methods and Methodologies in Education*. 2nd ed., edited by R. Coe, M. Waring, L. Hedges, and J. Arthur, 138–149. London: Sage.

Hammersley, M. 2013. *What Is Qualitative Research? What Is? Research Methods*. London: Continuum/Bloomsbury.

Harari, Y. 2015. *Sapiens: A Brief History of Humankind*. London: Vintage.

Harper, G. 2008. "Creative Writing: Words as Practice-led Research." *Journal of Visual Art Practice* 7 (2): 161–171.

Heller, M. 2008. "Doing Ethnography." In *The Blackwell Guide to Research Methods in Bilingualism and Multilingualism*, edited by Li Wei and M. Moyer, 249–262. London: Blackwell.

Hesse, D. 2010. "The Place of Creative Writing in Composition Studies." *College Composition and Communication* 62 (1): 31–52.

Hill, A. 2014. "Digital Storytelling and the Politics of Doing Good." In *Community-based Multiliteracies and Digital Media Projects*, edited by H. Pleasants and D. Sater, 34–46. New York: Peter Long.

Hymes, D. 1996. *Ethnography, Linguistics, Narrative Inquiry: Toward an Understanding of Voice*. London: Taylor and Francis.

Kahn, M. 2002. *Basic Freud: Psycho-analytic Thought for the 21st Century*. New York: Basic Books.

Klein, Sheri R. 2012. *Action Research Methods: Plain and Simple*. New York: Palgrave Macmillan US.

Koshy, V. 2009. *Action Research for Improving Educational Practice: A Step-by-Step Guide*. 2nd ed. London: SAGE.

Kress. 2003. *Literacy in the New Media Age*. Oxon: Routledge.

Light, G. 1996. "Towards a Theory of Creative Writing." https://www.researchgate.net/publication/328315754_Towards_a_Theory_of_Creative_Writing (accessed 30 April 2020).

Macleroy, V., and S. Hirsch. 2019. "The Art of Belonging: Exploring the Effects on the English Classroom When Poetry Meets Multilingual Digital Storytelling." *English in Education*. doi:10.1080/04250494.2019.1690394.

McMahon, K. 2019. "Writing the Cards." In *Story Makers Dialogues* [Goldsmiths' edition], Carnegie School of Education, Leeds Beckett University, 74–84. https://www.leedsbeckett.ac.uk/-/media/files/schools/school-of-education/smd-creating-possibilities-issue-2/story-makers-dialogues-the-benefits-of-creative-writing-issue-3.pdf?la=en (accessed 24 July 2020).

Mills, K. 2016. *Literacy Theories for the Digital Age*. Bristol: Multilingual Matters.

Muncey, T. 2010. *Creating Autoethnographies*. London: SAGE Publications Ltd.

Nahm, M. 1975. *Readings in Philosophy of Art and Aesthetics (The Century Philosophy Series)*. Englewood Cliffs, NJ: Prentice-Hall.

Pahl, K., and J. Rowsell. 2010. *Artifactual Literacies: Every Object Tells a Story*. New York, NY: Teachers College Press.

Pennebaker, J. 2000. "Telling Stories: The Health Benefits of Narrative." *Literature and Medicine* 19 (1): 3–18.

Pike, M. 2002. "Action Research for English Teaching: Ideology, Pedagogy and Personal Growth." *Educational Action Research* 10 (1): 27–44.

Rainer, T. 2004. *The New Diary: How to Use a Journal for Self-guidance and Expanded Creativity*. New York: Jeremy P. Tarcher/Penguin.

Reid, M. 2005. "Cinema, Poetry, Pedagogy: Montage as Metaphor." *English Teaching* 4 (1): 60–69.

Smallhorne, I. 2019. "Why I Write: Using Writing to Push Back Against Oppression." In *Story Makers Dialogues* [Goldsmiths' Edition], Carnegie School of Education, Leeds Beckett University, 92–103. https://www.leedsbeckett.ac.uk/-/media/files/schools/school-of-education/smd-creating-possibilities-issue-2/story-makers-dialogues-the-benefits-of-creative-writing-issue-3.pdf?la=en (accessed 30 April 2020).

Smith, J., and S. Wrigley. 2012. "What Has Writing Ever Done For Us? The Power of Teachers' Writing Groups." *English in Education* 46 (1): 70–84.

Smith, R. 2018. "Plato." In *Macmillan Interdisciplinary Handbooks: Philosophy: Education*, edited by B. Warnick. New York: Macmillan US. https://search-credoreference-com.gold.idm.oclc.org/content/entry/macuspe/plato/0?institutionId=1872 (accessed 20 May 2020).

Tymms, P. 2017. "Questionnaires." In *Research Methods and Methodologies in Education*. 2nd ed., edited by R. Coe, M. Waring, L. Hedges, and J. Arthur, 223–240. London: Sage.

Vygotsky, L., and A. Kozulin. 2012. *Thought and Language* (Rev. and Expanded ed., edited and with a new foreword by Alex Kozulin). Cambridge, MA: MIT Press.

Wenger, E. 1999. *Communities of Practice: Learning, Meaning, and Identity (Learning in Doing: Social, Cognitive and Computational Perspectives)*. Cambridge: Cambridge University Press.

Wordsworth, W. 1800. "Preface to the Lyrical Ballads in 'The Lyrical Ballads'," T. N. Longman & O. Rees, London.

Forms of illumination

This week, I was on the phone accepting a new job during the year's biggest thunderstorm – which made me wonder about the choice I was making. Call it a kind of atmospheric cross-examination! When the sky is clear and there is nothing rumbling it seems simple to take a next step; but, when it's stormy, and the air is unsettled, the ground beneath you seems less solid. Neither condition is definitive or any guarantee you're making the right choice, but both influence your thoughts and feelings. I had applied for the job online a few months earlier, during a bright, steady, sunny summer. Now, months later, in late afternoon, the windows of the house were being buffeted by rain and lightning flashing a different kind of light, in sheets across a dark sky …

I set the phone down with a half-hearted 'Looking forward to it!' and stared out into the darkening street.

'It's what happens when you go hopping around!' Phil piped, suddenly, seated behind me prying a nail from a board he was going to shape and carve into the remains of a nineteenth-century washboard. He liked to make imitation historical artefacts from contemporary domestic waste and to claim he had found them. It was something of a dishonest practice, but he did draw attention to the plight of preserving the past and the upshot was greater public sympathy for heritage, so we largely ignored the con.

'I'm hardly hopping,' I said.

He smoothed his hand over the broken board, pulling a sliver of thick, old, pale paint from one corner and examining it.

'Five years isn't hopping.'

'I guess not,' he said, absently.

The thunder rumbled.

'Anyhow,' I said, 'it's time.'

'I guess so,' said Phil.

'Right?'

'Sure,' he said, turning the board in front of him, inspecting it closely.

The lightning struck and spread out over the sky, which was so dark now that when the light spread it lit the clouds from behind and they formed an illuminated archipelago.

'Wild out there,' I said.

He looked at me directly, with the beginning of his artefact held out in his hands. 'Actually, I wouldn't have thought you'd change it up so … much,' he replied.

The thunder followed the lightning, closer now.

'Oh?' I said.

He stood up. 'You can't force good stuff to happen, you know?' he said. 'You can only create the circumstances for it. In my view.'

As he stepped into the laundry to submerge his counterfeit historical discovery into a bucket of vinegar and tea he was keeping there, to age it, he was lit by another sheet of lightning and his standing shadow sprang up thinly, all the way to the ceiling.

When we write creatively, drafting and revising and editing, we employ actions and aspects of change-making – creatively, perhaps structurally, perhaps thematically or in the interests of a renewed or new subject or subjects. We pursue the circumstances for the reader to explore something anew with us, and we do this also with our self-expression in mind, our own desire to express something, uniquely, individually – to illuminate something so far hidden or newly discovered.

Though as creative writers we often at least hope to predict something of how a reader (or audience, in the case of visual and aural texts) will react to what we present to them, we can't ensure much of it. Writing skill and experience notwithstanding, we have limited predictive ability, a relatively small chance of forecasting how one individual or another will react to aspects of our novels or our poems or our scripts. Individual psychology, language, culture, all play a role. We can speculate on the reaction, but we can hardly be sure of it. And that is in fact part of the joy of writing creatively – the interchange (even the clash) of individual imaginations, ours as writers, those of our readers/audiences, our own feelings and thoughts, those of others – each individual connecting in a not entirely predictable way.

All this is elemental and illuminating – whether that illumination is bright, steady, and sunny or it is abrupt flashes of lightning in the dark (followed by thunderous concern about whether what we've done communicates what we desire to communicate!). The forms of illumination creative writing embodies and inhabits are empowering of human choice if not, given the vast range of humans, narrow in result.

Graeme Harper

Retooling workshops of empire: globalising creative writing with an edge*

Khem Aryal

ABSTRACT

The creative writing workshop has been questioned as the appropriate, signature pedagogy in the recent years more than ever for various reasons. While the discussions around the workshop reveal to us the consequences as well as the limitations of the traditional workshop, the pedagogy continues to dominate the teaching of creative writing not only in the United States but also around the world where creative writing programmes are burgeoning at a fast pace. In this context, it is pertinent to ask what kind of writing the workshop is perpetuating in other parts of the world where the workshop has been accepted as the default creative writing pedagogy, and what more those programmes can, and should, do to have an edge.

Creative writing in America, and elsewhere, gets unequivocally identified with a specific pedagogy, the workshop, often called the discipline's 'signature pedagogy.' In recent years, the workshop has taken some heat for having changed little since its emergence in Iowa and development in the 1930s–1950s. One major strain of critique of the workshop in the contemporary creative writing studies scholarship questions the validity and relevance of the traditional workshop's emphasis on the product rather than the process, hence casting all creative writing students of the twenty-first century, not just MFA students, in the image of the Iowa Workshop's 'cadre of graduate students, the 'polished' writers who populated the workshop as it took hold in creative writing mythology' (Vanderslice 2010, 32). Stephanie Vanderslice's argument that 'the traditional, product-centered creative writing workshop gives little to no attention to invention and creativity, to how poems, short stories, essays or plays are actually *constructed*' sums up this strain of critique (33). Another strain of the workshop critique deals with the traditional workshop's impact on the kind of literature that is being produced in the United States. This is more of a literary approach (than the process and skills approach) to studying creative writing, which in recent years has culminated in works like Mark McGurl's *The Program Era* and Eric Bennet's *Workshops of Empire*. While these discussions reveal to us the consequences as well as the limitations of the traditional workshop, it continues to dominate the teaching of creative writing not only in America but also around

---

*An earlier version of this work was presented at the 28th Annual Conference of GASI in Morocco and published in the proceedings of the conference.

the world where creative writing programmes are expanding at a fast pace. In this context, it is pertinent to ask what kind of writing the workshop is perpetuating in other parts of the world where the workshop has been accepted as the default creative writing pedagogy, and what more those programmes can, and should, do to have the edge.

Since the founding of the first creative writing programme in the United States, the University of Iowa Writers' Workshop, commonly known as the Iowa Workshop, in 1936, the teaching of creative writing has expanded exponentially in the country. There were 244 Creative Writing MFA and 50 Creative Writing PhD programmes in the United States in 2016 (Brady 2017). The Association of Writers and Writing Programs (AWP 2017) claims in its 2017 annual report to have served over 550 writing programmes across North America and beyond each year. Amy Brady reported in 2017 that a total of 20,000 applicants applied to MFA programmes that year and more than 3000 MFAs are 'minted' every year (Brady 2017). The AWP annual conference brings together more than 12,000 writers and professionals and more than 2000 presenters present in more than 550 different sessions (AWP 2017).

This development in America has had a direct influence on educational institutions around the world, and, as novelist Viet Thanh Nguyen (2017) notes, 'the American way of teaching writing is beginning to spread globally.' It is relatively hard to determine the exact number of programmes that teach creative writing around the world, but it is not hard to see that creative writing instruction has spread around the world at a fast pace, to universities in Hong Kong and India to Australia, the UK and Africa. This 'American way of teaching writing' which is spreading around the world is the way of the workshop, which, if we agree with Eric Bennett as he argues in his 2015 book *Workshops of Empire: Stegner, Engle, And American Creative Writing During the Cold War*, is a construct of the 'empire' perpetuating a certain ideology. Nguyen rightly contends that the workshop pedagogy is 'a model of pedagogy that is also an object lesson in how power propagates and conceals itself,' and there's a risk of this pedagogy being followed around the world 'with all its unexamined assumptions.'

The workshop as we know

Creative writing in America has its roots in a course in composition (Advanced Composition at Harvard), the progressive education movement, and writers' colonies, according to D. G. Myers (2006). In essence, the teaching of creative writing was a new humanist project, the idea that teaching and studying great books (of literature) was the path to knowledge, and ultimate salvation. Paul Engle, Wallace Stegner, and Norman Foerster, perhaps the most important figure in the history of creative writing instruction in America, were all committed humanists; it was their faith in literature that made space for creative writing in the university. Norman Foerster believed that creative writing was a way of studying literature from inside, i.e. studying literature by writing it.

The workshop was established as creative writing's default pedagogy in the 1920s as a result of the progressive education movement's enormous faith in children's ability to learn from nature and on their own. The workshop made space for students to come forth with their own ideas, hence become 'creative,' and learn. As Eric Bennett (2015) explains, this naturally helped confine their practices to what they – the classroom participants – thought and believed conducive to their learning, and New Criticism readily provided them a tool. As a result, Bennett further explains, the workshop helped the New Humanists, who established creative writing in the university, steer the programme toward the personal instead of the social and political, toward the individual author's 'earnest craft' instead of theory and ideology.

And creative writing 'gain[ed] a distinct character after 1945' (Bennett 2015, 16) as the 'empire' saw opportunity to manipulate its pedagogy to serve its own ends. Eric Bennett argues that in around the 1950s the workshops at Iowa and seminars at Stanford

> heralded a new academic discipline created by men who not only loved literature but also reacted to the pressure of political anxieties, felt the lure of philanthropic money, and placed enormous faith in the role literature could play in the peace that followed World War II. (32)

The 'philanthropic face or Standard Oil' from the Rockefeller Foundation, in the words of Bennett, 'ignited programs in education and public health around the globe' to contain forces that might 'endanger a national and international atmosphere conducive to stable markets' (58–59). 'Anxieties about totalitarianism, the containment of Communism, the repudiation of American radicalism, the newly powerful mass culture, and the nature of literature all contributed to the contours of the emerging discipline' (8), and it all got epitomised in its signature pedagogy, the workshop. The workshop became a space for the discussion of mere techniques in terms of writing skills and the personal in terms of the subject matter for the writers.

This helped turn the teaching of the writing of literature into a pacifist enterprise, resulting in the production and consumption of a specific kind of literature, 'a body of work that it is fair to describe as self-involved even when its interests are patently social and historical' (McGurl 2009, xi). Mark McGurl, in his study of post-war fiction as a product of the creative writing programme, *The Program Era*, doesn't quite see the ideological manifestation as Bennett does, but he concludes that 'the creative writing program produces programmatically,' and adds, 'but also in rich and various profusion, a literature aptly suited to a programmatic society' (xii). This consequence of creative writing programmes (namely, the workshop, and a synonym for the MFA programme) has become a subject of much critique in recent years.

Anis Shivani sums up the discontent about the new development in his near 'infamous' book among MFAs, *Against the Workshop: Provocations, Polemics, Controversies,* thus: 'Contemporary American fiction has become cheap counseling to the bereaved bourgeois. Its scope is restricted too much to the trivial domestic sphere. It promotes grief, paralysis, inaction: a determinism for the post-politics society, where ideology has no place' (2011, 12). He continues, 'The vacuum in political ideology is being filled today by an anti-politics, or personality and charisma, leading to gradual submission to authoritarianism among all potential sources of resistance' (19). Shivani declares, 'The MFA programs are killing writing in this country' (19), and claims, '[A]ll American fiction is minimalist in a sense – there is no European or Asian or Latin American-style maximalist pursuit of the indefinable' (23).

The MFA (hence, the workshop) has mostly come under fire from authors coming from outside the 'mainstream' (i.e. white) American authors. Junot Diaz, the 2008 Pulitzer winner, lambasts the lack of attention in workshops to issues that matter most to authors of other races and cultures. He writes in an article for the *New Yorker*,

> In my workshop we never explored our racial identities or how they impacted our writing – at all. Never got any kind of instruction in that area – at all. Shit, in my workshop we never talked about race except on the rare occasion someone wanted to argue that "race discussions" were exactly the discussion a serious writer should not be having. (Diaz 2014)

Diaz impersonates the standard, 'mainstream,' white contentment: 'I don't want to write about race, I want to write about real literature.' That 'real literature' is the anti-political voice of the workshop. He quotes one of the MFAs complaining about one of her peers saying, 'Our workshop is about writing, not political correctness.' The US-exported creative writing programme tends to lack what Diaz says most MFAs in the US, without diverse faculty, lack – 'the tradition of resistance.'

Bennett argues in his 2014 article, 'How Iowa Flattened Literature,' that the Iowa Workshop rose to prominence by capitalising on the fears of communism and the hopes in the midst of the Cold War. The pedagogy took to a set of distinct features that would not only be easier to teach but also avoid questions of bigger consequences. He contends,

> In our workshops, we simply accept it as true that larger structures of common interest have been destroyed by the atomizing forces of economy and ideology, and what's left to do is be faithful to the needs of the sentence. (Bennett 2014)

Nguyen rightly takes issue with the signature pedagogy, and the ideology it propagates, which is 'the nobility of craftsmanship' – he qualifies it – 'physical (not intellectual) labor – and masculinity' (Nguyen 2017). This 'nobility of craftsmanship' is supposedly achieved by excluding 'political and historical concerns' that Nguyen would be worried about as he participated in workshops.

The creative writing that has been practiced in America and is being exported is the workshop, which to a large extent equals craft, which equals textual analysis and study and the 'surface manipulation of language' (Mayers 2018) at the cost of bigger issues of literary study and production. Though not explicitly acknowledged, New Criticism is the pedagogy of the workshop, in which, Nguyen (2017) sums up, 'Politics and the spirit of collectives would not be in fashion.' Nguyen continues, 'What would be in fashion: voice, experience, and showing rather than telling. So it is that workshops typically focus on strategies of the writing "art" that develop character, setting, time, description, theme, voice and, to a lesser extent, plot.' This is codified, practiced, and expressed as 'craft' and/or 'technique.'

Graeme Harper makes a distinction between the act of creative writing and the final product – poems, stories, novels. The workshop disproportionately focuses on the final product, and neglects the politics of the process, the act. When are too focused on the final product, we end up making the 'craft' our tool. Harper writes, 'Those completed works might indeed be an important reason a creative writer begins writing (2013). They might inspire a writer, provide wonderful … models, suggest solutions to creative writing problems … . But they are not in *essence* creative writing' (2). He argues that all those products are the result of creative writing, the *event*. This can be a helpful way of further explaining why the traditional workshop finds a natural ally in craft, instead of making space for what goes into the production, circulation, and consumption of literature, the 'politics and the spirit of collectives,' to use Nguyen's (2017) words.

Creative writing at Ashoka University: an anecdotal look

Ashoka, a new Liberal Arts University in India, offers a minor in creative writing. The programme offers four different courses in creative writing: Introduction or Creative Writing (two genres), The Craft of Writing (genre specific – poetry, fiction, and nonfiction), Creative Writing Workshop ('A laboratory for working writers'), and Critical Thinking Seminar in Creative Writing. A cursory look at the course description will tell us that, to a large extent, the courses function within the ideology of the workshop and tend to teach the craft of writing.

The description of 'Introduction to Creative Writing' situates the course more within the process approach to teaching writing. It reads: 'The emphasis will be on generating a lot of raw material, and advancing a chunk of this work toward completion.' It adds, 'At the end of the course, students will learn how to look at literature from the point of view of a practitioner and apply writing techniques to a variety of rhetorical situations.' The rest of the courses move in the direction of the lab. The description of the second course, 'The Craft of Writing,' says, 'Exercises in the technique of writing, such as rhythm, metre, point of view, voice, narrative, pacing, will be combined with discussion of student writing and texts selected by the instructor.' 'Creative Writing Workshop' is described as 'a laboratory for working writers' which implicitly focuses on technique, as the main task will be to 'write in each class, share new work with peers and help each other to develop early drafts with honest, critical feedback.' The last course is titled, interestingly, 'Critical Thinking Seminar in Creative Writing' but the goals and pedagogy are not any different (of course, it is yet another creative writing course): 'The goal is to reflect on writing methods, techniques, and reading literature with the eyes of a writer' ("Minor"). But to the programme's credit, though, it also offers courses in theories though not within creative writing.

My purpose here is to only hint at how the creative writing programmes fashioned after US creative writing programmes can end up with a little too much focus on craft, the technique, with only a little or no room for theory of literature and literary production, issues of socio-cultural and political ramifications. In the true fashion of New Humanism, students may be treated as just individuals and encouraged to develop their skill sets to write their stories, at the most with the help of each other, in essence, functioning within the epistemology of the traditional workshop pedagogy, with its roots in the progressive education movement that relied on the individual's experiment with truth and inherent talent.

So the question today is – what do we want from creative writing? If we stick to the pedagogy of the traditional workshop, whether in the U.S. or outside, we will end up helping certain political ideology and power to prevail.

Alternative practices

Encouragingly, alternative models of the workshop are emerging in other parts of the world. As Vanderslice states, '[C]onsidered, thoughtful, even vanguard programs are beginning to dot the landscape,' in places like UK and Australia, 'where much exciting work is being done overall in postsecondary creative writing theory, education and curriculum' (Vanderslice 2011, 10). Although US creative writing programmes were instrumental in the establishment of creative writing in Australia and the United Kingdom, the programmes in those countries have taken a direction, away from the traditional workshops of empire.

Unlike the American model, the Australian model (if we can call it a model at all), as outlined by Paul Dawson in his book *Creative Writing and the New Humanities* (2005), erases the line that exists between creative writing and literature, and presents creative writing not as a solely craft practice devoid of theoretical and 'intellectual' dimensions. Dawson contends that creative writing should become the new torch-bearer of the English department and creative writers should be the new public intellectuals. According to Dawson, what distinguishes creative writing in Australia is the programme's scholarly dimension. Creative writing in that country is no less academic and theoretical enterprise than any other university discipline. It is not removed from literature, and it doesn't limit itself to New Critical analysis of literature and techniques of mastering the craft of writing, devoid of socio-political and cultural dimensions of literary production and consumption.

By placing creative writers squarely at the centre of the university's intellectual life, Dawson re-imagines of a New Humanities in which creative writers assume the position of public intellectuals. This re-imagining not only requires literature to be placed at the centre of what creative writers practice but also expects creative writing to be an interdisciplinary enterprise. What makes it all possible is making space for theory in creative writing. Dawson argues, 'Creative Writing needs to answer the critique of authorship and of the category of literature offered by Theory, rather than simply rejecting this critique as unhelpful or deleterious to literary culture' (2005, 161). He suggests three models of theory application in creative writing: (a) integration model, (b) avant-garde model, and (c) political model. Of the three, the political model gives creative writing the most radical departure from 'craft' based writing pedagogy. I quote him at length:

> The focus [of this model] is not on formal experimentation but on the pragmatics of production and reception within the framework of Cultural Studies. In this model of teaching, the workshop is not a neutral zone for the development of literary craft, but a site at which critiques of the poetics of representation and analysis of the circulation of literature across different institutions become part of the ethical and professional training of students who will emerge, not as writers who know the avenues of commercial publication, but as professionals who have a critical awareness of the power relations at work in the field of writing. (172)

In this way he espouses the 'sociological poetics' of creative writing in which we not only discuss craft but also employ 'oppositional criticism precisely to interrogate the assumptions about literature underpinning these responses and then to consider how the work in question differs and interrelates with a range of non-literary (scholarly, political, journalistic, legal) discourses of gendered power relations' (206).

How much is Dawson's model being practiced in Australian creative writing programmes? A more extensive study would show us the exact picture, but a quick look at some of the programmes from Australia show that direction.

The overview of the University of Sidney's Master of Creative Writing programme reads:

> Explore and develop your skills in fiction, non-fiction, poetry and other forms of writing. Gain a deep understanding of theories and histories of writing and develop the core skills of writing, structuring and editing. We give you intimate access to Sydney's literary life, including a constant calendar of readings, performances, major literary and cultural events, and a host of celebrated visitors. ("Master of Creative Writing")

The 'core skills of writing, structuring, and editing' are, of course, part of the deal, but what is equally important in this approach is the 'deep understanding of theories and histories of writing.'

The University of Adelaide offers degrees in Bachelor or Creative Arts, which includes both fine arts and creative writing degrees, has required core courses called 'The Inquiring Mind,' 'What is the Thing Called Art,' and 'Creativity and Adelaide Festival.' Together with elective courses in specific Creative Arts courses, the programme aims to 'create a unique academic space to develop individual creativity' ("Bachelor"). The course description of 'What Is the Think Called Art?' states that the course 'will encourage students to think critically about the very notion of art and to begin to question their own practice as makers of art in contemporary culture' ("Bachelor").

As expected, teaching the craft of writing, and teaching the skills of writing, is also part of the programme, and they do it through the introductory creative writing course, and genre specific courses teach the craft of their particular genres, but that it is not hard to see that the programme place those courses within a broader theoretical framework. And this introductory course, called 'Creative Writing: The Essentials' is the only course that used the term 'craft' among the course details available online. Equally interestingly, the programme also offers a course called 'Boundary Riders: Creative Critical Writing.' The courses, the syllabus says, 'will introduce students writing that brings together theory and creative practice' ("Bachelor"). In this course, students produce 'critical creative works and an exegetical work discussing process and form' ("Bachelor").

The University of Melbourne's "Master of Creative Writing, Publishing and Editing" has clearly an outcome based programme which states that this degree 'if you want to build your project management, research and critical thinking in writing, editing and publishing projects, or develop sound knowledge of the commercial impetus of the global publishing industry.' The creative writing courses offered by the programme have the theory aspect integrated to them in addition to craft. The course description for 'Short Fiction' reads: 'In this subject students will explore principles of the craft and theory of writing short fiction including graphic narrative.' Similarly, the description for 'Novel' reads: 'It will introduce students to theoretical and historical approaches to the understanding and practice of extended narrative or novel writing. Students will read a variety of narrative-based and theoretical texts with emphasis on contemporary works.'

The UK model comes closer to the Australian model in that it also promotes critical approaches to practicing creative writing. Diane Donnelly explains it in terms of UK creative writing programmes' requirement of a substantial critical introduction to accompany a creative dissertation, like in Australia (2012). (One important thing to note here: many creative writing programmes in the US are also requiring this introduction.) Michelene Wandor, in her book *The Author is Not Dead, Merely Somewhere Else,* claims, 'Despite the immediate influence of the US, explicitly evident in the MA at UEA in 1970, and still a prevalent presence, the preconditions for CW were very different in the UK' (2008, 81), and she credits the UK's 'social and educational histories' (81) for this difference. Wandor also places theory and literature squarely at the centre of creative writing to distinguish it from the programme in America.

Vanderslice explains this distinction as a result of a UK government initiative toward an outcomes based education through a 1997 study, commonly known as Dearing Report. Vanderslice concludes that because the 'UK creative writing programs were founded or necessarily revised during post-Dearing era, their curricula and programs of study reveal concrete connections to intended learning outcomes, learning outcomes ... ' (Vanderslice 2011, 12). This happened in the UK because, she goes on, the programmes

> emerged from a great deal of reflection and interrogation on the teaching of a subject that many in the US continue to resist interrogating on the grounds that creative writing cannot be taught – even as they make their livelihoods by teaching it. (Vanderslice 2011, 12)

The 'MSt in Creative Writing' at Oxford University requires both creative and critical writing right from the beginning and the emphasis of the course is 'cross-cultural and cross-genre, pointing up the needs and challenges of the contemporary writer who produces their creative work in the context of a global writerly and critical community' ("MSt"). It also calls 'research placement' a 'distinguishing feature of the course.' In fact, workshop in the genre that a student chooses is not the focus on the whole first year, but 'critical reading and analysis.' Students specialise in their chosen genre only in the second year of the programme.

Another worth-noting feature of UK creative writing programmes, like some programmes in Australia, is that creative writing has been linked to other, more professional, fields, like journalism and professional writing. University of Portsmouth offers a degree called 'Journalism with Creative Writing' ("Journalism"), University of the West England offers a programme called 'Creative and Professional Writing' ("Creative"), and the University of Strathclyde Glasgow has even a programme called 'English, Creative Writing and Law,' in addition to the English and Creative Writing degree and other courses in which Creative Writing has been linked to journalism, French, and even History ("Explore"). This believe has to do with the focus on the intended programme outcomes as mentioned above.

This is not to mean that craft is not part of the creative writing. But in both the cases, theories of literature and literary production take the central stage and the traditional workshop ceases to be a neutral zone for honing the craft of writing. Equally important, if not more, is the value placed on preserving and building on local literary traditions and aesthetics, which is in fact seen in many other programmes around the world, including at Ashoka through the offering of courses in local vernacular literatures and critical theories.

Moving forward

The expansion of the teaching of creative writing at universities around the world is an encouraging and a welcome development. Because of creative writing's potential to reconfigure the teaching of literature and its potential impact on our students' creative and critical faculties and the socio-culture life of a society as a whole, this development should be embraced with open hearts. However, the traditional workshop pedagogy after the American creative writing model, which is still predominantly craft-based, needs to be reconsidered, and more space should be made for the theoretical and critical understanding of literature production and consumption. Every time we fall back to the workshop pedagogy, we need to mindful of the history and the practices it perpetuates.

It would be unrealistic to expect all writing teachers to be well-versed in the history and the ideological underpinnings of creative writing pedagogies, especially because one, it is not part of the academic training in creative writing in the US as yet, and two, it is common for many writers to be teaching creative writing without related academic training. These issues can be of particular concern outside the US where the US creative writing programmes represent the best of what creative writing can be. As much as we try to learn from and replicate the successes of the creative workshop pedagogy, we should be highlighting the discussions that have started problematising the workshop in the US in the recent years. Creative writing programmes building on the US programmes and the workshop pedagogy should be mindful of the critical discussions happening here.

In fact, the universities around the world introducing creative writing degrees are in an advantaged position to have to build not only on the traditional workshop model of the US but also on the programmes in Australia and the UK, with a special attention to theories of literary production, circulation, and consumption as well as to local literary traditions and heritage that students bring to the creative writing classroom. Even the programmes in the US should not wait any longer to learn from programmes around the world and speed up the process of transforming the workshops of empire for the new age, something that has certainly started happening. So, as a practical first step, creative writing programmes around the world can incorporate theories of literary production and consumption in their courses. Incorporating local aesthetics into those discussions will help them redefine and practice craft as contextual and ideological. Embracing the developments happening through the newly emerging field of creative writing studies can lead to self-reflectivity about our practices in term of power relations, who we are benefiting and who we have put in the position of disadvantage through our pedagogies. The creative writing of tomorrow, the global creative writing, can, and should, have the edge on critical reflection.

Acknowledgements

The author expresses sincere thanks to Dr. Stephanie Vanderslice for her invaluable feedback on an earlier draft of this article.

Disclosure statement

No potential conflict of interest was reported by the author.

References

AWP. 2017. *AWP 2017 Annual Report*. Association of Writers and Writing Programs. https://www.awpwriter.org/application/public/pdf/AWPAnnualReport17.pdf.

"Bachelor of Creative Arts." University of Adelaide. https://calendar.adelaide.edu.au/aprcw/2020/bca_bcrarts.

Bennett, Eric. 2014. "How Iowa Flattened Literature." *Chronicle of Higher Education*, February 10. https://www.chronicle.com/article/How-Iowa-Flattened-Literature/144531/.

Bennett, Eric. 2015. *Workshops of Empire: Stegner, Engle, And American Creative Writing During the Cold War*. Iowa: University of Iowa Press.

Brady, Amy. 2017. "MFA by Numbers, On the Eve of AWP: Danielle Steele Doesn't Have an MFA, And other Shocking Numbers." *Literary Hub*. https://lithub.com/mfa-by-the-numbers-on-the-eve-of-awp/.

"Creative and Professional Writing." BA(Hons), UWE Bristol. https://courses.uwe.ac.uk/W81F/creative-and-professional-writing-with-foundation-year.

Dawson, Paul. 2005. *Creative Writing and the New Humanities*. London: Routledge.

Diaz, Junot. 2014. "MFA vs POC." *The New Yorker*, April 30. https://www.newyorker.com/books/page-turner/mfa-vs-poc.

Donnelly, Dianne. 2012. *Establishing Creative Writing as an Academic Discipline*. Bristol: Multilingual Matters.

"Explore Our International Programs." Study at Strathclyde, University of Strathclyde Glasgow. https://www.studyatstrathclyde.com/programmes/undergraduate-programmes/.

Harper, Graeme. 2013. "Introduction." In *A Companion to Creative Writing*, edited by Graeme Harper, 1–6. West Sussex: Wiley-Blackwell.

"Journalism with Creative Writing." BA Hons with Creative Writing. University of Portsmouth. https://www.port.ac.uk/study/courses/ba-hons-journalism-with-creative-writing.

"Master of Creative Writing." Courses. University of Sydney. https://sydney.edu.au/courses/courses/pc/master-of-creative-writing.html.

"Master of Creative Writing, Publishing and Editing." Study. The University of Melbourne. https://study.unimelb.edu.au/find/courses/graduate/master-of-creative-writing-publishing-and-editing/what-will-i-study/.

Mayers, Tim. 2018. "Re(Crafting) Craft: Amending the Cultural, Institutional, and Scholarly Conceits." Critiques and Revisions: Examining Ideologies of Craft in Creative Writing, 4th Annual Creative Writing Studies Conference, 17–18 October, Montreat, NC. Conference Presentation.

McGurl, Mark. 2009. *The Program Era: Postwar Fiction and the Rise of Creative Writing*. Harvard: Harvard University Press.

"Minor in Creative Writing." Ashoka University. https://www.ashoka.edu.in/pages/creative-writing-61.

"MSt in Creative Writing." Graduate. University of Oxford. https://www.ox.ac.uk/admissions/graduate/courses/mst-creative-writing.

Myers, D. G. 2006. *Elephants Teach: Creative Writing Since 1880*. Chicago: University of Chicago Press.

Nguyen, Viet Thanh. 2017. "Viet Thanh Nguyen Reveals How Writers' Workshops Can Be Hostile." *The New York Times*, April 26. https://www.nytimes.com/2017/04/26/books/review/viet-thanh-nguyen-writers-workshops.html.

Shivani, Anis. 2011. *Against the Workshop: Provocations, Polemics, Controversies*. Texas: Texas Review Press.

Vanderslice, Stephanie. 2010. "Once More to the Workshop: A Myth Caught in Time." In *Does the Writing Workshop Still Work?*, edited by Dianne Donnelly, 30–35. Bristol: Multilingual Matters.

Vanderslice, Stephanie. 2011. *Rethinking Creative Writing in Higher Education: Programs and Practices That Work*. Cambridge: The Professional and Higher Partnerships.

Wandor, Michelene. 2008. *The Author is Not Dead, Merely Somewhere Else*. Hampshire: Palgrave Macmillan.

New types of intelligence relevant to creative writers

We generally recognise that creative writing involves a number of intelligences. Linguistic intelligence is the ability to learn and use language. Throughout history, creative writers have sought to have and to improve upon their linguistic intelligence. Interpersonal intelligence is related to effective communication, and while creative writing is an art it has always also been a form of communication. Creative intelligence is of course fundamental to creative writing – creative intelligence being the ability to imagine the new, the distinctive, the unusual, the different, the previously unimaginable. Creative writers often do what they do to in order to apply their creative intelligence. Audiences seek out works of creative writing because of wanting to engage with that application. This exchange creates an individual bond in what is often a communal exchange. For example, an individual writer writes a novel and we buy that novel in the expectation of it appealing to us individually, even though dozens or thousands or even millions of people will buy that same novel.

Greater and more immediate access to information for those located across much of the world, and the impact of new technologies (Artificial Intelligence, for example, advanced remote conferencing technologies, the Internet of Things) along with evolving forms and fields of knowledge, raises questions about what new types of intelligence might be emerging – new intelligences with which creative writers can become engaged. These might take on both the character of creative writing as a pursuit and the character of our current historical moment. For example:

Butterfly intelligence. The ability to believe you can work on more than one writing project at a time, not get blown off course on any of them, and be equally happy with the bright and lively appearance of all of them. Butterfly intelligence conjures up visions of you on a sunny day, dancing in a flowery field. It is also topically very much like working 'remote', at home, sometimes, and sometimes working elsewhere (say, an office in a university, for example, at other times). You happily flitting between these locations. Despite the reference to nature, the foundation of butterfly intelligence is the unnatural speed at which you can now move from one thing to another, confident you're not merely madly flapping.

Thumb intelligence. Related to butterfly intelligence but more dexterous, this intelligence is about knowing which device you happen to be depending on at any given moment. This saves you, in your half-awake morning state, trying to look for the redial function on your '90s digital alarm clock, or expecting to be able to send your draft poem to your laptop from your refrigerator. Thumb intelligence is being enhanced by the arrival of the Internet of Things or IoT – in which not only can you express emotions in the direction of inanimate objects (such as shouting at a chair when you stub your toe on it) those inanimate objects can now get emotional with you. Thumb intelligence is also the mysterious and impressive ability to immediately know where to place your thumbs when told something is 'entirely autonomous and hands-free'.

Sorting intelligence. So much information is available today so quickly. The development of 'Artificial Super Intelligence' is an increasingly significant reason for this. Artificial Super

Intelligence is advanced AI that exceeds any individual human brain power. Sorting intelligence is the ability to arrange, order, classify and choose from an impossibly large number of choices provided increasingly via Artificial Super Intelligence. Those possessed of exceptional sorting intelligence can detect the absence of any real relevance in the 33,000 search results you just received, mined by Artificial Super Intelligence. Additionally, with sorting intelligence you are able to determine which of the goods and services chosen anonymously for you based on your previous internet searches are actually more appropriate for your cat or your goldfish or relate to the internet searches conducted by the kid next door who recently hacked your WIFI.

Emotive intelligence. Increased access to information relating to good *and* bad events locally, nationally and internationally has also meant an increase in what is generally (though not medically, as it happens) referred to as 'catastrophizing'. A constant digital stream of death notices and obituaries of other humans, known and unknown, regular news of natural and person-made disasters and updates on the aftermaths of those disasters, and a frenetic reporting of constant change in every part of human and natural life, has led to increased instances of catastrophising. Catastrophising is a mental distortion where the worst possible outcome is always thought to be the most likely outcome. Catastrophising might manifest itself in creative writing in the grimness of your themes and subjects or in the predominance of declarative sentences and a preponderance of exclamation marks! Repeatedly! Those with emotive intelligence avoid catastrophising. Emotive intelligence is not emotional intelligence because it is not only a general reference to emotions. Rather emotive intelligence is about knowing *exaggerated* feeling does happen, but infrequently, and therefore we should not be constantly catastrophising.

At which point we pause in our exploration of these new mock 'intelligences' (yes, those were satirical inventions, believe it or not!) because this final one comes close to being real enough to be worthy of its own final reference. Emotive intelligence is about correspondence, not blandness or poise, necessarily, but correspondence – the ability to get outside of your own head so that how you create is as much about who might read or experience your creation as it is about your own thoughts and feelings. As the world changes – which it does regularly, of course, more than it stays exactly the same – we encounter it as writers not with a fixed intelligence but with evolving intelligence. We apply our thoughts and abilities to observe and consider what we experience, and our imaginations, and our feelings to create works that most often aim to communicate with fellow humans. We build one-to-one relationships this way, even in mass audiences (such as in the viewing of films based on our screenplays or theatrical performances based on our scripts) and we do so with the aim that human intelligences are many and varied by type and by person and by circumstance; but, at the core, and importantly, they are all fundamentally human.

Graeme Harper

English-language creative writing in a Chinese context: translation as a supplement

Xia Fang

ABSTRACT

One of creative writing's contributions to knowledge is made through writers themselves reflecting on their creative practices, otherwise termed 'practice-based research'. Based on this concept, this essay delves into creative writing research in a Chinese context. The majority of my 'practice-based' research, including several translation projects and a writing project that I undertook, took place during my Ph.D. study. English-language creative writing in the Chinese context is in many ways linked with the unique identity of the practitioners, who are bilinguals in both English and Chinese. In reference to unique features of creative writing in non-anglophone regions and the writers themselves, I consider several key issues here, including the position of translation in creative writing and the writer's responsibility regarding the creation of literary works, which has been palpably distinguished from a similar kind delineated by Paul Dawson in anglophone contexts. I believe these issues can map out fundamental premises and questions of this particular research, which ultimately aims to expound the potential link between translation and creative writing.

1. Creative writing research: literary translation and self-penned writing project

The issue of just what creative writing truly is as either a practice or a discipline has proven the fundamental enquiry of creative writing studies. Harper (2013) describes the nature and core of this discipline as revolving around 'a creative writer exploring their own creative writing, through doing it, and through considering how they are doing it' (278). Even though this statement is somewhat disputable considering that 'creative writing research can also be research about creative writing, not involving the practice itself' (285), this direction of 'practice-led research' has justifiably gained authority in higher education, with increasing numbers of creative writing programmes being established around the world and being recognised for academic credit. At universities, a portfolio thesis consisting of creative work and critical writing is the conventional requirement for the completion of a degree in creative writing. It is thus justifiable to say that in this discipline one of the dimensions of creative writing research is focused on conducting 'practice-led research', also referred to as 'research through practice', 'practice-based research', or 'arts practice research' (279). This is usually where critical commentary (reflection) is built. In short, this particular discipline enables creative writers to critique and research their own work.

In Harper (2013)'s review of the scholarly attitudes towards 'reflection' on creative writing work, some scholars attest that contemplative reflection on the creative writing process is favourable, whereas others contend that excessive critical thoughts might hamper creative practice, as Harper explains further when saying, 'perhaps reflection denies some of our more spontaneous, instinctive, unpremeditated human actions' (283). Reflection involves creative writers scrutinising their practices, with the ultimate goal of facilitating a clearer comprehension of both their own work and creative writing in general. Harper (2013) contends that individual cases of creative writing can have wider scope of application and greater significance (278–291). McLoughlin (2013) attempts to extend the significance of reflection as far as to generating new knowledge, when he says:

> poets reflect critically on their poetics and on their processes. These may be further subdivided into reflection on elements of craft and how these elements may be experimented with, and reflection on elements of theoretical poetics and what the author believes makes a good text. The author reflects critically on the imaginative processes of making text; their influences and how those have been assimilated; and on their critical processes and the theories that underpin them. All of these critical reflective processes may generate new knowledge of the phenomena to which they relate as well as to the nature of 'being in the world' (Heidegger) in relation to the poet. (49)

Despite these varied perceptions of the creative writing process, 'practice-led research' as the most prevalent approach in creative writing studies has therefore become a basic component of creative writing research in general (Harper 2013, 279). In line with Harper's argument, Webb and Hetherington (2016) approach this issue from a slightly different angle by distinguishing and identifying 'when the making of art is research, and when it is just the making of art' (11). They stress the significance of constructing knowledge through practice by citing the poet Ian Wedde, who says that:

> knowledge has nothing to do with facts, or with empirical theses. They are just evidence of work ... if you think of the writing of poetry as a mental exercise as well as physical exercise, as the exercising of thought in writing – knowledge comes from that. (11)

This perspective resonates with what Harper (2013) demonstrated in his discussion of 'situational knowledge', which stresses individual experience and other related dynamics. Webb and Hetherington (2016) have also critiqued the faulty phenomenon that writing as research is generally underestimated due to the bias of the poet whose primary responsibility is at variance with that of the researchers, the former rather being 'more interested in making complex meanings out of language', thus resulting in his/her being less interested in contributing to new knowledge in the research field. This phenomenon can largely be justified due to poets' subjectivity and 'their circumstances and interests' (15). In other words, poets don't make efforts to systematise their creative works and make a contribution to knowledge. Creative works have long been perceived as lacking research value in academia, and this partly explains why creative artists have displayed a tendency to maintain distance from the research field, either voluntarily or reluctantly. It is somehow flawed in nature. This traditional perception is corrected by Webb and

Hetherington (2016) who claim that creative works can be treated separately, and some of which can be utilised as 'knowledge statements' (12). This is aligned with the ultimate goal of this research. The production of creative works and a critical investigation of the creative writing process that ensued can be validated as ways of building new knowledge.

Ramifications of creativity and the creative process behind it are investigated and then reflected in my own written work. The writing project (*A View of the Sky Tunnel*) and several translation projects (*Great Wall Capriccio and Other Poems*, *City of Dead Stars*, Classical Chinese Poetry translation Project, etc.) conducted are interrelated in various ways and contribute to reveal the connection between translation and creative writing in practical terms. Theoretical investigation and discussion in this research primarily are based on my writing project, *A View of the Sky Tunnel*, a bilingual poetry collection of 73 poems written in both English and Chinese.

Considering the substantial research previously undertaken on creative writing educational methods and approaches, it has become necessary to draw upon teaching concepts in order to shed insight into the research of creativity and its relationship with and the ramifications through engaging in translation. What should be considered as the criteria in the investigation of creativity in creative writing? How has students' role in education been perceived up till now? What are the possible innovative ways of reconsidering this issue? Workshop as the signature pedagogy of creative writing has been previously researched in terms of its dynamics and constituent elements (such as the students and the underlying theory), as well as the nuances of contextualisation in which the methods are utilised, taking into consideration the particularity of the target students. In contrast to the well-researched and established concept of the workshop, a new concept, the 'unworkshop', proposed by Harper (2017), is labelled as a 'destructive construct' of the conventional perception of the pedagogical practice of workshop:

> the unworkshop does not assume rules; rather, it assumes networks and synapses. In other words, while compositional studies might suggest a rhetorical decree, a regimen or guidelines, the unworkshop, focused as it is on the actual individual acts and results of creative writing, suggests intrinsic and extrinsic value will be related to the creative writer's decisions on what is fit for purposes, as well as an accompanying sense of what constitutes nodes of exchange. (24–25)

It can be inferred that this innovative method is even more student-centred in that the practitioner has the flexibility to adopt methods which are suitable for each one's own individual case, rather than force-feeding knowledge in a passive, generic manner. As a result of this force-feeding, students are generally taught via structured seminars or workshops, which focus more on a specific set of rules or skills as the primary teaching goals. Unworkshop is oriented towards the individual learning needs and the results of the learning process, through which the students are motivated to utilise a variety of materials, resources, and theories, which are 'drawn not from one disciplinary or epistemological perspective but most often from many' (22). Echoing Freire (1968)'s pedagogy of the oppressed, this liberating pedagogical method simulates this theory in spirit, reinforcing what Freire (1973) advocated as 'practice of freedom'. The students are given the freedom to use their own initiative in the learning process and mobilise the resources at their disposal to reach that result. Unworkshop is closely linked with the concept of 'situational understanding' and 'situational knowledge', proposed also by Harper (2013, 107). It is defined as 'knowledge that is generated by and applied to the situation or circumstance that ensues ... if a creative writer is pursuing the completion of a task, whatever knowledge they explore, employ or produce will be defined by that aim of completion ... ' (107). This definition reinforces the idea that unworkshop is not only an individualised but also a situation-based construct. Being a pedagogical concept on the surface, 'unworkshop' can be alternatively treated in reference to its critical value.

Individualisation is also a principle advocated in the educational precepts of Confucius who paid attention to students' individual characteristics. It was recorded in the *Analects* that Confucius would give comments and suggestions based on each student's difference and faculty and that different students were judged on their individual merits (Palmer 2001, 2). While it is not necessary to elaborate further on Confucius' educational theory here, it is nonetheless important to note that we can see examples here of individualisation. In actuality, the individual characteristics of each student tend to be overlooked and overshadowed by existing educational methods. In view of the aforementioned concepts in the area of creative writing studies, *A View of the Sky Tunnel* is taken as a task-based project, and the process of completing this project relies on identifying and resolving various situation-based obstacles I have encountered. The individuality of this project is also exhibited in the liberty and autonomy I exercised in deciding which topics I would elect to explore in my own poetry and what resources I would then utilise to assist my writing project. The significance of this singular project lies also in the way that it experiments with a creative approach, and its viability and potential to have wider applicability are put to the test through the singularity of this project. The implications of this research also lie in the way that specific methods are used to stimulate the proposed concept of unworkshop.

Practice-based projects mainly serve as a method of inquiry in this research to investigate the interplay between translation and creative writing. Practice-based projects I undertook bring to the fore several aspects, such as the inner mechanism of conducting these projects, which emerge from and rely on certain situations and individuality. Prior to and throughout this project, I actively engaged in the practice of translation. The role of practising translation has effectively served as 'literary apprenticeship'. Dawson (2005) demonstrates the notion of 'literary apprenticeship' when discussing the establishment of workshop as 'merely a formalization of writers' groups or of individual mentoring relationships which have developed between famous writers' (48). Workshops are the contexts where literary apprenticeship, one of the widely accepted underlying principles of creative writing teaching, is forged. A workshop creates a space where a community of writers can gather and through which the experienced writers give advice to the younger (83). In this study, literary apprenticeship was demonstrated by means of several translation projects, which were conducted in collaboration with a literary community composed of a hierarchy of veteran poets, novice translators, and more experienced translators. During the process, the majority of time was spent working with the experienced poets on poetry translation. The term 'literary apprenticeship' is focused on utilising the practice of literary translation, and facilitating a network of social dialogues which involves people of both the veteran and the novice groups (a concept that reflects the inner mechanism of workshop), ultimately aiming at enhancing individual literary growth in poetry writing.

In this research, literary apprenticeship is also conducted in the form of group activities where some undergraduates or postgraduates who enrolled in a creative writing course have actively participated. I have also benefited from being a participant and a project leader at creative writing classes where some time was allocated for translation activities. More particularly, poetry translation was utilised to facilitate creative writing, during which the lecturer (who also serves as the editor) actively workshopped with the students on their translation productions. The first project I designed as the supplementary element of creative writing classes is titled 'Classical Poem Translation: Flowers, Seasons and Festivals'. This project has been conducted with a number of groups from different classes, with the express purpose of composing poetry at creative writing classes. This project represents the inception of my attempt at forging the link between translation and creative writing in practical terms and at a theoretical level.

The final project in my portfolio thesis consists of a collection of poems, a selection of which have been published as my first book of poetry through a local publisher in 2017. The writing process of the mentioned creative works benefited from the practice of translation. All the translation projects that I have engaged in, either for publication or simply as a practice, have collectively contributed to the creative writing endeavour that follows. The process that began from engagement with translation has gradually led me onto a more progressive track in terms of my creative writing. This process also involves exploring the homogeneity between translation and writing, observing empirically how other practitioners who take creative writing courses participate in the translation-and-writing project I facilitated, as well as exploring the questions of how well they perform in activities of different natures, and what role translation has played in inspiring their creative writing. Based on a number of completed translation projects, my own writing project is analysed to reflect on how the practice of translation has influenced my own creative writing process.

As Harper (2013) said, 'creative writing exploring knowledge *for* a situation and *for* an individual does not mean this knowledge cannot be shared ... have wider "impact"' (280; emphasis original). Hence, an individual case of the creative writing process also creates wider scope for creative writing in general and contributes to an understanding of this discipline and its practical value, as a whole. It is these practice-based projects that form the foundation of this research. Various scopes entailed in the creation of my poetry, such as translation, reading, self-translation, and influence of life experience, culminated in generating new knowledge regarding the creative writing process and creativity research. This thorough reflection subsequently stimulates a further inquiry regarding the interplay between translation and writing, which also constitutes the main theoretical and practical inquiries under scrutiny in the essay. These projects, including several translation projects and a writing project, the latter being both place-based and inspired by translation, may collectively and uniquely contribute to new knowledge, and it is these that serve as the source of originality of this essay. In the following sections, I will conduct a survey of creative writing practice/research that occur generally in tertiary institutions and particularly in international contexts. This investigation will ultimately lead to a revelation of the catalyst of using literary translation in the context of creative writing in Asia.

2. Creative writing in institutions

Considering that this research is dedicated to creativity and the interface between translation and creative writing, it is thus inseparably linked with aspects of creative writing education. This is due to the fact that, in the modern context, creative writing studies have been increasingly concerned with the teaching of this subject/practice in institutions. Thus, several teaching concepts will be unavoidably dealt with, so as to examine creativity.

Teaching of creative writing, and of its various approaches that help guide the poets, can be found in a plethora of tutorial materials. The available materials provide training exercises and useful channels that encourage amateur poets to express their ideas (Addonizio and Laux 1997; Finch 2012; Herbert 2010; Bugeja 2001). Michael J. Bugeja informs readers on techniques on how to recognise and produce ideas, as well as on methods of recording them for later use. For instance, through keeping journals, notebooks, or files containing raw ideas, from which ideas can continue to develop and grow. Generally, the pivotal components from which poetry composition is built include rhyme, metric, forms, patterns, and motifs. Bugeja categorises poetry craft into three key sections: journals and genres; the elements of poetry; and formats and forms. The second section is subdivided into analysis of voice, lines, stanzas, titles, metre, and rhyme. The last section includes various modes of expression, such as narrative poem, lyric poem, dramatic poem, free verse, and sonnet. Bugeja's book is exemplified here as *the* teaching tutorial for creative writing. However, there are various other handbooks in this discipline that explore slightly different dimensions. For instance, W.N. Herbert offers concise and practical guidance on key writing skills in *Writing Poetry* (Herbert 2010), which also includes dialogues with eminent poets; Jane Spiro, in *Creative Poetry Writing* (Spiro 2004), provides resourceful activities placed in different categories of poetic features ranging from sound, words, to the entire text.

An alternative method to creative writing transpires in the classroom at schools or universities. Dianne Donnelly (2010, 4–10) suggests that there is a number of topics that can be explored in creative writing studies, such as topics and/or courses discussed and used before in its history; the theoretical underpinnings for pedagogical approaches; research methodologies; contemporary issues concerned; and, possibly, curriculum design. In this section, I will focus on the theoretical underpinnings for creative writing pedagogy, so as to single out aspects that are related to the uniqueness of creative writing in a Chinese context. Donnelly summarises four basic taxonomies for creative writing pedagogy: (1) objective theory: highlighting the meaning of the text; (2) expressivist theory: emphasising explaining the meaning from the author's perspective; (3) mimetic theory: 'to discuss the imitable functions of the writer's world that emphasize that meaning lies with the "universe"' (19); and (4) pragmatic theory: characterised by reader-response pedagogy in which meaning is with the reader. As Donnelly asserts, the rationale for any approaches adopted relies on what teachers prioritise at their creative writing classes. Mimetic theory is relevant to the topic of my essay, and it is this that I will be expounding further in the following analysis.

The causality that exists in mimetic theory means that students must familiarise themselves with writing strategies, styles, and structures if they are to effectively mimic them. On a fundamental level, mimesis is the main principle in the creation of art. Socrates enlightens us to the conception that mimes s is palpable in 'the arts of painting, poetry, music, dancing and sculpture' (quoted in Donnelly 2010, 57). According to Patrick Bizzaro, cognitivists 'saw writing as a cognitive activity – that is, as a process of intellection students could learn how to do by imitating the behaviours of good or experienced writers' (57). Mimetic practices are particularly useful for students in practising various styles and genres of creative writing. As Nicholas Delbanco claims, the principal motive of the mimetic approach adopted by the teacher is that 'if you understand the way another's story has been built you can set about building your own' (59). The viability of this principle is bolstered in Finch's (2012) assertion: 'for centuries, all the way until the early nineteenth century, the accepted way for beginning poets to learn to write was by direct imitation of the great poets of the past, usually the classical poets' (36). In this sense, imitation becomes the most widely adopted principle of the teaching approach in creative writing. While the particular mechanism in a writing workshop varies from country to country (adaptive to differing teaching contexts), the underlying principle of the mimetic theory remains universally applicable. Due to its underlying mimetic feature, the practice of translation (seeking equivalences on various levels with a source text) is proposed as an effective method for creative writing.

What are the fundamental functions of creative writing that form it into a subject that is widely studied at schools and in institutions of higher education in anglophone countries? Myers (2006) traces the origin of creative writing through a survey of its antecedents, namely, the courses of English Composition, Rhetoric, Philology, and English Literature (35–56). Myers' historical scrutiny of this subject has also helped reveal its evolving educational functions in university, which originally laid emphasis on the correct use of grammar and other rules of language use. The teaching focus began to shift towards nurturing students' expressiveness in a creative writing course.

Compared with its antecedents, a creative writing course includes several different functions. According to Dawson (2005), creative writing is built on four institutional trajectories: creative *self-expression, literacy, craft*, and *reading from the inside* (48–80). Here I will focus on the first two trajectories as they are more pertinent to my research. 'Creative self-expression' constitutes the theoretical underpinning of creative writing being adopted at schools for the benefit of 'self-cultivation' on the part of the students (58). In Dawson's account, as a replacement for English composition, creative writing offered at schools helps promote children's personal growth through self-expression, whereas Creative Writing at universities tends to emphasise 'the finished product and the development of critical standards rather than on the enrichment of personality with which the high school teacher is primarily concerned' (quoted in Dawson 2005, 56). I contend that Dawson's discussion of 'creative self-expression', which underpins creative writing taught at schools, can apply to creative writing at universities in a Chinese context, where writing for publication is not the primary goal of a creative writing course. In explaining the trajectory of 'literacy', Dawson refers to a composition course offered by Harvard University for freshmen, which involves writing about the 'daily theme' as a means of self-cultivation (58). He cites Myers in explaining that the course of English composition as a precursor to a creative writing course has the same features as creative writing, both of which are operated by '"intrinsic" demands,' and students' expressions of their own experience (59). In this trajectory of 'literacy', creative writing becomes a means of enhancing literacy through a verbalisation of personal experience.

Kroll (2013) in 'Creative Writing and Education' explains what she deems to be the significance of creative writing education in a teaching context. Kroll wrote that 'this understanding of the benefits of writing as a process conditions how it is integrated into school curricula, with goals such as enhancing creativity, supporting self-expression, and increasing self-esteem' (247). Kroll's opinion is similar to Dawson's in this respect. I contend that promoting self-expression, boosting self-empowerment, and enhancing literacy are the most valuable and fundamental traits in reinforcing creative writing in non-anglophone contexts, and it is these that are held as the underlying principles of my writing project and critical investigations.

Generally, self-expression has become a fundamental trait in creative writing. As an underlying principle of the act of creative writing, how does self-expression engender creativity? Another more pertinent and more urgent demand to be addressed is, how has creativity been scrutinised in creative writing studies? Dawson reviews various scholars' attitudes and opinions on creativity, and begins from the question of just what can be counted as 'creative writing'. Creative work is defined as work that is 'original, unconventional, expressive' (Dawson 2005, 21). On that account, creative writing was originally seen as an act that can only be achieved by a relatively small number of prestigious writers. Dawson (2005) has traced the development of creative writing as a discipline and the key concepts it concerns, such as creativity, creative power, and imagination, among which:

> creative power was the capacity of a poet's imagination to mimic the divine act of creation by producing in fiction characters which did not exist in nature, or events and ideas which had not previously been contemplated. (29)

And that 'creative power springs from within rather than being breathed in from without' (29). Firstly, creative power that comes from the human being is placed on an equal footing with the divine act of creation. Secondly, this power is valued as a source that comes from within, which unriddles why creative writing is advocated at schools for the promotion of students' self-realisation and personal growth.

Generally, the understanding and development of creative writing as a school subject have experienced a shift to 'a democratization of concepts of authorship in particular and human productivity in general' (22). This prevalence of authorship is formed thanks to a more democratic view of creativity. This idea is reiterated in Andrew McCallum's (2012) historicised review of creativity, in which he distinguishes the more traditional definition of 'creativity' from the more contemporary definition of 'being creative', the former of which is a faculty only demonstrated in 'the actions of an elite few, those who can offer an image of the world in keeping with its previous connotations of a divine presence', whereas the latter refers to 'more humble attempts to replicate this creativity' (9). The faculty embodied in the latter concept has assumed a more democratic attribute, as opposed to being restricted to a few intellectually privileged groups. Because of the wider application of 'being creative', creativity becomes extensively used in a wider context, particularly in education. Due to its exploitable potential, the concept of creativity has been manipulated by educators to carry out student-centred teaching, aiming at a more comprehensive development.

What should be the purposes and the articulated agendas of creative writing courses, with particular reference to English-language creative writing in China? To answer this question, I will explore in the following section second-language writers' responsibility in terms of how they position their creative work in relation to other English-language literature created in an anglophone context. Further on, I will address what role translation, a unique edge possessed by bilingual writers, plays in creative writing in China.

3. Writing in a Chinese context: issues to consider

Creative writing has undergone two divergent courses of evolvement in both an anglophone and a non-anglophone context, with the former having become more advanced than the latter in terms of education and research. In regard to the English-speaking context, 'professionalisation' is a term explained by Dawson (2005) when he examines the causes of the emergence of creative writing in Australia, which is attributed partly to the crisis in the teaching of literature (4). The professionalisation of creative writing as a discipline is achieved through the increasing number of creative writing courses offered in institutions of higher education at both undergraduate and postgraduate levels, along with Bachelor's, Master's, and doctoral degrees in Creative Writing. The institutionalisation of this discipline is stimulated and fortified by postgraduate research, as said by Dawson: 'establishing the theoretical and institutional parameters of "research" in a particular area is a major means by which disciplines are established, and it is around disciplines that professional bodies are organized in the academy' (157). The institutionalisation of this discipline sets itself on a path towards professionalisation in anglophone contexts.

In non-anglophone contexts, creative writing has been largely marginalised. According to Kroll (2013), 'outside Anglophone countries, the integration of creative writing into education poses linguistic and cultural challenges' (248). She explains that in the past decade, creative writing education has begun to develop in Asian countries, where its undergraduate courses lay emphasis on second-language competence, whilst M.A. degrees aim beyond this for betterment in creativity, producing writing workshops that promote local literature and culture (245–263). As previously mentioned, improving and enhancing literacy has proven to be one of the most preliminary purposes of creative writing education, and this is especially true in the non-anglophone context.

Lam (2014), the author of *Becoming Poets: The Asian English Experience*, provides a thorough look into the development of poets and poetry in Asian countries, through a five-stage model, namely, emergence of English literacy, apprenticeship, publishing, poetic identity, and mentorship. She garners and examines writing and writers' cases from many Asian places, including Macao. Where Macao is concerned, the apprenticeship is mainly taken in the form of literary translation, particularly in poetry translation projects. Poetry translations that have been published range from classical work to more contemporary work, from English to Chinese and vice versa. The unique identity of bilingual writers makes translation a necessary tool. Taking into account the cross-cultural and cross-linguistic features embedded in translation, we can observe that translation generates a space, enabling the acquisition of literary competence through this particular engagement on the part of a translator. In this part, I want to investigate the following lesser-explored questions: what is the function of English-language creative writing in China? Has translation become necessary in creative writing? What role does it play in writing: empowering or counter-productive?

3.1. Professional writing or self-expression?

Similar to the frequent inquiry of 'whether or not creative writing can be taught' that is raised in anglophone settings, it is equally dubious as to whether the product of creative writing created in non-anglophone contexts can be deemed as professional writing. In other words, to what extent can creative works written in a Chinese context be valued as serious work?

Dawson (2005) discusses the scenario of English-language creative writing, where his stance on the cognation of creative writing with various other elements can be summarised in three aspects. Firstly, the emergence and development of creative writing is aimed at reinvigorating English studies. Secondly, creative writing is an artistic endeavour that helps to shape a society. Thirdly, a creative writer plays the role of the 'public intellectual' who engages in reading and critiquing contemporary literature and cultures in a society. Referring back to the first aspect, Dawson (2005) argues that creative writing is 'an element of Literary Studies that developed as a series of pedagogical responses to the perennial crisis in English' (205). He reiterates the significance of 'dialogic junction of literature and criticism' at universities and states that in order for creative writing to gain authority in institutions of higher education, literature should not only be approached as an 'influential agent in the cultural life of a society which demands critical attention' (205), but should also be encouraged as a practice with which to contribute to English studies. Regarding the second facet, Dawson refers to Nadine Gordimer's article 'The Essential Gesture: Writers and Responsibility', in which he asserts that 'society's right to make demands on the writer is equal to the writer's commitment to his artistic vision' (149). This aspect of responsibility is in fact one of the primary traits of being a writer. Lastly, a writer's responsibility towards the creative works they created also hinges on social and literary affiliations, and:

> great emphasis is placed on the position of the writer in society. This position is one of critical engagement, and it is for this reason that writing is studied in conjunction with a broad array of reading and analysis in contemporary cultures. (149)

It can be inferred that creative writing in an English-speaking context, either theoretically or pedagogically, has been injected with the concept of relying on and being deemed as a continual effort to reinvigorate the discipline of English studies. The role of writers in creative writing education is conceived as that of a 'public intellectual' (214). For instance, when I was on a visiting programme to Bangor University, I observed that the creative writing programme offered there adopts the basic approach of reading from a writer's perspective, which directs the student-writer to engage in criticism of culture and art in the form of creative writing. In conclusion, creative writing in the western context both plays a crucial educational role at institutions, whilst also serving as a social and cultural commentary. These trilateral responsibilities delineate the role of the creative writer, and also determine the underlying principle of creative writing teaching in higher institutions of the anglophone context.

The following example can further demonstrate the advancement of creative writing teaching in an anglophone context. Kroll and Dai (2014, 77–91) compare writing workshops in China and in Australia respectively, focusing on the course of Life Writing (non-fiction). In the former case, Dai Fan as the course facilitator at Sun Yat-sen University bases her workshop on the principle of 'reading from the writerly perspective' (77), a mature approach well established in the English creative writing context. In the end, Jeri Kroll, representing the Australian side of creative writing teaching, points out that a lack of instruction on ethical issues in the workshop at Sun Yat-sen University is the most striking difference between these two cases of workshop in question. In Kroll's life writing workshop, students are asked 'not only to write personal stories but to consider the ethical implications if those stories were published' (87). An awareness of the ethical issues, that prepares the students to go forward in the publishing industry, is what Kroll considers to be the preliminary and requisite component of the workshop. This demonstrates the essential difference between creative writing in the context of a first language and that of a second language, where the former assumes the responsibility of nurturing future writers, and the latter is aimed primarily at improving students' second-language proficiency.

English-language creative writing in a non-anglophone context, on the other hand, possesses different features with regard to its intellectual and social functions (Disney 2014; Dai 2015; Kelen 2011, 2014). In *Exploring Second Language Creative Writing: After Babel*, manifold topics revolving around second-language creative writing are investigated by multiple scholars, but each of them unanimously hinges on the relationship between languages, literature, and identity. Similarly to subjects such as translation studies, linguistics, and literary studies, creative writing also serves as a means of English teaching. According to Disney (2014), creative writing serves as a means of enhancing creative literacy through opening 'dialogical conversation with literary artefacts' (3). This can be achieved through emulating literary work in the manner of making story or poetry. Disney proposes poetry as the genre that can activate interpersonal and intrapersonal learning outcomes while advancing lexical, systemic, and creative literacies. In another chapter of the book, Chin (2014) explores second-language (L2) identity formation through the medium of playwriting. The writer's identity, language, and place are interrelated to form a learning process that involves considerations of postcolonialism, bilingualism, and their specific sociocultural contexts. Chin draws the conclusion that L2 creative writing can be effectively used for personal exploration and self-expression.

Self-expression is the underlying principle of any creative writing, whether it be in the west or the non-anglophone environment, as any writing essentially directs to the writer's self and selfhood. How has self-expression been defined in different creative writing contexts? According to McCallum (2012), self-expression 'is not about students using language creatively in pursuit of their own essential selves, but about them being co-opted to move towards a notion of completeness exemplified – though never fully delineated – in the creative force of literature' (14). McCallum believes that self-expression gains significance in creative writing through the practitioner's understanding of previous literature. This also helps to explain why 'reading from a writer's perspective' is the underlying principle that informs the creative writing workshop in western countries (see Kroll and Dai 2014). For Chinese students who write creatively in English, the concept of self-expression in their learning and teaching context tends to represent an entitlement of greater freedom in verbal expression and idea construction. I contend that the phrase 'self-expression' has been understood differently by scholars and creative writing practitioners alike, both at home and abroad. In the non-anglophone context, the self-expressiveness of creative writing is tantamount to a perfunctory expression of the writer's self, the emphasis of which in creative writing education possibly subordinates other equally important requirements, such as the writer's social, intellectual, and literary responsibility as elaborated in Dawson's treatise. This can largely be explained by the differing functions of English-language creative writing elaborated in different contexts. However, under the guiding principle of self-expressiveness, the seriousness of the creative works composed by Chinese writers may resultantly be watered down; these works are then relegated to an inferior status in the world of English-language literature. From another perspective, due to the lack of sufficient contact with western literary traditions (such as poetics, aesthetics, stereotypes, and motifs) in and outside of the educational system, English creative writing in China is concerned more with creativity studies and using creativity to facilitate the practitioner's English proficiency, a viewpoint that has initially been explained by Dai (2010).

The aforementioned opinions on creative writing do not imply that second-language creative writing should be taken lightly or has underachieved. Regarding Chinese writers who write in a second language, the most successful examples include Lin Yutang, Ha Jin, Guo Xiaolu, and Li Xiangyun, among others. Guo Xiaolu, educated in Beijing, is the author of the English novel *Twenty Fragments of a Ravenous Youth*, a somewhat autobiographical piece of writing that drew the attention of English media, and was longlisted for the Man Asia Literary Prize. Li Xiangyun is another author native to China who writes in English. Her writing career commenced after she moved to the U.S.A. to undertake a Ph.D. degree in immunology. During this time Li developed a real passion for writing. In spite of her writing in a second language, one she developed during high school, Li has been awarded the MacArthur Foundation 'Genius Grant'[1] for her work, and her name has been placed in the list of best American young writers. Ha Jin, born in 1959, is one of the most prestigious Chinese-American writers, who has published 18 English novels and won a number of American literary awards, including the Pen/Faulkner Award. Most of his stories and novels are set in China. All these aforementioned writers could be considered as immigrant writers, despite their having only begun learning English as part of their education starting from high school or university.

Due to the scarcity of successful Chinese writers writing in English, it can hardly be said that they are representative of the average level of Chinese writers in general. The creative writing programmes offered at universities often profess to impart transferable skills that are applicable and adaptable to the needs of different professions. The educational purpose of improving literacy and language proficiency should be and indeed generally still is prioritised as the top agenda in creative writing teaching in the context of English as a second language. Creative writing tends to develop as a means of improving language proficiency, through the practice of structuring ideas for story, or through creating poetry. Creative writing has been established as a course at schools and other educational institutions in English-speaking countries, largely built upon the premise that self-expression encourages personal growth. It is under such conditions that means of creative writing are otherwise explored.

So what responsibility should Chinese writers assume? English-language creative writing is an undertaking that has manifold functions and purposes. As English gradually has developed into a global language, intermingling with diversified languages and cultures, the mission of writing in a global context has been contextualised in different cultures and language systems. Writing in English is not only an enterprise to gain a competitive edge with English, it is also an inevitable act of mingling with this globalised language, its culture and literature, through asserting the uniqueness of one's native language and literary tradition. The aforementioned is also the responsibility of the Chinese writers and their education, apart from the primary aim of improving language proficiency. In the global context, where the mainstream literature is still written within the segregation of different languages, translation has built bridges linking literatures of different languages, which has not only enriched one literary system, but also has served as a tool to improve the literary growth of an individual translator. Here, I want to emphasise the connection between literary translation and creative writing. Due to the uniqueness of Chinese writers writing in English (their second language), culturally, they do not align themselves with English literary tradition, nor do they necessarily follow Chinese literary tradition in a strict sense. It is often the case that the production is a result of hybridity, mixing cultural and linguistic elements from two domains. As discussed in the previous section, English-language creative writing in China lays emphasis on creativity, which inscribes a different agenda compared with those set in anglophone contexts, particularly in the way that the work produced in the former normally is not generally regarded as being sufficiently professional to be positioned in the wider context of English-language literature. In this essay, translation is an element promoted in creative writing where English is used as a second language. Translation helps fill in the knowledge gap between English and Chinese, so that the practitioner can develop a certain degree of familiarity with the two languages in terms of culture and literature.

Although creative writing enjoys greater freedom compared with the restrained freedom in the practice of translation, I contend that the practice of translation and its effect hinge on the content a translator obtains from the source text, and that serves as the crucial step or inspirations for preparing a translator-writer to begin a writing process. This is ideally similar to the workshop approach of 'reading from a writerly perspective' adopted in western settings. Likewise, translation is viewed as being close reading, and this is also an underlying principle of the majority of literary translation workshops available in different countries across the world. Translation facilitates understanding, infiltration, and integration of literatures across nations (see Literature Across Frontiers, https://www.lit-across-frontiers.org). In the following section, I aim to explore the following question: can creative writing, as 'new' literature, be integrated with translation in an actual learning process?

3.2. Translation in creative writing: empowering or marginalised?

Translation has long been adopted as a tool in language learning and acquisition. The fundamental interrogation that needs to be addressed here is, does translation facilitate/ enhance language learning or hinder it? How does literary translation differentiate from other genres of translation? In *Translation in Second Language Learning and Teaching*, various issues related to translation and its implications for language learning/teaching are discussed. In answering the first question, drawbacks to the use of translation in language teaching have been identified also, such as 'the dreariness of rather monotonous exercises, focusing on grammatical and morph-syntactical correctness rather than communicative or functional aspects of the language' (Witte et al. 2009, 5). Translation is criticised there as being a rigid linguistic activity. This same aspect is seen as a merit by Arnd Witte et al. who state that 'it has always played a role in enhancing grammatical, syntactic and lexical awareness, albeit on a largely implicit level' (3). In this book, the ways in which translation can be integrated into language teaching are addressed from various perspectives. Witte contends that the influence exerted by translation on learners enables a 'subjective intercultural third space' (7), through which an opportunity is generated for learners to develop their own 'intercultural competence' (7). In this sense, translation bridges between two cultures and serves as a means of cross-cultural communication. Apart from the aforementioned pros and cons of validity and effectiveness of translation as a teaching tool in language learning, the value of translation has also been explored in Loffredo and Perteghella's (2006) treatise. Forsaking the traditional concept of translation, Loffredo and Perteghella audaciously rethink translation as a form of 'creative writing' and examine how translation has generated a creative and interactive space between L1 and L2. They assert:

> [I]ndeed we call for the use of translation, in particular of a creative, literary translation, as a useful tool in L2 acquisition. By using translation – and its different strategies and forms – in a creative way, engaging for example with the materiality of language itself, exploring different spaces where the text can be reshaped to transform the source text into something different, indeed opening up a 'dialogue' between the source text and the ensuing target texts, students gain awareness of how languages function. (68)

Fundamentally, they believe that literary translation can help people gain a better comprehension of language. Loffredo and Perteghella investigate the use of translation as a writing approach for the L2 classroom. The authors cite McCallum's concept of 'transformation' which is defined as 'self-conscious manipulation of source material to bring something new into being' (61). Creative production is seen as 'Freirean: a dialogical and emancipatory engagement' (57). They claim that 'translation cannot be reduced ... to just a linguistic 'skill', but must be understood as an experiential, transformative, explorative creative writing practice, with all the complex processes and decision-making this entails' (67). They establish two forms of workshops: a live workshop and a virtual/e-workshop. In these workshops, the students are encouraged to 'be creative and explorative with both L1 and L2 language texts', rather than aim at an equivalent translation that is linguistically correct and satisfactory. This particular approach thus 'ultimately enhances their confidence with L2' (57).

The live workshop focuses on 'initial reading, interpretation of meaning, exploration of new meanings, and the refashioning and recreation of the form and/or mode, and eventually, to the final revision of the text' (72). The structure of the live workshop provides examples of creative strategies, including transgeneric translation, intersemiotic translation, and dialect adaptation. These strategies are taken principally as aiming to 'engage students with the learning of L2 by exploring and transforming literary texts in creative ways' (72). Multimedia equipment, which could include 'tape recorders/paintbrushes/cut out images from newspapers or magazines', are encouraged for use in translating (73). These are ways in which the writer can engage with 'intersemiotic/multimodal translation' (73). We can infer from this structure of workshop that the methods adopted are not the traditional methods of interlingual translation that emphasise linguistic transference, but are rather a transference between different semiotics, modes of expressions, artistic forms and genres. The drawback of their paper is that it lacks detailed case analysis to support this new standpoint. However, we can deduce that a practice of transference that is motivated by crossing genres and modes of expression can greatly encourage creativity and creative use of the language. Based on the aforementioned multimedia equipment that are encouraged for use, we can presume that different artistic forms, such as voice, picture, and painting, are utilised to help express ideas that are generally only verbally expressed. In the second type of workshop, the virtual workshop, students are required to 'produce more than one translation by following a different brief each time' (73). Multiple versions of translation, presumably, create an opportunity for students to experience 'the idiosyncratic workings of language' (74) in a literary text.

Loffredo and Perteghella's investigation displays their efforts to adapt translation as a creative practice in an unprecedented way. However, one drawback to their work is that although two modes of workshop are designed, built on this 'creative translation' they have corroborated, they have not provided any case analysis of students' production in these workshops. A lack of empirical evidence to some extent weakens their theoretical construction. As the primary tool advocated in this approach, literary translation is not explicated in terms of its unique advantage for the purpose of engendering creativity that could differentiate itself from other types of translation in their paper. Similarly to their argument and attempts at 're-thought literary translation as creative writing' (57), my essay also focuses on literary translation and its creative potential for the facilitation of creative writing. Creative writing is a subject taught at both schools and universities, but it is a solitary, sedentary work by nature. Because of this nature, how could translation be an effective tool in the acquisition of creative writing skills? In my study, I will discuss the role of literary translation in different contexts (as an individual practice, in a literary community, and in workshop) evidenced with examples of projects conducted, i.e. several literary translation projects and a poetry writing project.

In reference to empirical evidence garnered from creative writing courses (2013–2015) offered at the university where I conducted my Ph.D. study, translation may not always positively serve creative writing, due to either students' misconception of this practice or its catalytic effect on activities of creative writing, where translation was only attempted as a supplementary element in the class. Once translation enters the domain of creative writing, it, however, unavoidably faces the likelihood of being marginalised and subdued in order to highlight the precedence of creative writing. To be more exact, when translation is adopted for the purpose of learning creative writing, the notion of translation tends to be appropriated so as to amplify and stress its creative tendency and potential. Due to the unique features of poetry translation, including its openness to interpretation and the constraints of form, this practice engenders a higher degree of flexibility in recreating a comparable aesthetic effect in the target language, conveniently allowing and necessitating itself respectively to be adopted to foster creativity.

In the discipline of creative writing, where the practice of translation is incorporated as a minor element for the purpose of writing skills acquisition, translation inevitably drifts from its original scholarship focus, turning away from the perpetual discussion revolving around its mediating role between two different cultures and languages. Instead translation is positioned on a continuum, with faithful translation at the one end, emphasising fidelity to the original text, whereas at the other end, we have the polar opposite. Original writing is positioned here in such a way that it stresses originality produced by the writer. On this continuum, translation assumes a new role in aiding the translator to be a creative writer. To this end, the student-writer (also a translator at the same time) becomes fully aware of the creative dimensions in terms of the learning objectives and motivations. Thereupon, the practice of translation is relegated as inferior and secondary in its importance. The subordination of translation in this particular context entails its being practically stretched, distorted, appropriated, and rewritten as methodologies. Consequently, the specific strategies adopted are subversively liberating. Gentzler (2002) in the article 'Translation, poststructuralism, and power' discusses 'the power turn' in translation studies by saying that 'some translators feel so empowered that they deliberately subvert traditional allegiances of translation, interjecting their own worldviews and politics into their work' (197). In Gentzler's opinion, the translator gains the power in appropriating the original text out of political considerations. This power can be generally applicable in a literary context for the purpose of asserting certain poetics, or exists simply because the translator gains greater right in interpreting the original text based on his/her personal misunderstanding.

The adoption of translation can either be empowering or occupy a marginalised position in the creative writing learning process. The student-writer's motivation and their focus skewing towards creative writing skills culminate in the marginalisation of translation and its shifted status of being deemed as lacking in validity and seriousness in a creative writing workshop or class. But if properly designed, translation can play an effective role at creative writing classes. Take the creative writing classes at the university where I was for instance, where translation was adopted as a class activity for the purpose of introducing the specific poetic form, haiku. During these classes, students were instructed to translate English haiku into Chinese. It offered a chance for students to briefly brush up their translation skills, while also developing their understanding of the concept of haiku through English examples, and motivating them to translate them into their first language. Through engaging in translating a few short poems, the students very quickly got a grasp of this particular form, and would later be better equipped to create their own haiku in English, their second language. In the follow-up instructions for creating haiku, the practice of translation was frequently interjected to create bilingual text for the English haiku they wrote. However, translation can only be adopted to such an extent in a manageable manner.

Translation adopted in the process of creative writing skill acquisition places students in a situation of identity negotiation. Where translation becomes involved at a creative writing class, students are likely to face the issue of struggling with their identity and may have to decide whether they view themselves more as translators, or as poets. At creative writing classes dominated by writing exercises, students generally consider themselves more as creative writers. Based on my observation of creative writing classes at my university, either at the undergraduate or at the graduate level, the student-writers generally saw the role of translation as counteracting the learning motivations they expected from an English creative writing class. A chunk of the class time was assigned to storytelling and commenting; along with that, the translation project, upon pre-discussion with the lecturer, was conducted as a supplementary and experimental activity carried on outside of the creative writing class or in class. During the second semester of 2014/2015, students enrolled in the creative writing course participated en masse in the translation project 'Flowers, Seasons and Festivals'. Each week they were assigned several Classical Chinese poems to translate, which have rarely been translated. This increased the level of difficulty for the students who were thus expected to translate with fewer or almost no notes or background information to refer to. It was observed that much of their translated work became appropriation of the original text, particularly in places where the archaism was liable to cause misunderstanding and, as a result, the practitioners rewrote to replace what was supposed to be handled with linguistic rigour. These translation activities thus involved a greater degree of rewriting. Translation in question here instead is deemed as a source from which student-translators feel free to transfer or deviate from meaning where they feel this is necessary (particularly when the meaning of the source text is beyond their comprehension). This type of supplementary role of translation serves to increase its marginalised position in the process of acquiring creative writing skills. Evidently, this somewhat constrained activity (translation), which relies on the switching between two languages, becomes obstructive and counter-productive for students' self-expression in English. In addition, the restrained nature of translation seems to contradict writing tasks designed to encourage creative ideas and freedom of expression.

Does this mean that translation is not a suitable tool to be used to facilitate creative writing? In this light, although translation has been purposefully designed as an extra-curricular activity, the reification of translation would be stretched and expanded by students as a result of the negotiation of their primal identity as a writer in this particular context. Translation is appropriated, subverted, and recycled as manifested in specific strategies utilised by the students. It has become marginalised in the sense that the practice of translation was utterly appropriated from a traditional perspective, yet at the same time it was also empowering for students to adopt translation for creative purposes and to obtain some knowledge of either English poetic forms or inspirations for poem ideas. This is the catalyst for adopting translation at a creative writing class.

Considering the marginalised position of translation in creative writing classes, further research should be conducted to investigate the matter from a different perspective and in different forms, i.e. as an individual practice or in a group, in order to test its creative potential and to explore whether or not it could be used in creative writing learning with validity, and if so, how. I suggest more research should be conducted to consider the writers' engagement in the practice of literary translation and the resulting impact on their individual writings, within and beyond the context of workshops or seminars at educational institutes.

4 . Conclusion

The key issues examined in this essay include practice-based research conducted in the field of creative writing and the salient features Chinese writers are concerned about, aiming to provide the background for the issues discussed in the remaining part of the essay. It is contended that creative writing is not just an undertaking to express oneself so as to foster personal growth, but also a discipline that partly builds on practice-led research, which heightens the professionalisation of this subject. For the Chinese writers, cross-linguistic and cross-cultural dilemmas in writing are unavoidable issues to be reckoned with. In such a case, the assertion of the uniqueness of one's own culture and literature demarcates the primary responsibility being undertaken in creative writing in a Chinese context.

Note

1. This award, also known as the MacArthur Fellowship, is given to 20 to 30 people each year from all walks of life who show exceptional creativity and perseverance in their creative endeavours and a significant capacity for self determination.

Disclosure statement

No potential conflict of interest was reported by the author.

Funding

This work was supported by Yangzhou University [grant number YZLYJF2020PHD052].

ORCID

Xia Fang ⓘ http://orcid.org/0000-0002-4741-4505

References

Addonizio, Kim, and Dorianne Laux. 1997. *The Poet's Companion: A Guide to the Pleasure of Writing Poetry*. New York, NY: W.W. Norton & Company.

Bugeja, Michael J. 2001. *The Art and Craft of Poetry*. Cincinnati, Ohio: Writer's Digest; David & Charles.

Chin, Grace VS. 2014. "Co-constructing a Community of Creative Writers." *Exploring Second Language Creative Writing: Beyond Babel*, 119–139.

Dai, Fan. 2010. "English-language Creative Writing in Mainland China." *World Englishes* 29 (4): 546–556. doi:10.1111/j.1467-971X.2010.01681.x

Dai, Fan. 2015. "Teaching Creative Writing in English in the Chinese Context." *World Englishes* 34 (issue 2): 247–258. doi:10.1111/weng.12136

Dawson, Paul. 2005. *Creative Writing and the New Humanities*. New York: Routledge.

Disney, Dan. 2014. *Exploring Second Language Creative Writing: Beyond Babel*. Philadelphia: John Benjamins Publishing Company.

Donnelly, Dianne. 2010. *Does the Writing Workshop Still Work?* Bristol: Multilingual Matters.

Finch, Annie. 2012. *A Poet's Craft: A Comprehensive Guide to Making and Sharing Your Poetry*. Ann Arbor: University of Michigan Press.

Freire, Paulo. 1968. *Pedagogy of the Oppressed*. New York: Seabury.

Freire, Paulo. 1973. *Education: The Practice of Freedom*. London: Sheet & Ward.

Gentzler, Edwin. 2002. "Translation, Post-Structuralism and Power." In *Translation and Power*, edited by Maria Tymoczko, and Edwin Gentzler, 195–218. Amherst, MA: University of Massachusetts Press.

Harper, Graeme. 2013. *A Companion to Creative Writing*. New York: Wiley.

Harper, Graeme. 2017. "The UnWorkshop." *Creative Writing Innovations: Breaking Boundaries in the Classroom*, 27–38.

Herbert, William N. 2010. *Writing Poetry*. London: Routledge.

Kelen, Christopher. 2011. "Community in the Translation/Response Continuum: Poetry as Dialogic Play." In *Collective Creativity*, edited by Gerhard Fischer, and Florian Vassen, 281–298. Leiden: Brill.

Kelen, Christopher. 2014. "Process and Product, Means and Ends, Creative Writing in Macao." In *Beyond Babel: Exploring Second Language Creative Writing*, edited by Dan Disney, 75–102. Philadelphia: John Benjamins Publishing Company.

Kroll, Jeri. 2013. "Creative Writing and Education." In *A Companion to Creative Writing*, edited by Graeme Harper, 245–263. New York: Wiley.

Kroll, Jeri, and Dai Fan. 2014. "Reading as a Writer in Australia and China: Adapting the Workshop." *New Writing: International Journal for the Practice and Theory of Creative Writing* 11 (1): 77–91. doi:10.1080/14790726.2013.849743

Lam, Agnes. 2014. *Becoming Poets: The Asian English Experience*. Bern: Peter Lang.

Loffredo, Eugenia, and Manuela Perteghella. 2006. *Translation and Creativity: Perspectives on Creative Writing and Translation Studies*. London: Continuum.

McCallum, Andrew. 2012. *Creativity and Learning in Secondary English: Teaching for a Creative Classroom*. London: Routledge.

McLoughlin, Nigel. 2013. "Writing Poetry." *A Companion to Creative Writing*, 40–55. doi:10.1002/9781118325759.ch3

Myers, D. G. 2006. *The Elephants Teach: Creative Writing Since 1880*. Chicago: University of Chicago Press.

Palmer, Joy A. 2001. *Fifty Major Thinkers on Education: From Confucius to Dewey*. London: Routledge.

Spiro, Jane 2004. *Creative Poetry Writing*. Oxford: OUP.

Webb, Jen, and Paul Hetherington. 2016. "'Research Active' vs 'Practice Active': Re-Imagining the Relationship Between the Academy and the Creative Arts Sector." In *Old and New, Tried and Untried: Creativity and Research in the 21st Century*, edited by Jeri Kroll, Andrew Melrose, and Jen Webb, 1–20. Champaign, IL: Common Ground Publishing.

Witte, Arnd, et al. 2009. *Translation in Second Language Learning and Teaching*. Oxford: Peter Lang.

An agreeable crest: the *New Writing* 20th anniversary year

When in the 17th Century Edward Shin Yentre and Millicent Caracaccio unknowingly and almost simultaneously invented creative writing neither expected it to last. The notion of it, by its very nature, was preposterous and even more so in a century in which electricity and calculus were invented and gravitation discovered. And yet, somehow, a hundred years passed, and it was still around. The Age of Enlightenment, the Scientific Revolution, Imperialism, Rationalism – none of these could shift it. So still it persisted. In 1876 the world's first phone call did nothing to dislodge its popularity. In fact, if anything it enhanced it. And when in 1878 electric light was invented it shed enough light on paper and quills that it set in motion the invention of the fountain pen and, subsequently, the ballpoint, which followed. Both empowered the fatuous scourge of creative writing.

Undeterred by the ridiculousness of it, and unmoved by actions against it, which included powered flight, globalization, popular music, video recording and quantum physics, by the arrival of the 3rd Millenium it had all but reduced commonsense to an afterthought and unsettled such emotions and thoughts as could never have previously been imagined. Around then – well, to be entirely accurate, three years hence – *New Writing: The International Journal for the Practice and Theory of Creative Writing* was slung out into the world with the kind of abandon that is mostly reserved for high dives from concrete platforms and for wrestling venomous snakes. Appropriately, it promised to sink like a stone – in the sparkling blue pool water below that platform, most likely, surrounded by those grinning serpents. Nonsensically, instead, it swam.

It is an affront to decency and clear thinking, of course, that any publication, never mind an entire eminent journal, could devote itself to a practice so ridiculous, so speculative, so unconscionable and so imprudent as this one. More so, that it might flourish and grow. And that it should ever in any reasonable lifetime be *read*! More so still, that while flourishing that it should chart the absurd nuances and preoccupations of the practice, a practice so irrational that domestic animals run from it and leaders of certain political parties condemn it. And yet, such a journal here exists and it persists.

I am reminded of the time, in the Summer of 1963, when wandering along a beach in the Molacanacan Islands two young shellfish farmers saw that the sky was filled with something approximating crustaceans in a deep sea pond and came to the conclusion, right there, that the universe was, to all intents and purposes, upside down. The Moon was therefore a glistening puddle and the soil and seagrass around them were the textured celestial sphere, teaming with life. The result, of course, was the utter ordinariness, six years later, of human beings landing and walking on The Moon, and brought about a rejection of any interest in those islands of that event or any other involving leaving the terrestrial. No one flies there. There are no airports. No seaplanes, even. In the Molacanacan Islands they get around in boats. Everything is reversed. The animals live in houses and the people in the jungles and the streets. The night is morning, and the morning is night. People sleep for entertainment, and they keep themselves awake to rest.

AN AGREEABLE CREST: THE *NEW WRITING* 20TH ANNIVERSARY YEAR

It is amazing, that here in 2024, the reversal of understanding and good sense seen on those remote tropical islands is reflected in the lack of corrective action history clearly demands be taken concerning this very publication. And, now entering its 20th year, that without such action this outrageous publication continues to exist and to impact.

'Nay!' I hear you shout, 'Nay! In fact, its impact *extends*!'

So true.

After 20 years, what lies ahead of us here is therefore abundantly, outrageously and disturbingly clear. As Edward Shin Yentre wrote, now some 348 years ago, or 4176 months as it is on the Grenoble Calendar, in the first stanza of the world's first poem, 'The Agreeable Crest':

Wilt thou forgive that stone where we began
In gardens each contemplating yet
An agreeable crest (Yentre 1676: 1)

A sentiment Millicent Caracaccio's opening sentence of the second paragraph of her third chapter perfectly echoes 12 years later:

So fearful a place, among such strange Creatures, yonder, a moment
of life will pass, and pass, and pass again (Caracaccio, 1688: 9)

And so it went also with two young shellfish farmers observing, there at night on a remote warm island beach, a clear night sky with an openness of mind that was not so much overanxious as unequivocal. In all this comes the message of what lies ahead for us, 20 years from now.

Voila! Firstly, in the next 20 years in the life of this preposterous journal Artificial Intelligence will productively remove any need of human involvement in the practice of creative writing. Lord knows we'll all be celebrating that day! The labour will no longer be of any interest, because of course, it will no longer exist.

'AI AI AI, it's off to work it goes.'

Further, new tools will emerge that mold and mightily empower our human brains – with small batteries implanted strategically, I believe - vanquishing the random bizzarery of imaginative speculation and the uncertainty of barbarous conjecture that makes up the majority of creative writing - if not all of it, to be frank. We will conquer by eliminating and eliminate conqueringly. Gone will be the unsettled! Dismissed with be the unknown! Neural networks will be manufactured, and expert systems perfected. Prediction, or what psychologists brilliantly call 'Prospectism', will disappear and surety will thereafter prevail. Informed by big data, the need of analysis will grow less as our faultlessness grows greater.

In these things, reason will finally prevail.

That is the second and final thing, of course.

As a hundred, a hundred times hundred hundred human events have made clear to us, there is no merit in emotional outpouring and none in the ingrained consideration of chimera and figments. With that in mind, the next 20 years will eliminate these completely. Beyond that lies the shore onto which we will crash, rocky perhaps, and distant no doubt, but oh so much more agreeable than the tempestuous sea we have been sailing so far.

20 years since this journal's foundation what follows, building on previous and current generations of the preposterous, the ridiculous and the imprudent, is now surely certain demise. It is premature to celebrate. The destruction needs to be complete, the demons put to bed (as Dostoevsky or Updike, one of those amateur philosophers, once said), the dragons slayed, if you like, the hunting wolves, the Midgard serpents, the Tooth Fairy, the Cheshire

Cat. At least evidence suggests we won't have to wait long now. We have reached that 'agreeable crest', and now will come crashing down as all crests mightily must.

I have included here in this first 20th anniversary year issue, an interview with poet, biographer and novelist, Sir Andrew Motion, to show there is occasional resistance, in some quarters at least. But we all can see the direction this is heading. Of course, Andrew is such a romantic, as by nature poets tend to be.

20 years ago this journal was launched with no understanding of what a real discipline of study might look like, of course. It might as well have been a late-night bus service to Croyden or a painting competition for sea lions. Then something possessed people, as the published evidence here suggests. Who knows why? Old beliefs die hard, I suppose. Hearts and minds persist in their ludicrous ways. Folks speculate. Rabbits, mice and spiders jump out. The imagination goes its own way, looting and gathering. Empathetically, we can but offer a platform for whatever survives. Humans will be humans, the saying goes. I sometimes wonder if, had we not been flawed enough to invent the electric light and the phone call, we would all be far better off. At least then we would have no reason to see or speak.

References

Caracaccio, Millicent, *Barber of a New World: A Novel*, London, Maxwell: 1688
Yentre, Edward Shin, 'The Agreeable Crest' in *Reliques Poemutam*, London, Chivas and Gulliver: 1676

Graeme Harper

Conclusion

Intentional Echoes

Graeme Harper

Practice-led research in creative writing research has evolved considerably and internationally now for well over half a century. While we can trace such research in creative writing back to national origins (Andrew Cowan in his chapter "The Rise of Creative Writing", Nigel Krauth in his article "Evolution of the Exegesis" and Richard Moody in his article "The Creative Thesis" offer examples), we also find global variation in the ways in which this research is described. In the USA, "English with a Creative Dissertation", for example, in the UK "Creative and Critical Writing", and in Australia "creative work and an exegesis". These are reasonably accurate descriptions, contractions, or conflations of what are varied attempts, worldwide, to name what happens when we research creative writing through the practice of writing creatively and, along with this, critically articulate the themes, subjects, hypotheses, theories, or contexts of this research. There are also local variations. In essence, individual universities and particular creative writing programs have also chosen nomenclature for practice-led research.

That said, of course not all research in creative writing is, has been, or needs to be practice-led; even if research in creative writing begins in recognizing our actions – the movements, the emphases and focal points, the styles, the tempos of our writerly activities. From that logical beginning, however, we have seen and we see here in *New Writing Explorations: Researching Creative Writing* a focus by some researchers on pedagogy, the ways in which we attempt to pass on knowledge and skills and understanding about creative writing. We have also seen explorations of conceptual knowledge in creative writing and ways of thinking as a creative writer might think – often examined by considering what creative writers have said about their actions, in interviews, and in memoirs and diaries, for example. Creativity, the imagination, textuality, cultural context, and societal history all have emerged as topics of interest to creative writing researchers, and they have generated research and researchers who, over considerable time now, have delved deeply into these subject areas. These among a myriad of other topics too, because with such complex, latticed, stream of practice and research as creative writing, the vibrancy is considerable and the epistemological reflections are many. Additionally, the field of creative writing research draws on what are often considered cognate disciplines – the study of literature, of composition, of other arts – and does so by its recognition of the echoic presence of writerly actions and results in these fields of study. Similarly, creative writing researchers delve into content-related academic areas widely across the

Humanities, the Social Sciences, and the Sciences, from action-based explorations in areas such as ethnography and sociology, to the evidence trails examined in social history and the considerations of aesthetics, and including the inward focuses of psychology and neuroscience. These academic areas to name just a few. So goes our "poking and prying with a purpose" (Thurston: 127).

Our research is not constricted by the boundaries of university departments or marshalled by demands of academic paradigms fixed so firmly over time in institutional environments. Rather, creative writing research is intentionally echoic in its embracing of both personal thinking and individual emotions, fluid and attentive to the needs of the researcher, in time and in the place in which they are researching. It is also communal, coming about because written language is shared in literate cultures, and in that way embodies cultural and societal needs and desires. Personally and publicly, such research is therefore a fascinating corollary to creative writing, the adventurous practice with which many of us engage. Its aim is to be a revelatory contributor to our greater understanding of what we humans do when we use writing simultaneously to communicate and create art.

References

Cowan, Andrew, "The Rise of Creative Writing" in Ann Hewings, Lynda Prescott and Philip Seargeant (eds), *Futures for English Studies; Teaching Language, Literature and Creative Writing in Higher Education*, London: Palgrave Macmillan, 2016, p.39

Hurston, Zora Neale, *Dust Tracks on a Road*. 1942. New York: Harper Perennial, 1991.

Krauth, Nigel, "Evolution of the Exegesis: The Radical Trajectory of the Creative Writing Doctorate in Australia." *TEXT*, 15.1, 2011. Last Accessed date: December 24, 2024.

Moody, Richard. "The Creative Thesis." *Educational Theatre Journal*, 10.3, October 1958, pp. 223–232

Index

Note: *Italic* page numbers refer to figures and page numbers followed by "n" denote endnotes.

academic context 65, 86–88
academic language 87, 102
academic research 32, 102, 117
academic training 130–131
action research methodology 37, 104, 111–113, 118
agreeable crest 154–156
America 123–124, 129
anglophone contexts 143–144, 147
Antilogikê 5, 7–9, 10n1
apprentice writers 5, 9–10
Aristotle 5, 70–71, 77–78, 106, 115; workshop 5
Aronson, L. 33
artifactual literacies 114
Artificial Super Intelligence 133–134
artistic forms 148–149
Association of Writers and Writing Programs (AWP) 124
Atherton, Cassandra 19; poem 20–21, 26
Australia/Australian 35, 40, 124, 127–131, 143–144, 157; model 128–129; Research Council 37–38, 71, 86
authority 5, 7–8, 75, 93–94, 96–98, 135
authority-conscious pedagogy 93–94
auto-ethnography 103, 104, 109–111, 118; research methods 110

banking model 94–95
Barker, George 15
Baudelaire, Charles 15
Bennett, E. 125–126
Berlant, Lauren 36
bilingual writers 143
Bizzaro, Patrick 141
Boireau, N. 78
Brien, D. L. 35
Brophy, Kevin 17

Caldwell 37
Chinese: context 135–151; writers 146–147, 151
Chin, G. 145

classes 6, 26, 46, 50, 54, 56, 92–99, 108, 127, 139–140, 149–151
classroom 55, 57, 93–97, 131, 140, 148
cognitive poetics 62–63, 65; and creative practice 62
Cohen, L. L. 106
communities of practice 105
components 68–69, 140
Conor, Bridget 36
contemporary cultures 129, 144
contemporary literature 14, 144
content 31, 33–34, 37, 41, 68, 78, 96, 147, 157
contexts 33, 35–37, 39–41, 65, 70, 94, 96, 124, 130, 138–139, 145–146, 149, 151
contradiction 4–7, 9, 94, 110, 115
Covino, William 8
craft 9–10, 34, 38, 40, 53–54, 57, 70, 75, 93, 95, 126–130, 136, 141; analysis 53–54; choices 53–54; focus question 96; practices 5–6, 128
creation 10, 25, 37, 50, 64, 134, 139–140, 142
creative/creativity 46, 50–51, 87, 94–95, 118, 123, 137, 140, 142–143, 146–147, 149; arts 35, 129; component 69–70, 84; dissertation 129, 157;-exegetical form 73, 75;-exegetical genre 69, 79, 87; explorations 66; intelligence 133; labour 36; literacies 145; nonfiction 87; piece 70; poetry writing 140; possibilities 36, 38; power 142; practitioners 35; processes 34, 36, 58, 65, 118, 137; product 69, 71–72, 75, 85, 87; research 137, 139; screenwriter 40–41; self-expression 141; spaces 20, 26; studies 50, 146; ways 37, 148; work 20, 66, 68–71, 73–87, 92, 97, 130, 135–137, 139, 142–144, 146; writers 13, 51–52, 61, 71, 91, 101–105, 107–108, 110, 114–116, 118, 128, 133, 135–136, 144, 157
creative practice 19, 36, 38–39, 41, 62–65, 71, 75, 117, 129, 136, 149; impact on 36; research 33, 35, 37, 39, 41; researchers 2, 40
creative writing 49–50, 71, 73, 79, 84, 92–95, 98–99, 124, 127–130, 141–143, 148, 154; action of 12; act of 63, 126, 142; in America

160 INDEX

123–124; in Australia 128, 143; in China 143,
146; development of 142; discipline 70,
85, 149; and education 103, 110; research
45; significance of 101, 142; teaching 93;
translation 151; workshop 7, 127
critical approaches 38–39, 57, 129
critical explorations 46–47
criticism, history of 71
cultural productions 55–56

Dawson, P. 141, 143, 144
decentre power 93, 95–96
Degenaar, Anna 115
deictic centre 64–65
deictic projection 64–65
Delville, Michael 27
dialogic character 94, 97, 99
Disney 145
Dissoi Logoi 5, 7, 9, 11n1
Donnelly, Dianne 140
drama/dramatic 75, 77–78; dialogues 76–77
Dryden, John 71, 73, 77–78, 85; essay 77–78, 85

education/educational 44, 49, 94–95, 97,
103–104, 110, 112, 125, 127, 137, 140,
142–144, 146–147; institutions 124, 146;
settings 94, 98, 113
emotive intelligence 134
empathy 65, 68
English language 137–151; creative writing
in China 142–143, 147; haiku 150; literature
86, 141, 143, 146–147; -speaking context
143–144; studies 144
enhancing literacy 141–143
ethical issues 74, 106, 145
exegesis/exegetical 46, 69–75, 78–79, 85–87;
components 69; work 70, 129
existing knowledge 37–38
explicit knowledge 2

Field, Syd 33
finished product 104, 141
flight 12, 60–61
formalized curiosity 3
Freire, P. 137
Freud, S. 115
Frow, John 16, 26

generative creative writing *6*
generative magic 8
genres 2, 15–17, 22–27, 35–36, 39, 53, 68, 71,
85, 87–88, 127, 129–130, 145, 147–148; of
creative writing 75, 141
global context 146–147
Graff, Gerald 24
Greenbaum, Andrea 7, 11n2
Grosser, Emmylou 15

Harper, G. 35, 136, 139
Hart, Henry 24
Hauge, M. 33
Hecq, Dominique 23–24
Hetherington, P. 136
higher education 4, 49, 135, 141, 143–144
Hill, Geoffrey 14
Hirsch, Sara 114
Horace 70–75, 77–78
how-to screenwriting manuals 36
human creativity 2, 44
Hurston, Zora Neale 1, 3

ideological scripts 55–56
imaginary worlds 63, 66
indeterminacy 5–6, 9–10, 21
industry 33–37, 39–40, 44
institutions 4, 8, 45, 128, 140–141, 143–144
instruction 4–5, 36, 48–49, 124, 126, 145, 150
instructor 4–5, 7, 10, 92–99, 127; work 98–99
intelligence 133–134
International Journal 16, 33, 154
interpretive communities 54–55
interrogate 8, 33, 54, 114, 128
intertextual references 18, 21–22
intervention 108, 111
Iowa Workshop 4, 123–124, 126

Jarratt, Susan 11n2
Johnson, Peter 16
journal 3, 25, 32–33, 38, 50, 80, 82, 140, 154, 156

Kaplan, Edward 18
Kearns, R. M. 97
knowledge 2–3, 7, 9, 33, 37–38, 40, 60–61, 81,
84, 91–92, 133, 136, 138–139
Krauth 69–70, 157
Kristeva, Julia 21
Kroll, J. 142, 143

language 7–8, 16–17, 21, 24, 51–52, 63–65, 68,
71, 133, 136, 145, 147–149, 151; learning
147–148; proficiency, improving 146–147;
teaching 147–148
Lawrence, D.H. 21–22
Leahy, A. 7, 93–94
learning process 137, 145, 147, 150
Lee, Jason 36
liberating pedagogy 94, 98
linguistic intelligence 133
literacy 8, 114, 141
literary/literature 22–24, 35, 51, 55–57,
70–71, 88, 123–130, 143–145, 147, 151,
157; apprenticeship 138–139; community
51–52, 138, 149; craft 53, 128; critics 71, 74,
104; cultures 2, 158; forms 15, 18, 25, 28,
85; history 55, 85; history of 71; production

51, 55, 57, 127–128, 130–131; scholars 91; studies 33, 36, 126, 144–145; teaching of 130, 143; texts 56–57, 148–149; traditions 103, 147; translation 135, 138–139, 147–149, 151; works 17, 145
lived experiences 63, 110–111, 117–118
local literary traditions 130–131
lyric poems 21, 53, 140

Maclean, Marie 18
manuals 33–37, 39–41
marginalised position 150–151
master narratives 55–56
McCallum, A. 145
McGurl, Mark 123
McKee, R. 33
McLoughlin, N. 136
meta-knowledge 48–57
methodological holism 61
methods and methodologies 106–107, 118
MFAs 124–126
mimetic theory 140–141
model 2, 31, 37, 46, 64, 93–94, 99, 124, 126, 128, 130; of education 94
modes of expression 140, 148–149
module 92–93, 96–99, 103
Monte, Steven 16
multimodal research approaches 114
Murphy, Margueritte S. 23
Myers, D. G. 141

narrative poetry 17, 70
narrator 20, 22–24, 26, 65
National Association of Writers in Education 49
Nelmes, J. 33–34
neosophistic workshop 8–10
new knowledge 36–38, 41, 84, 136–137, 139
Newton, Isaac 12–13
non-anglophone contexts 142–145
Norton Anthology of Theory and Criticism 71
notebooks 24–26, 79–80, 82, 84, 140

objects 12, 51, 64, 105, 114
O'Leary's cycles of research 112
oral examinations 45–46
original text 22, 149–151
Oxford English Dictionary 84

Paiva, Daniel 3
participant: model 92–93, 96–97, 99; workshop model 93, 96
pedagogy 36, 41, 46, 55, 94, 97, 113, 123–128, 130–131, 137, 140
personal histories 20, 116
Petersen, David 16
Phaedrus 76–77
Plato 5, 7, 8, 71, 76–77, 106, 115–116

poems/poetic/poetry 3, 14–17, 19–28, 38, 53–54, 68–70, 72–73, 75, 85–87, 96, 98, 103, 105–106, 114–115, 122–123, 127–128, 137–141, 145; imagery 18–19; language 27; and prose 14, 16–17, 28; translations 138–139, 143, 149
political model 128
portfolio approach 40
power 7–8, 44, 51–52, 72, 74, 93–95, 99, 113, 118, 124, 127, 150; dynamics 92–97, 99; of poetry 103
practice 2–3, 8, 32–41, 57–58, 60–61, 66, 71–74, 81, 83–84, 94–97, 102–103, 105, 110–113, 115–116, 129–131, 135–136, 148–149, 154–155, 157; -based projects 138–139; -focussed texts 37, 40–41; of literary translation 138, 151; and research 34, 84, 135–136, 151, 157; of translation 138–139, 141, 147, 149–151
problem-posing model 94–96, 99
processes 50–51, 54, 62–65, 73–74, 76–80, 85–87, 93–94, 103–107, 109–112, 114–117, 123, 129, 131, 136–139, 141
programmes 45–47, 55, 103, 124–131, 135, 144, 146
progressive education movement 124, 127
propositions 31, 45, 50
prose 3, 14–17, 21–25, 28, 66, 72, 75, 77, 86, 110; fiction 19, 85–86; genres 23; poem/poetry 3, 14–28, 38; poets 14–15
psychology of creativity 50
psychology of screenwriting 36

qualitative research methodology 109, 118
quantitative research 107, 117
Queensland University of Technology 38
questionnaires 107–108

Ramazani, Jahan 25
recreational activity 104–105
refereed journals 82
reflective essay 79, 85
reflective practice 37, 112–113
research 2–3, 34–41, 49–50, 54, 65, 69–71, 83–86, 99, 102–118, 135–141, 143, 151, 157–158; approach 109–110, 114; artefacts 37, 41; in creative writing 50, 157; definition of 37–38; legitimate form of 35–36, 38; methodologies 3, 41, 50, 103, 106–107, 109, 115, 140; process 87, 109, 112; questions 106–109, 111, 114–117; statement 71, 86; submission 69–70, 86
researchers 2, 34–35, 37, 40, 48–49, 103–110, 112–114, 118, 157
rhetorical modes 5, 7–8, 49, 57, 70, 87, 141
Richards, Kent Harold 16
role translation 139, 143
Rooms and Spaces project 14–27, 46, 51, 68, 80, 82, 127

INDEX

Salvadoran community 103
Santilli, Nikki 18, 20
schema theory 62, 64–66
Schneider, Pat 94–98
scholarly research essay 70, 79
scholarly work 69–87
screenplay 12, 32–35, 38–39, 134
screenwriters/screenwriting 32–36, 38–40; authors 33, 37, 39–40; manuals 32, 34–41; pedagogy 40–41; poetics 33; practice 32–34, 37–40; research 33–36; studies 32–41
second language 145–147, 150
Seger, L. 33
self-expression 54, 122, 141–142, 144–146, 151
shadow self 117–118
Shakespeare, W. 75–76
Shapiro, K. 73–75
shared language 2, 104
Shivani, Anis 125
signature pedagogy 123, 125–126, 137
situational knowledge 136, 138
Smallhorne, loney 111
Smith, Ali 17, 18
Socrates 76–77, 140; workshop 5
Sontag, Susan 25
sorting intelligence 133–134
Spencer, Dr. Darrell 9
Stegner, Wallace 11n2
Sternberg, Claudia 34
Still Movement of Prose Poetry 18
story worlds 63
structured empathy 68
students 4–5, 7, 9–10, 37–38, 46, 48, 50–58, 81–82, 92–99, 103–104, 109–110, 112–117, 123–124, 127–131, 137–142, 145, 148–151; in creative writing 52, 55–56; critique 98; space for 54, 124; -teachers 94–97
subject matter 39, 77, 86–87, 125
submission 9–10, 79, 85
Sun Yat-sen University 144–145

teacher-student 94–97
teaching contexts 141–142, 145
theoretical underpinnings 140–141

theories of literary production 131
threshold concepts 48–52, 54, 58
thumb intelligence 133
Todorov, T. 85–88
traditional workshop 4, 5, 123, 126–128, 130; model 95, 97, 131; pedagogy 127, 130
translation 72, 78, 135, 137–141, 143, 147–151; activities 139, 151; and creative writing 137–140; projects 137–139, 150; in second language learning and teaching 147; studies 145, 150
translators 143, 147, 149–150
truth 7, 46, 52, 76, 111, 127
Turco, Lewis 17

unconscionable mystification 14–28
United States (US) 123–124, 126–127, 129–131
universities 7–8, 39–40, 69, 71, 86–88, 92–93, 124–125, 128–131, 133, 135, 140–141, 144, 146, 149–150
unpredictability 44–47
unworkshop 137–138

Vanderslice, Stephanie 123, 127, 129
Vogler, C. 33
vulnerability 92–93, 95–97

Waldeback, Zara 38, 40
Wandor, Michelene 129
Webb, Jen 136
Williamson, R. 35
Woolf, Virginia 19
workshop 4–10, 50, 92–99, 112, 123–128, 130–131, 137–138, 141, 143–145, 148–151; conversation 10, 55; facilitator 6–8, 10; instruction 4–5; leaders 5, 8, 94–95, 113; model 93; participants 95, 97; pedagogy 124, 130–131; setting 93–98; submission 5–6, 9
writers 6–7, 34–37, 48–57, 62–65, 68, 71–79, 86–88, 95, 104–106, 108–112, 116–118, 124–128, 138, 143–146, 148–151; perspective 144–145; and reader 63; responsibility 144
written language 60, 158